David Engstrom

Under the Cover of Kindness

KNOWLEDGE:
Disciplinarity and Beyond

SERIES EDITORS
Ellen Messer-Davidow · David R. Shumway · David J. Sylvan

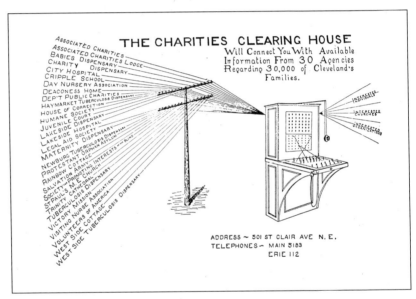

Illustration from *The Confidential Exchange* by Margaret F. Byington (1912)

Under the Cover
of Kindness
The Invention of Social Work

LESLIE MARGOLIN

Foreword by Eileen Gambrill

UNIVERSITY PRESS OF VIRGINIA

Charlottesville and London

Acknowledgment for previously published material appears on p. xiv.

THE UNIVERSITY PRESS OF VIRGINIA

© 1997 by the Rector and Visitors of the University of Virginia
All rights reserved
Printed in the United States of America

First published 1997

⊗ The paper used in this publication meets the minimum requirements of the American National Standard for Information Sciences—Permanence of Paper for Printed Library Materials, ANSI Z39.48-1984.

Library of Congress Cataloging-in-Publication Data
Margolin, Leslie, 1945–
    Under the cover of kindness : the invention of social work / Leslie Margolin.
      p. cm.—(Knowledge, disciplinarity and beyond)
    Includes bibliographical references and index.
    ISBN 0-8139-1713-1 (cloth : alk. paper)
    1. Social case work. 2. Social case work—United States. I. Title.
  II. Series.
  HV43.M295   1997
  361.3′2—dc21   96-47986
                                                   CIP

Frontispiece: Illustration from *The Confidential Exchange* by Margaret F. Byington (1912)

FOR MY MOTHER, PEGGY MARGOLIN,

with love

The judges of normality are present everywhere. We are in the society of the teacher-judge, the doctor-judge, the educator-judge, the "social worker"–judge; it is on them that the universal reign of the normative is based; and each individual, wherever he may find himself, subjects to it his body, his gestures, his aptitudes, his achievements. The carceral network, in its compact or disseminated forms, with its system of insertion, distribution, surveillance, observation, has been the greatest support, in modern society, of the normalizing power.

Michel Foucault, *Discipline and Punish*

CONTENTS

EILEEN GAMBRILL

T his book is a revealing, masterful analysis of social work based on the case records and professional writings of social workers themselves. Author Leslie Margolin is concerned with the core of social work that he defines as a type of power played out in social work's commitment to service to the poor in community-based nonprofit agencies. He traces this core work from the early days of charity visiting, focusing on the "fiction of voluntariness" in all endeavors falling under this definition of social work. The analysis shows a deep respect for clients and for their rights as individuals to be free of disguised penetration into their private lives. Margolin suggests that social workers live by two great contradictions: to help, to do good, but simultaneously to investigate and to impose society's values on poor clients. Through social work's own case records and professional literature he illustrates how these contradictions are played out and what their effects are on both clients and social workers. Like a scientist who discovers heretofore unrecognized pathogens, Margolin detects hidden pathogens in the very writings of social workers—ones that are missed by those caught in the profession's rhetoric. He notes that the "inspirational quality" of writing in social work gives it an "almost a miraculous mythical status that obscures recognition of the play of unequal power." He argues that social workers' calls to attend to structural and economic sources of poverty do not match what is done in their daily activities, where they focus on the individual and the family as a source of problems. He argues that in order to disguise a judgmental role entailing unequal power relationships, there must be extensive, ongoing discourse in the professional literature and in case records to justify this and to cloud the vision of all participants about what is happening. On this level, *Under the Cover of Kindness* is a fascinating analysis of the implicit functions of case records and professional writings.

A hallmark of a penetrating analysis is the linking of seemingly disparate events. Margolin suggests that, to maintain an impossible alliance between judging and doing good, a steady series of different strategies has covered up what is really happening. Social workers use friendliness, warmth, and empathy as techniques to pursue investigatory and judgmental aims. Similar functions are played by an ever-changing collection of technologies used in the service of an ever-constant cluster of aims: investigating, classifying, and judging. He suggests that only by portraying the target population as even more cognitively and socially impoverished could new levels of penetration into the private lives of the poor be justified. Indeed, today hundreds of psychiatric labels are used to classify clients. The coded language of these labels is a means of making judgments without appearing to do so, thereby removing any possibility that clients have a say in what is written and said about them.

Like masterful magicians who distract us from what is really happening, Margolin suggests that social workers distract clients from what is occurring—coercion and unwarranted trespass into their private lives by appeals to sincerity and *doing good.* However, master magicians are aware of how they create their illusions. Margolin argues that social workers as well as clients are mystified concerning the true function of their work. He argues that, far from empowering clients, social workers do the opposite; Margolin's point is that the very notion that you can empower someone in fact places the power in your own hands. He suggests that key coercive elements in social work include ambiguity regarding the goals of intervention (a healthy family) combined with an unambiguous set of constraints for those who refuse to be cooperative (e.g., increased visiting). He highlights the lack of choice clients have. If clients are resistant, social workers double their efforts to win their cooperation (e.g., more visits, more telephone calls).

The analysis presented in this book sheds light on many of the paradoxes in social work such as claims of positive effects in the absence of evidence, the embracing of an ever-changing parade of fads, and the addiction to emotive buzz words such as "empowerment" and "multicultural." This explains why social work goals are often so vague (e.g., promote healthy families). It explains why process (what is done) rather than outcomes (what is achieved) is the focus; both distract attention from a candid recognition of implicit functions of social work intervention. This explains social work's antiscience stance coupled with an eager embrace of pseudoscience (the use of the trappings of science without the substance of science such as use of the term "scientific charity"). The essence of science is criticism: critical discussion and testing of claims is viewed as essential to the growth of knowledge. Criticism may reveal contradictions between what is said and what is done to what effect. It may reveal hidden sources of power, which Margolin argues are everywhere, out into the open.

This book will help social workers understand the discomfort they often feel in their work. Here is a deep analysis of the causes of burnout at the level of the profession itself (its core mission). Margolin argues that the root cause of burnout is the constant work required to balance an intent to do good with a coercive, controlling, investigatory function. He does not view social workers as bad people. They want to help, but working with resistant, hostile clients is draining. Only if social workers are convinced that their actions are to help could they put up with rejection (e.g., doors slamming in their faces). Margolin suggests that one incentive to change is that social workers are victims, too.

Under the Cover of Kindness will have a secure place among books that help us understand the hidden functions of professions. It is in the tradition of books by writers such as Thomas Szasz, Michel Foucault, and Erving Goffman. Such books bring to our attention the soft underbelly of professional helping—its dark, unrecognized side—actions and consequences that we may reject if we care enough to recognize them. Readers will have to ask "is the view presented accurate?" Professionals who value comfort rather than enlightenment and critical appraisal will no doubt pretend neutrality while continuing to manipulate clients.

This book has a dual purpose: on the one hand, an examination of how social work uses power; on the other, an attempt to analyze the mechanics of social work language, to show how what is said to be in clients' interests, in their language, is really in social work's interests, in social work language. My hope is to go beyond some solemn show of unmasking and probe the mystification that transforms social work into a power that is seamless, invisible, and ubiquitous.

The starting point of this book, as well as my earlier book, *Goodness Personified*, is a feeling that virtue is neglected as an academic topic. We have all sorts of journals and courses on problems, deviance, and violence, but goodness gets little or no attention. Somehow trouble is "constructed," hence fascinating, the repository of all sorts of historical and ideological attributions, while charity and benevolence are "natural," hence dull, too obvious to warrant close scrutiny.

The story of social work as virtue, as helping and empowerment, may be familiar, but in my opinion it is neither "natural" nor obvious. The question I ask in this book is whether we can peer behind the familiar images to locate meanings more ironic than lofty, where self-interest poses as knowledge, and knowledge is an instrument of power. Of course, all this has a perverse effect: the language that attempts to deconstruct is seen as a polemic—"the author has an ax to grind"—while the language that purges consciousness of ideology is seen as neutral, objective. Let there be no mistake—this effort to track down the political tactics hidden within social work imposes a point of view: all the evidence was assembled specifically for the purpose of challenging the prevailing common sense of social work. At the same, I hope readers consider how not challenging the traditional appearances and motivations of social work (or any discipline) also imposes a point of view. I hope readers consider how social work's mild-mannered eclecticism may be the most presumptuous ideology of all since it pretends to have no ideology.

I selected social work because it seems to me that it has so far been dealt with very mildly. Also, I have some familiarity with the field: I have an MSW and worked in the profession for seventeen years before moving on to sociology and academia.

As the book's opening quotation suggests, the intellectual model and inspiration for this book comes from Foucault. The book's vision of social work also comes from the writings of several authors concerned with understanding the practices and assumptions underlying the relations between language and power: Friedrich Nietzsche, Creel Froman, George Orwell, Melvin Pollner, Murray Edelman, William Ryan, Stanley Cohen, Roland Barthes, Kingsley Davis, C. W. Mills.

Chapter 9 is based on a paper titled "Deviance on Record: Techniques for Labeling Child Abusers in Official Documents," which I published in *Social Problems* in 1992 (vol. 39, no. 1, pp. 58–70). I gratefully acknowledge the University of California Press for extending permission to use that material.

I wish to thank the people who read drafts and offered direction: Joel Best, Thom Carlson, Tom Corbett, Norman Denzin, Paul Durrenberger, Nancy Essig, Eileen Gambrill, Richard Hilbert, Donileen Loseke, John Nelson, Fred Redekop, David Shumway. Virginia Travis and Reta Litton from the University of Iowa were extremely helpful in getting the manuscript typed and formatted.

I cannot imagine writing this book without the feedback and advice from my wife, Mary. I thank her for giving this text so many patient readings.

Under the Cover of Kindness

O n a warm summer day in 1993, a five-year-old boy, Jamie Brown, wan-
dered away from his farm home in rural Iowa and managed to get to a
nearby highway. Joy Brown, the boy's mother, did not notice his departure
because she was busy laying her infant daughter down for a nap. She thought
he was watching a video with his older brother. As things turned out, there
was no cause for alarm: a motorist picked young Jamie up and immediately
took him to the police station. He was returned home in about an hour. End
of incident.[1]

Beginning of investigation. A social worker was dispatched to the Browns'
home, asked several questions, inspected the premises, and shared her findings with her supervisor. The social worker learned that Jamie is an autis-
tic child and ordinarily is well cared for. He has three siblings, his father is
a welder, and his family is new in the community. The final determination:
Jamie's mother was cited for child neglect. "The fact that the child suffers
from communication disability is in no way a factor in this finding," the letter from the social service agency explained. "No child of that age should be
unsupervised in traffic upon a busy highway." Joy Brown's penalty: her name
will appear for ten years on a state-run child abuse registry, sharing space
with those who torture, molest, and kill children. Also, she is not allowed to
adopt a child, be a foster parent, or work in a child-care business.

This was not done in a hostile or punitive way. Quite the contrary. When
the case was reviewed, social workers acknowledged that "the mother of this
child has been an exemplary parent-under very trying circumstances caused
by the child's disability. . . . He took advantage of the mother's momentary
distraction to wander away." In the words of the social services adminis-
trator, "There are good people on the Child Abuse Registry. People don't

always do what they should do. That doesn't mean they're good or bad. It in no way reflects on them."

There is a temptation to treat this story as an example of bureaucracy gone berserk. I offer it instead as a parable in which each element refers to what Foucault called the "carceral network": the solemn judgment, the evocation of normality, the false reassurance ("there are good people on the Child Abuse Registry"), the bringing of "the infinitesimal universe of unimportant irregularities and disturbances" into discourse.[2] All this, reproduced in any social work investigation, is here assembled, concentrated, organized in a very brief sequence of fact and gesture.

What are the social and cultural preconditions for this chain of events? What organic complexity underlies this simple tale? *Under the Cover of Kindness* is an attempt to answer such questions. The constellation of ideas and techniques that are expressed in the investigation of Jamie's family has a long history. It reaches deep into American culture and invites our serious attention.

This book examines how social workers developed the capacity to enter people's private spaces, to observe family interactions, and to record what they saw. It examines how the everyday existence of ordinary people became a topic of biographical writing.

My central premise is that prior to social work, political surveillance was more or less restricted to public domains—streets, businesses, schools. With social work, however, it became possible to keep track of marginal and common people in their homes as they pursued the most personal activities.[3]

What Is Social Work?

The meaning of *social work* has always been incredibly unclear. In social work textbooks, it appears as an umbrella term that encompasses the widest range of practice—individual, family, and group therapy, settlement work, community organization, service delivery of almost any variety. Given the fact that any of these vary to some degree depending on the nature of the sponsoring agency and funding source—public welfare, government initiatives, private charity, child protection, courts, corrections, hospitals, schools—the effort to define social work almost always ends in the greatest muddle.

A second complication is that the things social workers do cannot be restricted to any one profession or group of people. Physicians, psychologists, counselors of all kinds—even nurses, agricultural agents, home economists—can act as social workers because social work is a type of power, a way of seeing things, that traverses every kind of institution or profession, linking them, making them converge and function in a new way. Social work is not a thing that is possessed by social workers. Nor, to add to the confusion, is it a thing social workers always do. We see confirmation of this every day as more and more people trained and certified as social workers are calling themselves "therapists," focusing their attentions on middle-class clients who do not appear to need the kinds of protection and advocacy that social workers have traditionally provided.[4]

Surely an extraordinarily wide and elusive number of services and practices fall under the heading *social work*. Yet it is also true that a core technology and culture can be identified. It is this core, not the exceptions and deviations, that is the focus of my book.

Curiously, Harry Specht and Mark Courtney support the idea of a "core" profession in their book *Unfaithful Angels*, even as they appear to lament social work's loss of faith in its basic values and techniques. These authors note that as many as 40 percent of the members of the National Association of Social Workers (NASW) are in some type of private practice, performing some type of "popular psychotherapy"—psychoanalysis, reality therapy, humanistic therapy, neo-Freudian therapy, behavior therapy, gestalt therapy, Rogerian therapy, existential therapy—leaving a growing proportion of traditional social work positions in publicly supported social services agencies to be filled "by people who have, at best, only bachelor's level training in social work."[5] However, Specht and Courtney also insist that social work's traditional "core" continues as its defining concept. Their use of the passive voice, suggesting divine or natural origin, is instructive: "Most professionals who opt for private practice remove themselves from the problems, settings, and populations that *social work was created* to deal with. Psychotherapy practiced privately is not a bad or evil thing; it's just not social work"[6] (italics added).

For our purposes, it is important to keep in mind that despite the vast numbers of defectors, the overall number of social workers and social work positions has not declined. In fact, both are at record levels. In 1992, the National Association of Social Workers counted 140,000 members, and the 1986 U.S. Census counted between 365,000 and 500,000 people engaged in occupations classified as social work.[7]

That an increasing number of people with the MSW degree become "therapists" does not demonstrate a crisis in "faith" in the social work profession. It shows rather that social workers, like everybody else, make career decisions based on their self-interest. We should not be surprised that social workers leave their traditional field of practice when something more lucrative and comfortable, such as private practice, becomes available. This is just common sense.

The interesting question for me is not why social workers are "unfaithful" to some original calling but, rather, why they are so often uncomfortable practicing it. I want to know why social workers are so ready to bail out. But instead of blaming difficult work conditions, inflexible bureaucracy, uncooperative and unappreciative clients, as is true of other books addressing "burnout" in the social work profession, I point the finger at the profession itself—at a tradition that forces social workers into the most debilitating sorts of denial, hypocrisy, and double binds. My take on the matter, then, is that "the problem" is not that social workers are abandoning the core mission; the problem *is* the core mission.

So what is social work? What is this thing that so many people with MSWs are abandoning? First, to repeat, it is a commitment to service to the poor in community-based nonprofit agencies. Second, it is a commitment to reaching out: social work does not wait for clients to come to it (as is the case in the popular psychotherapies); it goes to them. Third, social work involves a deployment of techniques that are highly symbolic and personalistic: support, advocacy, affection, trust, empathy.[8] Fourth, it stands for a commitment to the case-by-case, social worker-to-client mode of helping identified with Mary Richmond—a type of helping that requires keeping the most prodigious files on individual cases.

This last point is controversial because it conflicts with the practice and philosophy of social work's central icon, the social reformer and founder of Hull House, Jane Addams. My point is that social workers may claim Jane Addams as their source of inspiration, but they *do* Mary Richmond. To put it in a nutshell, social workers attempt to change individuals and families, while social reformers such as Jane Addams aim to change institutions and culture. Here is how Richmond saw the difference: "Social casework does different things for and with people—it specializes and differentiates; social reform generalizes and simplifies by discovering ways of doing the same thing for everybody."[9]

For her part, Jane Addams did not support the professionalization of social work. She even disliked being called a social worker.[10] She refused to call the people she worked with clients or cases, preferring instead the term *neighbor*. Most importantly, she did not believe in keeping files on her "neighbors." In short, Addams was opposed to the way most social workers did social work, as illustrated by her assessment of charity visiting:

> Let us take a neighborhood of poor people, and test their ethical standards by those of the charity visitor, who comes first with the best desire in the world to help them out of their distress. A most striking incongruity, at once apparent, is the difference between the emotional kindness with which relief is given by one poor neighbor to another poor neighbor, and the guarded care with which relief is given by a charity visitor to a charity recipient. The neighborhood mind is at once confronted not only by the difference in method; but by an absolute clashing of two ethical standards.[11]

The social work examined in this book traces its lineage—its "core"—to the very charity visiting that Jane Addams so vigorously rejected. In sharp contrast to Jane Addams's mode of practice,[12] the social work examined here refuses to affiliate with social reform platforms, political agendas, political parties. And so, while there have been such things as radical and reformist social work, it is important to recognize that the history of radicalism and reform within "core" social work has been mostly fitful and discontinuous. In general, when social workers criticized the agencies that employed them, it was to decry the lack of funding and support. Rarely were social agencies, and their modalities of intervention, criticized *as such*.[13] In the words of Edward T. Devine, "It was the first duty of social workers to be persistently and aggressively non-partisan, to maintain such relations with men of social goodwill in all parties as well as insure their cooperation in specific measures for the promotion of the common good."[14]

This is not to say that social work is not political. In fact, it is social work's very rejection of political motive that makes it so politically effective. Precisely because its overall look and feel is nonexclusionary and nondivisive, it is able to create and reinforce popular beliefs about who is worthy and who is unworthy, who should be rewarded and who repressed.[15] It arouses little opposition as it establishes superior and subordinate roles because it does not explicitly stand for promoting one group over another—it simply wishes to "promote the common good."

As we shall see, the main functions of social work are not to alleviate poverty nor to train useful citizens. Rather, social work stabilizes middle-class power by creating an observable, discussable, write-about-able poor. Through social work, "the trivial ceases to belong to silence, to passing rumor or to fleeting avowal. All those things which make up the ordinary, the unimportant detail, the obscurity, the days without glory, the common life, can and must be said,—better, written."[16]

The Book's Strategy

This leads to what is probably the most provocative question about social work. To what degree was it (is it) intentional, calculating, consciously plotting? My answer is that it is absurd to speak of anyone inventing or formulating social work as a strategy of oppression. Social work does not understand itself creating or sustaining social divisions; rather, it depicts itself discovering and responding to such phenomena as independently established facts. Second, social workers are as much in the dark as anyone else. This is not because they are stupid or shallow or naive. The very opposite is true. Because social work is able to carry on its activities only by remaining oblivious to its use of power, a critical part of its survival involves creating new ways to keep itself oblivious. That is social work's ultimate sophistication: to consciously induce unconsciousness, and then to find ways to forget that unconsciousness is being induced in the first place.

What does all this mean for this book? If social work constitutes itself and its world by forgetting its constitutive work, and if part of that constitutive work includes that very forgetfulness, then we must address ourselves to the ways this vital incomprehension is perpetuated.[17] Only by understanding how social workers mystify themselves can we understand how their field of knowledge survives. And, moreover, only by recognizing that the processes of mystification are continually shifting, continually covering themselves in new ways, can we have any chance of identifying that which must always be hidden: power, self-interest, hierarchical domination.

This book is about how social work manages to keep both itself and its clients from being aware of what is taking place so that it can keep on doing what it has always done. In recognition of this ingenuity, I completely reject the perennial argument that social work is atheoretical—that its approach is more or less ad hoc, pragmatic, a method whose execution depends on coming to terms with the more or less circumscribed features relevant to the needed action; that it is no deeper nor more complex than common sense; that it exists only in the moment. Instead, I treat social work as if it were a meticulously coordinated and crafted construction. I do this by suspending conventional interest in the topics of social work's practical activities and emphasize instead how social workers use these activities to assemble evidences of the particular mythologies that support and legitimize their efforts.

Accordingly, unlike other studies addressing social work and social control, I do not make my case by bundling together all the most strident quotations I could find in which social workers proclaim the evils of the poor and the need to civilize and regulate them.[18] Instead, I bundle together statements on social workers' friendliness and sincerity, not to prove something about social work's essential friendliness and sincerity, but to illustrate that social work is able to carry on its activities only by continually elaborating its elevated motives and good intentions.

I am not interested in social work horror stories, evidences of brutality, or lapses and failures in social work technique. Rather, I am interested in how social work produces trust, conviction, ways of seeing things. Thus, I examine the methods by which social work creates and sustains subjects (persons with individual identities), relationships, statuses, and contexts of agency. In particular, I examine how positive imagery and "doing good" energize and direct this discourse.[19]

My goal is to show that we always have social work at the same time as—and precisely because—we have the belief that it is "doing good," and that the more intense the belief in social work's essential goodness, the more immune it is to criticism, and the less clients are able to resist its ministrations. This is why social workers are continually engaged in providing proof for themselves and their clients of the honorableness, sacredness, and utter veracity of their actions. Social workers are then able to appear to clients (and to themselves) as trustworthy—and can therefore enter clients' homes, make small talk, and hear the most shameful disclosures.

Other Strategies

In keeping with Foucault's view that genealogy "requires patience and a knowledge of details," I attempted to put together a broad accumulation of source materials, paying particular attention to the minutiae of social work stories: their central images and ironies, who takes the lead and who follows, how success and failure are defined.[20] There are essentially two sources of data for the book: social workers' case records, and the books, pamphlets, and articles written by and for social workers on how to perform social work—how to gain entry into clients' homes, to direct interviews, to gain trust, to question, to probe, to overcome resistances.

The documents that I have gathered together to illustrate social work's techniques are fairly homogeneous. In fact, they would be monotonous if it were not for the tension between what social work includes and what it excludes, between the things it recounts and its ways of recounting them, between what it does and what it says it does, between "those who complain and beseech and those who have the power over them; . . . between the minuscule order of problems raised and the enormity of the power set to work."[21]

In other words, the social work narratives that appear on the surface always seem to suggest underlying counternarratives: When social work describes its clients one way, all the other infinite ways those clients could be described are excluded. When social work establishes one reality, it necessarily blocks others: it is both positive and negative, simultaneously. What I constantly looked out for, then, is how social work denies, deflects, and silences at the very same time it produces, forms knowledge, and induces pleasure; how alongside all that makes it appear good and wholesome, all that makes it accepted, there is a subtle opposition threatening to undo it.

I pursued these counternarratives in a very self-conscious manner: Whenever I saw tradition giving a certain meaning to social work, I attempted to imagine the implications of the reverse or opposite interpretation. I consciously juxtaposed incongruous words, images, and motives onto social work. The master reversal, of course, was to interpret helping as domination.

Do such reversals create a biased (and negative) portrait of social work? No doubt, but to tell the truth, I do not think this is a fair way to state the problem. It suggests some natural dichotomy between biased and nonbiased writing, between texts that are pure (objective) and those that impose some viewpoint. I believe that social work, like everything else, is a story and can be told in different ways. I use *story* here to refer to the organizing theme that transforms any chronicle or history into a coherent whole. Stories weave facts together. And because this weaving is a mental operation and not an object available to direct observation, it cannot be described as true or false. It is rather a scheme we impose on facts to create order and meaning, for our purposes, not God's or Nature's. This is what I mean when I refer to the "invention" of social work. Although its meanings are cloaked in Truth, they are not "found" in the events of history but are planted there—imaginatively.

The story I tell in this book has storytellers as its central characters; its plot turns on the idea that they do not see themselves as storytellers at all but rather as "truth-tellers." Accordingly, social workers treat their world as a given rather than as an accomplishment. Their world and its exhibited properties are not constituted by virtue of their having been investigated, recorded, filed away. For social workers, the objects of investigation offer themselves as a priori, resistive, recalcitrant, and massively organized structures to which they must adapt themselves. What I bring to all this is simply the argument that social workers' methods of fact finding and fact display are themselves determinative, organizing, producing. This book's central question, then, is not how adequately social work's methods address society's "real" problems but how social work manages to claim it is addressing real problems, and how those claims become socially enforceable facts in their own right.

Social work stories are my topic. The case histories cited in this book are not used as evidence of larger events; they are the "events." By attending to the case histories themselves, I show how social work entails not only the imposition of surveillance and control in the heretofore closed space of the home but also the constant justification of this intervention as charitable and disinterested help. This book is about how social workers invent their field of knowledge as they simultaneously invent themselves.

What Follows

The book begins by describing the cultural climate in which social work emerged. In particular, I note the enormous demographic upswing in American cities during the second half of the nineteenth century, the rapid influx of foreigners, and the sudden appearance of an inspirational discourse on "the problem of the poor." That discourse provided a series of compelling explanations and justifications, what C. W. Mills called "vocabularies of motive,"[22] for investigating and writing about the impoverished foreigner: darkness and disease, murder and starvation, child abuse and neglect, wife beating, drunkenness, welfare fraud. These images together and singly stimulated suspicion and distrust sufficient for all manner of intrusions and monitoring, inspiring a second, technical discourse on how this monitoring should be accomplished. As the book proceeds, we examine the methods by which social work used power—the systems of information collection and surveillance, the use of archives, the rules that were or were not explicit, the arguments and reasons.

The overall organization of the book consists of three main divisions: in the first, *Basic Social Work*, consisting of chapters 1–4, my main purpose is to identify and illustrate social work's defining techniques—its methods of gaining entry, interviewing, and writing. Most of the references in these chapters are from the 1890s through the 1930s.

In the second section, *Aggressive Social Work*, chapters 5–7, I examine the years from about 1950 to 1975, a time when discourse on home visiting ("reaching the hard-to-reach") was particularly explicit and insistent. My purpose here is to exemplify the most aggressive and patronizing forms of social work in order to set up a contrast with the contemporary period in chapters 8–12.

The closing chapters, grouped under the heading *Empowering Social Work*, portray a profession that appears to represent a questioning or even radical reversal of the earlier "aggressive" social work. What I show instead is how the various innovations and reforms devoted to empowering clients, to equalizing and personalizing their relations with social workers, represent a continuation and, in some ways, an intensification of earlier patterns. This is not because the innovations failed. Rather, the changes that appeared so humane and progressive made it possible for social work to continue. Only by convincing itself and others that social work changed was social work able to stay the same.

That the book is structured chronologically is thus not intended to show that social workers from any earlier era were fundamentally different and/ or better or worse than the later ones. I do not make a case for change or progress. I make my case for constancy. Instead of describing social work history as one of linear, chronological development, as is usually done, I reverse the narrative. Instead of showing how the methods of the volunteers and do-gooders from earlier times were supplanted by the increasingly sophisticated methods of trained professionals, my story emphasizes continuity. I show that despite superficial shifts in claims and style, the basic practice is the same: people from one social class go into the homes of people belonging to another; they write biographies of these people; they judge what is normal and abnormal; they call it "doing good."

Part 1
Basic Social Work

CHAPTER 1

The Birth of the Investigation

> Look into any of these houses, everywhere the same piles of rags, of mal-
> odorous bones and musty paper, all of which the sanitary police flatter
> themselves they have banished to the dumps and warehouses. Here is a
> "flat" of "parlor" and two pitch-black coops called bedrooms. Truly, the
> bed is all there is room for. . . . One, two, three beds are there, if the old
> boxes and heaps of foul straw can be called by that name; a broken stove
> with crazy pipe from which smoke leaks at every joint, a table of rough
> boards propped up on boxes, piles of rubbish in the corner. The closeness
> and smell are appalling. How many people sleep here? The woman with
> the red bandanna shakes her head silently, but the bare-legged girl with
> the bright face counts on her fingers—five, six!
>
> **Jacob Riis, *How the Other Half Lives* (1890)**

At the end of the nineteenth century, the number of charity investigators in the United States suddenly exploded, tripling over a span of
ten years: from 1,419 paid agents and "friendly visitors" in 1882 to 4,202 in
1892.[1] How do we explain this?

It is hardly coincidental that the investigative impulse took off during the
years described as "the golden age of public health," the years when Americans finally accepted the idea that the human body is the host to millions of
tiny organisms that cause diseases such as tuberculosis, cholera, and plague,
and that there is a close connection between social conditions, living habits, poverty, and the spread of diseases.[2] Public health became a justification
for all kinds of inspections, home visiting, monitoring, and registration; in
particular, this involved the poor, who had always been seen as unsanitary,
unclean, diffuse sources of contagion. In the words of one public health ex-
aminer: "The medical history of a breakdown from tuberculosis, to be complete, involves a study of almost all that a man has ever done or has ever been
subjected to. . . . Tuberculosis is not a patch on the fabric of life—it is woven
into the warp and woof of life."[3]

The incredible pace of urban growth also promoted the impulse to investigate. The numbers are astonishing. Chicago had a population of 29,963 in

1850, 109,260 in 1860, 298,977 in 1870, 503,185 in 1880, 1,099,850 in 1890, 1,698,575 in 1900.[4] New York City and Brooklyn had a total population of 1,080,330 in 1860, 1,338,391 in 1870, 1,772,962 in 1880, 2,321,202 in 1890, and 3,337,202 in 1900.[5] Because faces and bodies of all backgrounds and classes were abruptly thrown together—"the beggar brushes against the millionaire, the rag-picker's cart blocks the way where the carriage of the Fifth Avenue belle would fain pass, and the ragged newsboy sells a paper to an Astor or Vanderbilt"—there was a craving for words that could be matched to the visual impressions.[6] Physical proximity unaccompanied by biographical information stimulated curiosity, "lonesomeness, . . . the feeling that the individual is surrounded on all sides by closed doors," and fears of unnamed violence and contagion.[7]

William I. Cole captured these anxieties in the opening lines to his introduction to *The City Wilderness*, a collection of essays published in 1899 on the newly emerged poverty ghettos of Boston. "Isolated and congested working-class quarters, with all the dangers to moral and material well-being that they present," he wrote, "grow along with the growth of our great cities."[8] The poor were threatening, according to Cole, because they lived so far from the established populations and their spheres of influence: "What chance . . . have American ideas and influences to penetrate these compact, self-contained groups, transported bodily, as it were, from a foreign world?"[9] But it was not just the geographic and cultural separation between the established and immigrant populations that created anxiety. Congestion was also a source of suspicion because it was associated with filth, disease, and, above all, sexual immodesty: overcrowding forced boys and girls, men and women, into the most dangerous proximity.[10] There was the general conviction that the moral atmosphere surrounding the poor was as pestilential as the physical.[11]

Given the sudden convergence in the metropolis of different races, classes, nationalities, languages, faiths, customs, and political ideas, it is not surprising that people were profoundly suspicious of one another, and that the monied classes were fearful of uprisings and mass violence, as if the entire community might at any moment erupt into a carnival of murder and crime. It is also understandable that the impoverished foreigner would be the focus of these fears.[12] Because the sudden accumulation of people mainly occurred among the foreign born and impoverished, because these people lived in separate districts and were mostly unheard and unknown, their very existence created economic, political, and medical panic.[13] Thus, the Haymarket Square riot of 1886 is significant, not so much because someone threw a bomb at a labor union meeting, killing and wounding many police and bystanders, but rather because a whole class of people—the poor, especially the immigrant poor—was held responsible.[14]

Broadly, one can say this fear originated from the well-to-do urbanites' recognition that they shared the city with unknown masses of people who lived on the fringe of starvation. Consider the story of "The Man with a Knife."

> A man stood at the corner of Fifth Avenue and Fourteenth Street the other day, looking gloomily at the carriages that rolled by, carrying the wealth and fashion of the avenues to and from the big stores down town. He was poor, and hungry, and ragged. This thought was in his mind: "They behind their well-fed teams have no thought for the morrow; they know hunger only by name, and ride down to spend in an hour's shopping what would keep me and my little ones from want a whole year." There arose before him the picture of those little ones crying for bread around the cold and cheerless hearth—then he sprang into the throng and slashed about him with a knife, blindly seeking to kill, to revenge.[15]

This story is important, not for what it reveals of some hypothetical or real impoverished man, but for what it reveals of the storyteller and his audience. It is a screen memory of their fear: "The man was arrested, of course, and locked up. To-day he is probably in a mad-house, forgotten. And the carriages roll by to and fro from the big stores with their gay throng of shoppers. The world forgets easily, too easily, what it does not like to remember." [16]

The story ends with the maniac locked in a "mad-house, forgotten," but this is not offered as a remedy or solution. Instead, this ending is a warning: forgetting, denial, and exclusion make it possible for such eruptions to recur. What is needed instead is knowledge, inquiry, heightened awareness of the offender's mind, environment, and motivations. This shift, this "master change," as Stanley Cohen called it,[17] emphasized that we should study not only the circumstances of the crime but also its causes, to know the story of the criminal's life, "from the triple point of view of psychology, social position, and upbringing, in order to discover the dangerous proclivities of the first, the harmful predispositions of the second, and the bad antecedents of the third." [18] The new emphasis on biography established not only the offender as existing before (and apart from) the offense, but also the hypothetical—what could happen, who might be to blame—as social control's central domain. Investigations, home visits, in-depth interviews, fact gathering, note taking, and maintaining records of all kinds thus assumed new importance because the object of correction was no longer a single act, or series of acts, but the sum total existence of the offender.

To place this shift in relief, we need only compare investigative literature from the 1870s with similar literature from the 1890s. Thus, when Charles Loring Brace examined "the problem of the poor" in his *Dangerous Classes of New York*, he devoted little attention to their domestic spaces, their homes, and their family relationships. Instead, "the problem" was almost exclusively the abandoned child or "street waif," the person living outside a "home" and away from a family—"ragged young girls who had nowhere to lay their heads; children driven from drunken homes; orphans who slept where they could find a box or a stairway; boys cast out by step-mothers or step-fathers; newsboys, whose incessant answer to our question, 'Where do you live?' rung in our ears, 'Do not live nowhere!' little bootblacks, young peddlers 'canawl-boys,' who seem to drift into the city every winter and live a vagabond life; pickpockets and petty thieves trying to get honest work; child beggars and flower-sellers growing up to enter courses of crime." [19]

By the 1890s, however, the "problem of the poor" was no longer restricted to the public domain of the street. A number of books and articles suddenly appeared that were devoted to describing and interpreting the domestic space of slum dwellers. Although the authors of these works came from a variety of backgrounds and professions, they had a common perspective. They each had a foothold of some type in the foreign colony—a settlement,[20] mission, church, newsbeat—that permitted continual observation of private places and domestic relations that until then had been completely unexplored.

Jacob Riis's investigations became legendary: the police reporter for the *New York Tribune* who was on easy and familiar terms with the immigrant poor, haunting their districts, uncovering their secrets, gathering stories such as that of a hardworking man and wife, a young couple from the country, "who took poison together in a Crosby Street tenement because they were 'tired,'" and of the mother of six who lived in two rooms with her husband, children, and an aged grandmother, the first room serving as parlor, bedroom, and eating-room, and the other, a small hall-room, serving as kitchen. She threw "herself from a window, and was carried up from the street dead. She was 'discouraged,' said some of the women from the tenement." [21]

These stories transmitted images of the poor that turn-of-the-century Americans accepted as self-evidently real. They silently organized perceptions of the poor, transforming them into objects suitable for study and writing, into objects that should be investigated and described by those who could carry out these tasks, the educated and well-to-do. Consider, for example, Jane Addams's story of a peasant woman "straight from the fields of Germany," whose "two years in America had been spent in patiently carrying water up and down two flights of stairs, and in washing the heavy flannel suits of iron-foundry workers. . . . Three of her daughters had fallen victims to the vice of the city. The mother was bewildered and distressed, but understood nothing. We were able to induce the betrayer of one daughter to marry her; the second, after a tedious lawsuit, supported his child; with the third we were able to do nothing." [22]

Because the stories were about the poor, and those who read and wrote

them were from the upper classes, a division was established between viewers and viewed, subjects and objects. To their new biographers, the poor became something to be experienced, judged; a group to which things must be
done, changed. Riis and Addams gave the slum dwellers a voice, it is true,
but organized that voice into something weak and pitiable—"the mother
was bewildered and distressed, but understood nothing." Although the slum
dwellers were now credited with speech, they had no immediate understanding of their own activities or relationships.

A contrast was thus established between the poor who are "without
leisure or energy for anything but the gain of subsistence . . . [who] live for
the moment side by side, many of them without knowledge of each other,
without fellowship, without local tradition or public spirit, without social organization of any kind," and the people who can provide the remedies, "the
people who . . . have the social tact and training, the large houses, and the
traditions and customs of hospitality."[23]

This emphasis on the passivity and nonreflexivity of the poor, and the
parallel agency and reflexivity of the well-to-do, found expression even in the
narrative style of these books. Helen Campbell, for example, in her *Darkness
and Daylight in New York*, took readers on visits to the homes of the poor,
treating the poor as stationary exhibits and the readers as tourists, enacting a
double objectification. Thus, Campbell and the doctor who accompanied
her tour the homes of the poor and gaze at them, and the reader, in turn, is
made to identify with their gaze, to see the poor as writers see them, as *these*
writers saw them, as parts of their environment rather than its inhabitants,
not as responsible for their own poverty but as a condition of it, blended
with it, as part of a single image:

> Our eyes, which had gradually accustomed themselves to the darkness,
> could now dimly make out doors here and there, one of which the doctor
> opened and passed through. A dim light came from windows crusted with
> dirt. It fell on little save walls in the same dirty condition, and with a mat-
> tress black with age in one corner on the floor; a tiny cooking-stove, one
> leg gone and its place supplied by a brick, a table propped against the wall
> for the same reason, and a single rickety chair. On a shelf were few dishes,
> and on the stove an old tomato-can held water. No wild beast's den could
> offer a more hopeless prospect for a human being, yet on the mattress a
> human being lay, and turned heavy eyes toward the doctor.[24]

Just as the images of sunlight and open air became identified at the turn of
the century as sources of health and well-being, as disease-fighting agents, so
in tours of the slums, darkness appeared as the alien element that had to be
penetrated and opposed for healthful relations to exist. Darkness was the
master metaphor for disease, filth, secrecy, foreignness; all that discriminated
the viewed from the viewers, the lower classes from the upper.[25]

All through the North End and some parts of the West End and "the Cove," there abound dark courts, often-times reached only by a tunnel, that are almost entirely barren of sunlight. For instance, there is a court off North Street, reached by a tunnel such as I have described, where the tenement houses are three deep from the street. The inside tenement, facing on the court, through most of the year is densely packed with people. For a large part of the length of the court it is only four feet wide, and the front windows of the house, which is three stories in height, look out on the dark wall which is only four feet away. On a dark day there is scarcely any light at all in these rooms; and on the brightest sunshiny day there is only a little light during the middle of the day, and never any direct rays of sun. I found, up in one of these rooms, a young woman with her first-born in her arms,—a pale, sickly little child, not yet a year old, that will certainly die before the summer is out, if it stays there. . . . Their faces look like potato-vines that have sprouted and grown in the cellar. They are dying for lack of sunshine and pure air.[26]

The critical point is that beside these images is a directive: to open, to expose, to let in the light of day. Yet the directive was never simply to overcome the darkness. It was to expose what the darkness hid: immorality, vice, neglect, abuse. Thus Riis's invitation for readers to peer into "hidden hovels," "unseen burrows," "pitch-black coops called bedrooms," is the invitation to examine a world "prolific of untold depravities."[27]

Child abuse and neglect, first of all. Contrary to what we have come to believe in the histories of social problems,[28] child abuse was not "discovered" in the 1960s but existed within turn-of-the-century texts as one of the most compelling of all justifications for investigating the homes of the poor, writing about them, judging them. In Campbell's 1891 text alone, an entire chapter was devoted to this topic, with four engraved photographs of scarred and bruised children:

> Here is a boy barely ten years old, whose left eye is nearly destroyed, and whose ears have been partially torn from his head by a drunken father, who at the same time threw the eighteen-months old baby across the room and beat his wife till she escaped and ran to the street for help. . . .
> Here . . . is a picture of the body of an eleventh-months baby starved to death by a drunken mother. The little frame is only a skeleton, and the pitiful face has a strange smile.[29]

Jacob Riis's *Children of the Poor* also contains some of the most graphic and emotional child abuse imagery ever produced. For example, at the end of his chapter on child abuse, there is a drawing of what appears to be a board. The caption underneath reads: "Club with which a four-year-old child was brutally beaten."[30] Earlier, there is the photograph of "case No. 25,745," a seven-year-old girl named Annie, "as she was driven forth by her cruel step-mother, beaten and starved, with her arms tied upon her back." In this profile shot, her dress is pulled down, exposing the scars on her arms. However, there is a second photo of Annie, posed in a silk dress and pearls, looking confidently into the camera "after six months in the Society's care."[31] The message: readers need not recoil from images of depravity and abuse because there are cures, reforms, remedies, solutions. In each of the before-and-after photos within these texts, the "before" shot shows someone dressed in rags, looking "poor," and the "after" photo reveals someone wearing newly pressed, expensive looking clothing, visual evidence of the healing power of class.

The whole point is that these cures do not occur by virtue of scientific knowledge or skill but by the grace and stewardship "of those who hold in trust the largest possessions of wealth and the larger possessions of heart and intellect."[32] In particular, it was the responsibility of upper-class women— they were the ones best suited to visiting the poor in their homes—because they had the specific sensibilities and education fitted to redeeming the degraded and low. "First," wrote Susan I. Lesley, "in most of our homes are servants and dependents, and the poor to whom they are related, and to whom, through them, we have been brought into relations. If we have been habitually just, kind, patient and considerate in these relations, inspired by a deep feeling of responsibility to *them*, as well as to ourselves, in exacting faithful service, we have gone far towards being educated for visitors."[33]

Some writers cautioned against drawing too negative a picture of the poor, against emphasizing debauchery and corruption at the expense of more ordinary and commonplace images.[34] Jane Addams, for example, regretted that the problems of the poor are often "confounded with the problems of the inefficient, the idle, and distressed."[35] But one dark image was present even among investigators seeking a more positive, balanced portrait: the drunken bum.

> There was a step leading down to a narrow cellar room lighted only by one dirt-encrusted window, and containing a dirty bed in one corner, a broken backed chair, a three-legged table, and a rickety stove. In the chair was seated a crying woman, with a deep cut across her cheek; a baby lay in her lap and five children huddled about her. In a corner, on some rags, groaning and telling her beads, lay an old woman, while across the bed was thrown the body of a man who breathed heavily in a drunken sleep. It is a frequent story, and he who runs may read. First, a carouse in any saloon of the neighborhood; then, on getting home, the agreeable pastime of beating his wife and children, throwing the few remaining dishes at the old grandmother, one of them taking the wife's cheek in flight.[36]

Drunkenness appeared not only as the root cause of child abuse, neglect, and wife beating but also as the cause of poverty itself. For charity investigators, it served as the all-purpose explanation, the condition that explained the problems accruing to poverty as well as what made the poor unresponsive to aid, what trapped them, leaving them incapable of bettering themselves.

But poverty was problematic not merely as a cause or consequence of depravity. It was a source of suspicion in its own right. The very existence of poverty was treated as questionable, a possible ruse, requiring the most cynical, minute investigation:

> It was only last winter that the officers of the Society for the Prevention of Cruelty to Children arrested an Italian woman who was begging along Madison Avenue with a poor little wreck of a girl, whose rags and pinched face were calculated to tug hard at the purse-strings of a miser. Over five dollars in nickels and pennies were taken from the woman's pockets, and when her story of poverty and hunger was investigated at the family's home in a Baxter Street tenement, bank-books turned up that showed the Masonis to be regular pauper capitalists, able to draw their check for three thousand dollars, had they been so disposed.[37]

Frauds and impostors, loafers and malingerers, were everywhere: "The poor man who preferred to work rather than to beg, was supplanted by the pauper, who preferred to beg rather than to work. It was a comparatively easy matter for a professional pauper to utilize the charity of several different societies, especially those which were religious, for the support of himself and his family; while shrewd knaves, who saw the market value of an infirmity or deformity, organized an army of cripples of every sort, whom they stationed at the corners of the streets, or through whom they invaded the homes of the compassionate."[38]

What remains is to recognize that the investigations these images inspired were defined and defended in terms completely different than those associated with detective work and police action. Again and again, social workers renounced the presumption that investigation was intended to exclude, repress, control: "Investigation is not as some may judge it to be, simply a contrivance to reduce the number of applicants. It is not a menace. Its purpose is kind. It is to obtain definite knowledge of those facts which may determine the relief to be given."[39]

No one disputed that the charity "investigation cannot be too thorough or extensive or painstaking or the record too careful" or that investigators must constantly be on the lookout for fraud, of unknowingly "giving to those that have already and are deceiving us."[40] Yet these imperatives were never seen as contradicting the core belief that the charity investigation is conducted "solely for the purpose of ascertaining whether and in what way help can be given."[41] Accordingly, even if investigations uncovered all manner of deceit, malingering, and vice, it was still possible to defend investigation as an expression of benevolence: "I only repeat the teachings of the great body of my instructors and fellows when I declare emphatically that the sole purpose of the investigation and the permanent record is the increase, and not the decrease, of charity."[42]

Visiting the poor was described as an exalted occupation, a "higher" calling, "divinely" motivated, a "revelation" that came when most needed.[43] And the visitors themselves were described as "a noble band of women," who "consecrated themselves to the sober task of binding them up that are bruised, and seeking and saving the lost." The point is that charity visiting had all the drama of religious conversion[44]:

> A suggestive account is given of a depraved family, with an invalid child, to whom a visitor presented some flowering plants. At her first visit she had seen no evidence of ambition, neatness or good housekeeping. Subsequent visits showed that, in order to benefit the flowers, the window panes had been cleaned so as to admit more sun and light. This was not only a great advantage also to the invalid, but it revealed to the mother the filthy condition of the apartment, and incited her to cleanlier habits. It showed, besides, the broken state of the furniture, and induced the drunken father to make repairs. This led him to remain with his family in the evenings, instead of spending his time and money in drinking. Thus, gradually, a desolate home was made cheerful, and a degraded family lifted to self-respect and independence.[45]

Religion provided a justification and model: "To be religious is not only moral but serviceable, not only clean but helpful, not only to 'be good' but to 'do good.' It is to serve society for 'God's sake.' Social service is thus of the essence of religion."[46] The social worker is a missionary, "whose mission is to teach not how to die but how to live, whose business it is to help the head of the family find work, if he desires work, and to inspire or shame him into desiring it, if he does not; to see that children attend school; to give tasteful hints on the preparation of food, the laws of hygiene and the modeling of garments; to help the growing boy or girl to a suitable situation, when the right time comes; to advise as to the expenditure of money; in short, to endeavor in every possible way permanently to uplift the *morale* of that particular home."[47]

And, like Christianity, social work could not be exercised "without knowing the inside of people's minds, without exploring their souls, without making them reveal their innermost secrets."[48] Both social work and Christianity were interested in "the minuscule world of the everyday, the banal faults, the even imperceptible failings."[49] Both Christianity and social work were enveloped in terminologies of benevolence and self-sacrifice, and so were not recognized as forms of power: "Christ came, not to be ministered unto, but to minister, to serve, not to be served."[50] And because they outwardly denied the wish to exclude, repress, or control, because both were outwardly friendly, they shared the capacity to create trust and to effectively solicit confessions.

The main difference was that for social work everything was registered in writing. Whereas the murmurings of the Christian confession were annihilated on earth at the very moment of their utterance, "conveyed to heaven by the scarcely audible confidence of the avowal,"[51] social work preserved its memory of misery and misconduct through the accumulation of records.

CHAPTER 2

The Social Work Gaze

> Our army of poor is made up of individuals, and must be met by individual knowledge and help. . . . Human nature is far too subtle a thing to be investigated in one or two interviews. . . . To understand character and the difficulties of getting on in life is a task that must require a personal knowledge and discrimination which can only grow out of intercourse akin to friendship.
>
> **Mrs. Glendlower Evans, "Scientific Charity" (1889)**

When Mary Richmond became the general secretary of the Baltimore Charity Organization Society in the early 1890s, she launched a campaign to figure out why some charity visitors were so much more successful than others: "Each case on file was broken down, analyzed, and interpreted step by step 'as though it were a new one.'" Cases that seemed similar were studied intensively to locate any hint of what occurred uniformly—to determine what worked and what did not. The main conclusion was that visitors' feelings toward clients—in particular, their sympathy and friendliness—were a key to the progress made.[1]

This was the epoch-making discovery, that sympathy and friendliness, not authority or station or physical force, were the most effective ways to gain entry into private places and access to the most personal, secret information: "The agent's deep unfeigned, educated sympathy leads the family to discuss things not spoken of to others. They reveal not only the amount of the supplies on hand, but also the remote cause of the physical want, and the family resources as well. There is no severe questioning. As a rule the family thinks he does not ask enough questions about flour and fuel and too many questions about life habits—not moral habits alone, but life habits. He delivers no lectures, . . . and his sympathy, fairness and thoroughness command their respect."[2]

Investigators avoided the mechanical, aloof methods of the public official or census taker. They were not to go monotonously and rigidly from house to house, filling out forms, asking intrusive questions. Instead, they appeared as neighborly callers. Rather than the massive, visible division between investigators and subjects, differences were submerged; rather than a system of fixed, centralized observation within enclosed spaces, observation could now move anywhere, becoming infinitely flexible, adaptable. And because investigators gradually came to know what went on in the homes of the poor, just as one friend comes to know about another friend, they were privy to confessions and anecdotes of the most personal kind and were able to make observations on the smallest, most shameful details: on cleanliness; sanitation; plumbing; drainage; light; ventilation; the size, number, and privacy of rooms; the care that is taken of them; the neatness and order of the home; where and with whom family members sleep; the food that is eaten and the manner of preparation; "the clothing they wear; the work they do; the wages which the bread-winners receive; the care with which the family income is spent; the various ways in which it is spent, the thrift, the cost of rent; the influence of intelligence and character, or the lack of it, upon the family."[3]

For this power to be exercised, for the poor to be transformed into a field of perception, observation itself had to be concealed. In other words, this is not a surveillance that features the equivalent of the panopticon guard tower, in which the observatory's size and central location lead prisoners to imagine they are being observed even when they are not.[4] This surveillance is not analogous to observation in which the observed are led to believe that everything they do can and will be held against them. By contrast, social workers attempt to convey that they are not seeing. Going further, they attempt to convey that even if they should happen to see, they will not tell. One mode of surveillance depends on the illusions of ceaseless observation and accountability; the other—the social work method—depends on the illusions of nonobservation and nonaccountability.

In sum, of the three functions of the panopticon—to enclose, to create the constant anticipation of surveillance, and to fix an anonymous gaze—social work preserves only the gaze. For example, during the home visit by the social worker, there is always the *fact* of surveillance, but there is also a concerted effort to divert attention from that fact in order to increase the opportunities of surveillance: "A medical-social worker says that if, after the immediate purpose of her visit to a home is accomplished, she has occasion to wait to make a train and busies herself with a book or some work meanwhile, the members of the family, ceasing to react to her, begin to react to one another, and she gets an impression of the home that she might miss altogether otherwise. Have the parents good control over their children? Do the latter seem afraid of either parent? Are they punished in anger, or is self-control exercised?"[5]

As for the gaze itself, social workers reject anonymity in favor of a highly personalized relation with the observed. Gone is the high drama of inspection, where the inequality between the observed and the observers is constantly on display, exaggerated through the administration of tests, roll calls, overt comparisons, restraint, and reward. In its place came a whole technology of obfuscation, variously identified as friendliness, rapport, trust, confidence: "We must go to them as 'friends' in the truest and broadest sense of the word; enter into their hopes and anxieties and give ourselves, not merely our thought and care in their affairs, but telling them from the first something of our own."

> Not what we give, but what we share,
> For the gift without the giver is bare.[6]

Friendship dramatically improves social workers' capacity to investigate by convincing the observed that surveillance is not occurring. In addition, it makes clients want to speak and act in the designated ways, the ways they imagine conform to social workers' wishes: "It is more and more the client's need to tell rather than the worker's pressure to extract."[7] Friendship, in other words, makes it possible to exercise direct supervision without anyone being aware that supervision is being exercised.

Home Visiting

In earlier times, charity societies usually conducted first interviews at their own offices, with the record forms before them and pen in hand. Questions were asked in the order they appeared on the forms, with each answer filled in before going on to the next: "Assistance asked? 'Coal and groceries.' Cause of need? 'Out of work.' Any relatives able to assist? 'No.'"[8] With the professionalization of charity work, however, the home visit became identified as the method that had the greatest chance of creating a personal linkage, a human relation, at the same time exposing clients to an inescapable, uninterrupted scrutiny: "All charity workers should take part in the visitation and investigation of the poor in their homes. It is simply impossible for people to get an intimate knowledge of the home life of the poor without visiting them frequently."[9]

Home visits made it possible to observe the most elementary details, to participate in the widest range of conversations, to notice personal relics and bric-a-brac, the most fleeting activities and shifts of mood, "the dust of events"[10]:

> (a) In the office, clients are on the defensive and justify their visits by their replies. In the home, the social worker is on the defensive; the host and hostess are at their ease. (b) Its avoidance of the need of so many questions, some of which are answered unasked by the communicative hostess and by her surroundings. To the quiet observer the photographs on the wall, the framed certificates of membership in fraternal orders, the pensioner's war relics, the Sunday school books, the household arrangements

are all eloquent. And far more revealing than these material items are the apparent relations of the members of the household to one another—the whole atmosphere of the home. (c) Its provision of natural openings for a frank exchange of experiences. "The great facts of birth and death alone are sufficient to make the whole world kin," and these and the universally interesting comparison of diseases form a good basis for that kind of informal intercourse which belongs to the fireside. Then, if some of the children are present for a part of the time at least, there is a good chance for comparing notes about brothers and sisters, their ages, names, namesakes, etc.[11]

This is not to say that there were not many problems associated with the home visit. There was always the chance that the interview in the home would be interrupted by the demands of children or the pressure of household duties, or other interfering circumstances: "One meticulous housekeeper admitted that she 'could not be herself' the first time the social worker called, for fear that her caller might be critically aware of the untidiness of her apartment—which was the quite pardonable result of nearly a week's constant attendance upon a sick child."[12] The central point is that social work was originally defined by the home visit; it is social work's totem technique, corresponding to the psychometric test of the psychologist or the physician's prescription. Other disciplines, such as psychology and psychiatry, also developed the capacity to probe into the details of clients' personal lives—but only social work understood the importance of checking to see how tidy or messy the client's apartment actually was, and if there was untidiness, was not too self-important or complacent to see for itself what was behind this—whether there really was a sick child who needed constant attendance or whether something else was going on.

Like all totems, the home visit supports a mythology of plastic powers: it can serve as both a treatment technique and as a method of diagnosis. It can serve as an alibi or a way of demonstrating power: "If you continue to miss appointments, perhaps it is better if I visited you." It proclaims to the client, "You cannot escape me." Yet the home visit is also a sign that the social worker cares and is committed; she is "reaching out." The rationale for its exercise is always unimpeachable: to best understand clients and their problems one needs to see how they function in their own environments. "The chief of these is usually the home. It is here that again and again the answer will be found to many of the difficulties in which a person finds himself."[13]

A social work text from the 1920s, *The Art of Helping People Out of Trouble* by Karl De Schweinitz, shows how a client's troubles (Mark Sullivan had recently been dismissed from his job because of marked apathy and sluggishness) could be correctly diagnosed only through the firsthand observations afforded by home visits: when the social worker whom Mr. Sullivan consulted called at his home, she found it in disarray and confusion.[14] Although Mr. Sullivan was married, he had to prepare his own breakfast in the morning, pack his own lunch, and assume responsibility for dinner at night. No wonder his effectiveness as a workman was impaired. At first it seemed that Mrs. Sullivan neglected her duties as housewife because she had health problems. She was always complaining of feeling too sick and listless to do anything. But when the social worker became acquainted with Mrs. Sullivan's mother, who made her home with the Sullivans, another explanation became available: the mother was actually encouraging her daughter's negligence. The social worker learned that the mother was always discussing her daughter's symptoms with her, casting them in the worst possible light. For example, if her daughter developed the merest suggestion of a cold, "her mother was sure to remark that this was just the most undesirable time of the year to have anything the matter with one; there was so much influenza, or there was so much pneumonia, or there was so much of some other kind of disease about." Because the social worker heard and saw what was going on with her own eyes, it was fairly easy to come up with a solution: she advised the Sullivans to place the mother in a home for the aged.

> This advice was followed, and Mrs. Sullivan, freed from the ever-present suggestion of ill-health, began to take an interest in other things. She regained her strength. Her housekeeping correspondingly improved, and her husband was able successfully to meet the requirements of the new job which he had obtained. Neither Mr. Sullivan nor Mrs. Sullivan had sensed the cause of their trouble, and the social worker herself had not discovered it until she had become intimately acquainted with the life of the family. The key to the problem lay there.

Because the home visit makes available amounts and varieties of information that are otherwise unseen, it also requires attention to issues and types of details that investigators had never previously considered. Accordingly, entrances, introductions, styles of address, and leave-taking became subject to the most minute analysis: Was the entrance too impersonal? Did the introduction contain a note of superiority? Were the family members addressed in the proper way? "It helps all about us to the right spirit, if we take pains not to say 'cases' when we could say 'families,' never to say 'your family' when we might say 'the Browns' or the 'Greens,' to speak of a woman as a friend of ours and not merely of ourselves as friends to her." [15]

Every movement, every gesture, every question asked, was assessed against the standard of friendliness: "The investigator must enter [the house] with care . . . (a hovel it may be), and the door should be gently wrapped before entering. The poor person spoken to should be very kindly approached; the rickety old rocking chair, which is very dear to the possessor, should be taken and used with politeness, as it is highly valued on account of its giver, who has long been missing, and whose picture hangs on the wall just over the place where the chair is kept."[16]

The visitor must always appear respectful: "She should avoid calling at inconvenient hours. She should make her poor friends feel that she fully recognizes the fact that she has no right to enter their homes, except that given her by their courtesy." The visitor who fails to take into consideration the time and schedule of her clients may rightfully be expected to be rebuffed: "The unexpected appearance of the worker immediately after the child, who has been referred to the clinic for inordinate fear of strangers, has awakened from a nap presupposes but one kind of reception. A father, working on the night shift, who has responded to the worker's thoughtless interruption of his morning sleep, is not in a frame of mind to take kindly to a discussion of the inadequate provision he is making for his family. And the worker who expects a conscientious and sympathetic mother to abandon her regular wash day to give detailed information for a social history, or a businessman to devote part of a busy morning to the discussion of a former employee's mental symptoms, must stand the consequences of her lack of consideration."[18]

Once the sacredness of the poor person's home is established,[19] "you will introduce yourself as the secretary, agent, visitor, or whatever title you may have, and to what society you belong, being careful not to deceive in any way the poor person or his family, who are in distress. You will then enter into a friendly conversation, by which, if you are experienced in the work, all the facts you need to report will be brought out, and if you will give the poor a chance to tell their story, you will soon be able to prove the statements already made in the office from which you were sent. If there is any doubt in your mind regarding their needs, ask to be shown what supplies they have on hand, and as you are already regarded as a friend and not a spy, you will be shown through the humble home, no matter how humiliating it may be to the poor family. You will then leave in as kindly and pleasant manner as possible, not making any very decided promises as to what you will do, lest further records being looked up might prevent what you have promised being carried out, as you are only an agent and must submit your report for action to others."[20]

Of course, none of this is as simple or straightforward as it appears. First, the poor must be shielded from any awareness that the visitor is uncomfortable or uneasy in their presence. As one social worker put it, "It was difficult for me . . . to sit down and have a meal with some of the immigrant families every time I came around, but if I declined it would have reflected upon the hospitality of the housewife. I ate and drank jam and tea, sipping the tea from a saucer. I broke bread and salt with many a host, and carried away many tokens of real friendship. Some of my most useful information was gained over a tea-cup."[21]

Second, investigators must cover or obscure anything that might make the poor reticent, tight-lipped, uncomfortable. Thus, to reduce suspicion, there should be no note taking during home visits; nor should the purpose of the visit be divulged. If the social worker is "hard-pressed for an excuse for calling, as for example when a landlord reports that the children of a certain family do not receive proper care, but says he does not wish his name mentioned," then an excuse must be invented: "In such case we may go with an invitation for Country Week, or some holiday entertainment, or through the school teacher we might get a message to bear." [22]

Third, the poor must always be kept from noting that facts are being gathered and judgments made: "Those to whom we go should be led to regard our visit not as one of investigation but as a friendly call." [23] The challenge here is "to gain access to a family without seeming to have come to visit it," [24] to "use all [one's] powers of observation . . . [without] appear[ing] to be doing so," [25] at the same time "being careful not to deceive in any way the poor person or his family, who are in distress." [26] It should always be remembered that "clients are quick to discern the forced smile, the pretended interest, the false assurance, or the feigned motive." [27]

The social worker must "put together all the suggestions of place, appearance, looks, signs, words, carefully spoken or carelessly dropped" to "see things not meant to be seen." [28] Yet "he should be frank and kind in demeanor and considerate," always displaying "a lively, loving, tender, courteous interest in [the visited] personally, not as part of the poor but as an individual with like feelings and like sensitiveness with himself." [29]

Consider the story of a social worker called to settle the incompatibility of a husband and wife. Both were Armenians. The woman claimed her husband neglected and abused her. Her relatives stood by her story. But the social worker needed to hear the man's side. So she visited the home of a friend of his, a woman named Mrs. Demoyan, also an Armenian. The interview did not go well at first. As soon as the social worker mentioned that she was trying to get some information "to help some friends of yours, Mr. Terian and his wife," Mrs. Demoyan replied, "I know nothing." To the social worker, "a mask seemed to fall down over the face of the woman." This is how the social worker managed to turn things around:

> After the two were seated, the visitor began, "You're an Armenian, aren't you? I have been so interested in Armenia because it has had such a terrible struggle. How long did you live there?"
> Simple and obvious though this introduction was, it immediately brought a response. The subject was of the greatest consequence to Mrs. Demoyan, and she began talking about her life in Armenia.
> "They have different customs about marriage over there, haven't they?" the visitor suggested after a while.
> Mrs. Demoyan replied by saying that she had not known her husband

until the day before she was married. She added that Mr. and Mrs. Terian had met each other only five days before their wedding.

A more desirable approach to the purpose of the interview could not have been found. In a very few minutes Mrs. Demoyan had told Mr. Terian's story and had promised to send him to call upon the social worker in order that he might talk with her about his marital difficulties.[30]

What lesson does this interview teach? That it is almost impossible for clients to refrain from revealing themselves once a personal connection is made. By simply stating, "You're an Armenian, aren't you? I have been so interested in Armenia because it has had such a terrible struggle," a highly resistive client was immediately transformed into a trusting confederate.[31] Although the objection can be raised that conversation upon subjects other than those of immediate importance wastes time, it is also true that clients often will not be open on the "subjects of immediate importance" unless they are assured that they are with someone who is safe.

Sustaining Rapport

If investigators are to be effective in gaining information and, at the same time, not appear to be seeking information, they need to refrain from pressuring or rushing: "How often, I wonder, does the almost pathetically earnest young visitor defeat her purpose by sitting upright on the edge of the wrong chair and proceeding directly to the heart of the matter!"[32] The social worker must find a way to blend into the background, to put herself aside and give her consciousness completely to the other person: "Listening of this character seeks the subtle meaning—hints of motivations, reaction to experience, interpretations painful to articulate—conveyed by nonverbal gestures (such as movements or expressions of eyes; posture; pitch, inflection and speed of voice; hand movements) as much as by speech."[33] Actual physical contact also has a place because it increases trust and smoothes the way for clients to make difficult admissions: "A touch of the arm, a linking of arms, or a handshake often serve to reduce tension."[34] In fact, simply agreeing with the client can dramatically lessen discomfort: "Are there not times when it is worth while appearing to agree, where nothing is at stake and a voiced disagreement by the interviewer will lead to a higher emotional pitch or perhaps even bringing about the termination of the interview?"[35] It also helps to do things with clients: "A lunch, a talk across a restaurant table, an afternoon stroll, may bring forth secrets that no interview in an office could produce. Again and again, the boy or girl whose reticence has resisted all efforts at conversation has been helped to self-revelation by the influence of an afternoon in a moving-picture show or a ride on a motor-bus."[36]

Doing things with clients is so effective because it creates the illusion that surveillance is not really taking place; it allows clients to forget that they are being observed: "Many people, no matter how much confidence they may place in the person to whom they are talking, prefer not to have him looking into their faces while they speak. To know that he is being noticed reminds a man of himself and makes him self-conscious. If he is seated by the side of his confidant instead of opposite, this sense of being watched does not become so strong. The idea that an individual is more likely to reveal his secrets when he is in the shadow than when he is in the full glare of light is not without its foundation in experience. We want to tell our secrets unobserved even by the person to whom they are being revealed."[37]

Another way to reduce clients' self-consciousness is to make their complaints appear less serious than they actually are: "A client was much wrought up because it was necessary for him to apply to the Family Welfare Association, and the interviewer said, 'But Mr. Crawford, it is not so terrible for you to come; why this society had twenty-five hundred families come to it last year for just the service you are asking!'"[38]

When clients visit the social worker's office, the "hostess technique" is also effective in creating the impression that observation and fact gathering are not the central purposes: "The interviewer may shake hands, invite the interviewee to sit in the most comfortable chair, face him away from the light and out of the draft, take his hat, ask him to put his parcels on a table, give him a newspaper if it is necessary for him to wait—in short, to do all the things the hostess does for the comfort of her guest."[39]

Flattery also has a role so long as clients are unaware that flattery is being used: "The right kind of compliment . . . gives them an increased sense of power, of achievement and self-confidence. It offers an effective way to influence them."[40] In the words of Marion Rannells, "use of flattery is not only legitimate and ethical, but advisable in order to gain rapport and confidence."[41]

Of course, it is absolutely forbidden to accuse clients of dishonesty: "To catch an interviewee in a deliberate misstatement will inevitably destroy rapport. It requires great tact and mental dexterity to overcome the resulting embarrassment and confusion."[42] It is especially important that rapport not be lost at the close of the interview. Accordingly, "in the last five or ten minutes of the interview we dwell upon hopeful and cheerful things, and leave in the mind of the client an impression not only of friendly interest but of a new and energizing force, a clear mind and a willing hand at his service."[43] Here are some additional injunctions and exhortations:

> Avoid unnecessary argument, contradiction, dictation.
> Detect, and then avoid the discussion of, "sore points."
> Never betray to the interviewee that his resistance is annoying.

Ignore excuses or agree with them as far as possible and then proceed with the interview.

Anticipate objections as far as possible and answer them in a few words.

Approve the interviewee's good intentions, ambitions, and resolutions.

Forestall negative answers by not giving the interviewee a chance to express them, so that they do not become established as a mental habit; start him in an affirmative direction.

"We never adopt a defensive attitude, and are willing to discuss misapprehensions and prejudices frankly."

Distinguish between sympathizing and patronizing.[44]

And because women are, in most cases, less clumsy and obtrusive than men, less likely to speak in loud tones and assume center stage, they should always be given preference when it comes to selecting investigators of the poor: A woman "can go, without offense, where men would not be welcome. She will see a great many things which ought to be considered, but which escape men."[45]

To illustrate how female social workers can gather the most detailed information without appearing to be doing so, how they can utilize the familiar and accepted norms of sympathy, support, and caregiving as information-gathering techniques—as if all their questions derived completely from these sensibilities—we consider a vignette from Mary Richmond's *Social Diagnosis*.[46] Here, "a young colored couple" referred to the social agency after the death of one of their children requested burial clothing and assistance toward the funeral expenses. Approaching the old wooden shanty where Mrs. Reynolds lived, the social worker heard a series of moans and groans. She found Mrs. Reynolds sitting on a tumbled bed, rocking her body back and forth. Even though her eyes were tearless, she moaned continually. The social worker rested her hand on the mother's shoulder and the latter, quiet for an instant, looked up questioningly.

"How do you do, Mrs. Reynolds? I am so glad I found you in, because Mrs. Miller would have been so disappointed if I had not."

"Oh, do you know Mrs. Miller?" asked the woman, immediately brightening, "Ain't she a fine woman?"

"Indeed she is," answered the visitor, and allowed the colored woman to run on for a few moments eulogizing Mrs. Miller, for whom she worked two days a week, as it seemed to take her mind off of her loss and to calm her. She explained that Mrs. Miller had known her husband and herself when they were first married, and had been very friendly to them ever since. By immediately following this lead, it was possible to learn where they were married, what her husband did for a living at that time, and the kind of employment he now wanted. In this way were also learned some of the places at which he had worked and the addresses at which the family had lived at the time.

What is illustrated here is the value of a mutual acquaintance for gaining the client's confidence. If the social worker had not named Mrs. Miller in this instance but had simply approached Mrs. Reynolds in some impersonal, officious way, her progress could not have been so rapid. It also illustrates how providing emotional support and gaining information (the investigative function of social work) are not separate processes but are actually part of the same function. Emotional support frees information:

> "Did you have two children when you were down on North Street?" asked [the social worker], knowing that a direct question about the names and ages of the children would probably start a fresh outbreak of grief.
>
> "No, I just had Willie. He was two then, and after we moved up here in 1910, Jessie came and poor Margaret would be two next month if she ———." Here the visitor interrupted quickly, "I imagine the children are very bright in school, are not they, Mrs. Reynolds? Do they go to public school No. 2?"
>
> "Yes," answered the mother, "and they bring home such fine grades."
>
> "Of course you send them to Sunday school, probably to the Colored Mission around the corner," continued the visitor.
>
> "Yes, we all go there," answered Mrs. Reynolds. "The funeral is going to be from there tomorrow afternoon."
>
> "Is the church going to help toward the expenses?"
>
> "No, but Dobson is very reasonable. He is only going to charge $38."
>
> "Well, perhaps the relatives will all contribute a little."
>
> "I haven't any relatives," was the conventional reply.
>
> "Won't you get a little insurance perhaps?" was the next suggestion.
>
> "No, the Metropolitan lapsed three weeks ago."
>
> "Do you get two carriages for the amount you are paying the undertaker, or just one?" inquired the visitor further.
>
> "Oh, we get two."
>
> "That's good," said the visitor, "because your own little family can go in one carriage, and then you can fill the other with just your nearest relatives, not people who come out of curiosity, but your own kin."
>
> "Yes, we have asked my sister and her husband to go and also Amos' brother John, with his wife and child," continued Mrs. Reynolds.
>
> "You are fortunate to have your own people living right near you. All of us are not that lucky."
>
> "I reckon we are, and they are pretty good to us. Of course we see more of my sister, Judy, for she lives just two doors from the corner. But Amos' brother lives down on East St., so he does not get up so often."

The chief point is that in the space of only one visit the social worker was able to get the names and addresses of this woman's relatives—despite her initial assertion that she did not have any. The social worker also learned about the client's marriage, how her husband earned a living, his prior work history, the state of the family's finances, where the children went to public school and Sunday school, and more. Although the client was in a grief-stricken frame of mind, this was not an obstacle to gathering data because the dialogue was strategically detoured away from the source of her trouble: "This is achieved by keeping up a rapid interchange of firm but kind questions and answers, allowing no time for lapses of attention on the part of the person interviewed. One would find it difficult to get a good first statement in a case like the foregoing, if the order were reversed; if the client were encouraged to speak of his trouble first in the interview, that is, before the background had been secured."[47]

In most instances, however, questions should not be asked in quick succession; such a practice makes the interview come off as too aggressive and one-sided. It is better to casually intersperse questions into the flow of conversation: "Instead of asking a woman directly how much rent she pays, it is perfectly easy to lead the conversation to the general subject of the expense of living in the city on account of high rents. She is quite likely to make some such reply as this: 'Yes, I pay $2.50 or $3.00 for these rooms, but they are not worth it.'"[48]

It is also unnecessary to ask anybody how old they are. Such a question might destroy the harmony that has been so carefully accomplished. Instead, it is better to ask a woman "how old she was when she came to this country, and perhaps ten minutes later ask how long she has been here; or get her age at the time of her marriage, and later find out how long she has been married."[49] Similarly, people are often sensitive about their inability to read and write, "and will deny it if questioned bluntly; but if we lead up to the question gradually, perhaps after talking about relatives and expressing our sense of the pity that they should lose sight of each other, we may perhaps bring out the fact that it is the result of the inability to write."[50]

Because small children are naturally trusting and friendly, "there is no limit to the amount of useful information that may be obtained from a bright child of six to ten years."[51] If such a child appears, "lose no time in making friends with him. . . . Ask him how many brothers and sisters he has, and . . . tell him how many [you] have. Then . . . compare names. If [you] have not the Christian names of the heads of the family, . . . ask which one is named after father and which after mother, and to whom the rest are named after, perhaps thus learning of an aunt in the country who helps sometimes, or of an uncle near by, or of other relatives, of whom mental note is to be made and the clues thus obtained followed up later. If [you] do not know the father's occupation, . . . perhaps ask the little fellow what he intends to do when he gets to be a man. The chances are that he will say that he does not know, and then follows most naturally the question as to what father does."[52]

When family members appear especially secretive or reticent, the best way to get through to them is to reveal something personal about yourself:

"Frequently it is helpful to match what the person in trouble is revealing with a revelation of something in one's own life."[53] Tell them about your friends: "If someone is sick, the mother or sister will be interested to hear about your friends who have recovered from the same disease. If there is an aged person, the story of the oldest man or woman you know will give them something to think about."[54] Simply put, if the client sees that the investigator gives trust, then trust is placed in the investigator: "If we wish to arrive at any real understanding of the people we are dealing with, we must give confidence for confidence."[55]

The directive, then, was for social workers to give their clients a special type of confidence—a confidence that appears as confidence to clients and feels like confidence to the investigators, that does what confidence is supposed to do in terms of eliciting information and trust, but a confidence that does not preclude the continuing recognition that "a family, under ordinary circumstances well-meaning and honest, under pressure of distress, may be tempted to deceive."[56]

George Orwell's name for such maneuvers is *doublethink*: "to know and not to know," to trust and not to trust, to give people confidence while holding them under suspicion, to be spontaneous and friendly while treating each statement secured in the interview not as a fact but as a point of departure for further inquiry: "Statements about employers and wages should be verified by consultation with employer; statements about illness and accidents, by inquiry of physician; statements about marriage, divorce, death, property ownership, naturalization, date of birth, court action, pensions, etc., by reference to public records."[58]

The central predicament for social workers is to hold contradictory beliefs about clients while satisfying themselves that they are not being inconsistent: "The practice has to be conscious, or it would not be carried out with efficient precision, but it also has to be unconscious, or it would bring with it a feeling of falsity."[59] The ultimate challenge is to go back and forth between confidence and suspicion, to forget the feeling of confidence whenever it is necessary to assume an investigative posture, then to reassert confidence when it is needed, and then promptly to forget it again, and finally, to apply the same process to the process itself: "Even to understand the word 'doublethink' involved the use of doublethink."[60]

CHAPTER 3

A Network of Writing

The purpose of case records is to put in permanent form the essential facts about the family, plans made and action taken, for purposes of reference for the visitor or any others dealing with the case, and especially for giving the new worker on the case the benefit of previous knowledge and plans; as an aid to the visitor in organizing her material and getting a clear picture, and as a record of progress.

Louise C. Odencrantz, *The Social Worker* (1929)

To fully understand how social workers used power during the early years of social work, we need to recognize that their "interventions" were not, in the strictest sense, imposed on the poor. In fact, one could easily argue that this was a cooperative relationship since, as often as not, social workers were invited into poor people's homes; their interventions were requested.[1]

Consider this message sent to the the Society of Organizing Charity (SOC) in early 1909: "Will you please call and see Mrs. Willem Sullivan Oakdail st I have two very sick children and my husband has no work and I am sick my self so I would like you to oblige me please for god sake not for me." Two months later, Mrs. Sullivan sent another plea for help to the same social service agency: "will you please call and see Mrs. Sullivan 2126 I have my boy home from the hospital and am very much in need of food for him oblige me."[2]

The SOC povided the material assistance Mrs. Sullivan requested. During the year and a half in which this social agency was involved with her, she was given food, cash, counseling, medical care, housing, job placement, legal assistance. Yet despite all the support and services provided her, she became increasingly unsure of herself. She seemed always to be apologizing to her social workers, always promising to do a better job. The more social workers became involved with her, the more she asked their opinion before doing the things she had previously done on her own—even seeking permission to visit her husband when he was hospitalized—and when she did not get a prompt reply, she became notably anxious and uncertain.

What I wish to emphasize now is that while social workers often stayed longer than their hosts preferred, their sheer presence was not the problem. Nor was the problem that social workers failed to come across with the assistance they promised. Rather, power came into this through an inequality in technology and writing. Because social workers possessed those new inventions, the typewriter and telephone, their words had special significance. To type an opinion and file it away is to separate words from human subjectivity; it is to transform them into facts and make them final. That social workers were connected to each other by telephones also made their version of reality uniquely compelling. It was a simple matter of social workers having the capacity to instantaneously share the contents of their records with schools, courts, clinics, or wherever clients' motives and past actions were subjected to official scrutiny.

For example, in the relatively brief span of time the SOC was involved with Mrs. Sullivan, its social workers shared her story with dozens of community members, doctors, police and court officers. There was record sharing with the Society for the Prevention of Cruelty to Children, the Children's Aid Society, the Children's Bureau, St. John's Home, St. Vincent's Home, the Bureau of Health, the Bureau of Charities, the local Catholic church, the municipal court. Then there were the hospitals: the Municipal Hospital, Philadelphia Hospital, Children's Homeopathic Hospital, Northern Dispensary, Episcopal Hospital, Women's Homeopathic Hospital, and Medic Chi Hospital.

So not only were Mrs. Sullivan's intimate details available to people she did not know and would never meet, they were typed, preserved, catalogued. My point is that social work's original clients, consisting largely of the foreigners who swelled American cities at the turn of the twentieth century, were not allowed to read what investigators wrote about them. They were not allowed to offer corrections, challenge interpretations, or monitor the uses to which their biographies were put. Entering into social workers' language "for their own good" made clients subordinate objects in it. They were engaged in a mass of records that captured and exposed them.[3]

Consider that in written language the message appears to survive on its own. No one is responsible for the document; its existence is independent of anyone's volition, self-sustaining, a monument to memory. Also, in written language, the words are visible. They are objects to be seen, grasped, manipulated. And because written words are more easily controlled than speech, fine distinctions can be drawn between those who should have access and those who should not, between those who can make additions and corrections and those who cannot. Recordkeeping, in other words, is the mechanism that assures the differential distribution of power.

In social work, for example, we can see that the objects of writing were completely excluded, while the investigators, the writers, were mandated to review prior records "without a moment's delay," to immerse themselves in dates, chronologies, locations, details, and gaps in details[4]: "In beginning the work on an old case . . . , it is not enough to read the record; it is necessary while reading to make careful notes of inaccuracies and omissions and to enter on the record card any items that had previously been overlooked, thus bringing the record up to a present-day standard of efficiency and orderliness."[5]

With the preliminary examination of the record completed, the social worker can approach the client's home calmly, confidently. Because the client knows nothing of the social worker's birth, family of origin, and work history, yet the social worker possesses an intimate awareness of these details in reference to the client, one party is anonymous to the degree that the other is individualized, exposed. Because the investigator knows, or has the potential of knowing, every earlier investigator's opinion of the client, yet the client is wholly uninformed by others' view of the social worker, there is always the guarantee of dissymmetry, disequilibrium, difference.

But the inequality between the "partners" was even more insuperable than this. Not only did social workers read what other investigators from their own agency wrote about each family, they learned what was written by investigators from all the other agencies throughout the district: "It is a universal experience that prompt consultation with the agencies listed as knowing the family, is often most enlightening and sometimes obviates the necessity of even leaving the office to make a visit, as the other agency is doing everything needed. With the rising standard of case work among all agencies, this is increasingly true, for the systematic registering of all cases by all agencies with the registration bureau makes it possible for a visitor to know exactly what agencies are working with a case."[6]

This practice began in Boston in 1879, where a registration bureau—the Associated Charities of Boston—was established for the purpose of pooling information on all persons receiving services from dispensaries, hospitals, almshouses, guilds, associations, missions, societies, and churches, and all persons known to the courts, police, and penal and reformatory institutions. Records from these various agencies were brought together in a central clearinghouse, grouped alphabetically by family name, and then immediately placed at the service of all forty-four participating community agencies.[7]

By 1906, the registration system in Boston was streamlined and simplified, quickly spreading to a number of other large cities, including New York, Philadelphia, Chicago, and Cleveland.[8] According to the new system, records and summaries of records were no longer kept in a centralized registration bureau; instead, only the names, ages, addresses, and occupations of the family group were retained at a central location along with the names of the various social agencies that had ever been involved with the client.[9] When a social agency took on a new client, the registration bureau—now called the

Confidential Exchange or Social Service Exchange—was consulted by mail, telephone, or messenger. If the inquiry showed that one or more agencies had past dealings with the client concerned, the inquiring agency consulted with these other interested agencies, resulting in a free exchange of information and cooperative planning, and "the nicest balance and adjustment of each part of the social machinery to every other part." [10]

The "confidential exchange" of records was not a method of observation but, rather, a strategy of sharing observation, of homogenizing it, making the same vision accessible to designated populations, privileging them with knowledge: "Skillfully manipulated by a group of people believing profoundly in the principle of social cooperation, it can win gradually the working together of a large group of social agencies. Through its aid no one of these agencies need take a step in any direction to benefit a human being without being assured of the advice and experience of all the others that have ever known the same person or any of his kindred." [11] The Confidential Exchange thus transformed social work records into an external memory that passed from one set of helpers to another, linking "that which has been done with what we are doing now, with that which we are sure ought to be done next year or the next ten years possibly and holds the thing in shape." [12] (See figure 1. for a breakdown of agencies associated with the Boston Bureau for the Confidential Exchange of Information.)

Because each social worker's point of view was coordinated with that of other accredited officials, power was automatized and disindividualized. The social worker never faced any given family as a single individual, nor even as the representative of a single organization; she became instead the point of intersection for all the remedial agencies in the community; she became the stand-in for an entire class of people: "Thus as the visitor approaches the neighborhood in which the applicant lives, she is in turn a representative of the garbage inspector, and of the street-cleaning department. Later as she views the exterior of the applicant's house, she becomes a representative of the Building Department and of the Bureau of Sanitation of the Department of Health. Carrying the same attitude from the physical aspect to the moral, she becomes in any undesirable neighborhood a representative of the Juvenile Protective Association or of the Juvenile Court." [13]

To sum up, when social workers visited the client's home, they were accompanied by many people. But only the social worker knew the identities of these uninivited guests. And only the social worker knew the uses to which these guests were put: "It is often best for interviewees not to know that an interviewer is in communication with outside sources of information as they might gain the feeling that he may be rendered prejudiced by someone else who did not quite understand them; they often feel that their past is trailing them wherever they go, and that they cannot make a new start in life." [14]

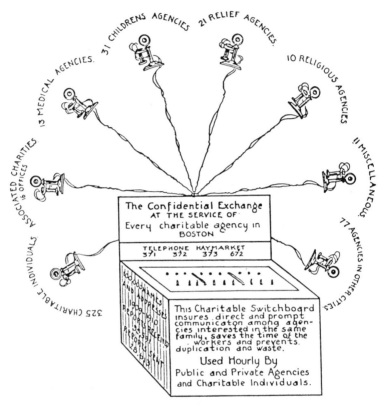

FIGURE 1. Cartoon used by the Boston Associated Charities to illustrate the Bureau for the Confidential Exchange of Information. (Published in Fox, 1911)

If the social worker needed to acknowledge facts taken from another agency or previous investigation, the accepted practice was to shield the source of information because "some interviewees might make it unpleasant for a person or agency which revealed information told in confidence." [15] Conversely, the utmost discretion was required at those times when the social worker needed to communicate with other social workers and agencies about the client: "If it becomes necessary to discuss a client's problems with a professional associate, it is never done where it is possible for the client himself to hear." [16]

In general, negative information about a social agency and dissention among social workers—regardless of what that dissention concerned—was kept from clients: "Agencies should not criticize each other except with constructive purpose or to responsible parties. This should never happen in the presence of clients. False impressions detected in the minds of clients towards other agencies should be corrected if possible."[17] The social worker's spirit of professional loyalty means "he does not discuss details of the other agencies' procedures, which is *their* business; he does not advise the client how to manipulate or 'wangle' a service or benefit; he does not tell the client how the other agency will treat him."[18]

Dependable, open, supportive relations between social workers of different agencies were not simply matters of good practice but were fundamental—they were ethical imperatives:

> The work of another agency should not be disparaged.
> Promises to other social agencies should be scrupulously kept.
> There should be no unauthorized discussions and public statements of plans made jointly with other agencies.
> If there must be some delay in carrying out plans made jointly with other agencies, the reasons for the delay should be fully explained.
> No agency should attempt to impose a plan of treatment upon another agency.
> Independent steps should not be taken by any social agency without first consultation with the agency primarily concerned.[19]

The Transformation of Records

The inequality between social workers and clients was possible only because of a transformation of recordkeeping itself. In earlier times, only the immediate circumstances of the poor and the practical activities of charity agencies were chronicled: "The old almoner went armed with a little notebook in which he wrote down what groceries and how much fuel would be needed in the ensuing month, or made an entry that no groceries or fuel would be needed. . . . The whole plan was calculated to the idea of material relief . . . to the total exclusion of every other idea."[20] To illustrate, table 1 presents entries taken from charity records for the years 1839 to 1841.

During the 1870s and 1880s, charity records began to include something of the client's story, the unfolding of events, a rudimentary description of character. But the primary orientation was still to the immediate time and situation. Such facts as were displayed could not be fitted into social and psychological theories. Tendencies, categories, or diagnoses could not be established on the basis of the detail provided. People had yet to become "cases" in which they were recognized and described in terms of a branch of knowledge:

> Nov. 24, 1879. *Vis.* Can teach music, crotchet, and knitting. Earns $3 to $4 a week in busy season. Has $10 a month from father's estate. No aid, but little from friends. Not accustomed to poverty; little ability.

> Nov. 25, 1879. *Vis.* Boys took mother's quilt for tent and then set it on fire. Teacher says Billy unruly and unreliable.

> Dec. 15, 1879. *Vis.* Boy set fire to shavings in an outhouse.

> Feb. 1. 1884. *Vis.* Mrs. K. C. Ingles asks to have something done about the rent. Mrs. X. has trouble with varicose veins and is therefore prevented from working. Two boys earn together $4 and family seem in danger of being turned out. Sent for landlord P.M. Mrs. X. comes, quite a ladylike person. Born in England and speaks like a Yorkshire woman. Says ownership of the building has been changed and settlement made with previous owner, but the advanced rent is called for by the present one. . . .

> March 16, 1885. *Vis.* Mrs. X asks more aid. A brother in Indianapolis in a large clothing store sends $5.00 or so every month. Another brother is in Minnesota traveling with a photographic company. John lives on a farm for board and clothes. Mary at home. $5 received on the 8th went partly for rent.[21]

It was not until the late 1890s that charity records discovered the meaning of complexity, causation, detail. Again, much of this was due to the influence of Mary Richmond. As general secretary of the Baltimore Charity Organization Society, she was struck by the difference in approach used within each charity district and even by each visitor. So to create more uniformity and make the case recordings more "scientific," Richmond decided that more background information was needed in the areas of household economics, child care methods, and health measures. Written reports on cases now had to be handed in daily, and long individual conferences were held in which workers were urged to tell minutely just how they went about their work.[22]

Richmond required a complete financial statement for every family that was investigated, including facts pertaining to: "Rent; landlord; debts; including installment purchases; beneficial societies; trade-union; life insurance; pawn tickets; has family ever saved and how much?; present savings; income; present means of subsistence other than wages; pensions; relief; sources, and amount." The heads of the family should have "a fairly complete brief biography, including a knowledge of their hopes and plans." Not only should statements be considered from "relatives and friends, their theory as to the best method of aiding, together with some definite promise as to what they themselves will do; the statements of pastor or Sunday-school teacher, of doctor, former employers, and former landlords; and the state-

Table 1. Charity Record Entries, 1839–1841

Name	Wood, feet	Cash	Residence	Remarks
Mary Peters	2	1.50	City	Sick with cancer.
John Robbins	2	2.00	City	Broken leg.
Josephine Adams	1	1.00	City	Partly blind.
Elizabeth Carter	2	2.00	City	And 3 children.
Margaret Riley	1	1.50	Ireland	Drunk H. 3 ch. under 8.
James Smith	2	1.50	City	Sick, wife & destitute child
William Jones	1	1.00	City	Large family.
Susan Miller	1	1.00	City	Widow, etc.
Marie Schmidt	2	2.00	Germany	Destitute
Martha Campbell	1	1.00	Scotland	Aged and destitute
Julia Williams	1	1.00	Maryland	Ditto
Mary Winston	1	1.00	City	Ditto
Walter Simpkins			City	Died this month
James Davis	1	1.00	Ireland	Injured by a fall from a horse.
Winifred Waters	2	1.50	City	Lame & has an idiot son.
Annie Flanagan	1	1.00	Ireland	Widow, 79 in March.
Jessie Bryant	1	1.00	City	Very aged.
Michael Sampson	1	1.00	City	Non compos.
Celia Cohen	2	2.00	Russia	Wife of Joseph. Left her.

Source: Ada Eliot Sheffield, *The Social Case History: Its Construction and Content*, 7.

ments and experiences also of others charitably interested may be needed before an effective plan can be made."[23]

Because social work dealt with the person in his entirety, in all his relations, anything that concerned those relations was of importance and should be a part of the record: "Everything pertinent is included; everything trivial, unimportant is excluded. This distinction is difficult to set down in words—although it is clear enough to the experienced case worker. The record should contain all the information about the client given by himself or his references, when given as information. The client's observations or his experiences are not important—belong to the trivial group—except when they bring out a state of mind or motive. A man said to one of our visitors apropos of her effort to get him into a sanitorium—'My father died coughing, and I shall, too.' That observation illuminates many dark and difficult passages of record. But, in general, it is the narrative alone which the record receives; the story of the client in action, present or past."[24]

Here is the rub: before social work, poor people were mainly vulnerable to starvation, disease, homelessness; with the advent of detailed record-keeping, however, they became vulnerable to judgment. In recordkeeping, people are not forced to do anything against their will, they are not killed or incapacitated in any way. It is all very discreet. But because social work records contain page after page of the most intimate description—the result of so many inspections, visits, interviews—the stability of people's moral universe is placed up for grabs.

I am not referring to the magical power we associate with capturing some-one's likeness. This is not about spells cast by voodoo dolls, nor the fear some people have of being photographed. This argument is much more mundane. It is simply that social work records or, rather, the details they hold make it possible to describe clients as any variety of "types" and their activities as "maladjustments." They make it possible to destroy reputa-tions—to blame with bitter words not just for one moment but for the days to come.

Describing someone in a case record is not usually recognized as a mode of dominance. This dominance is almost invisible. Once this is under-stood, we can see why social work investigation and recording—biography construction and preservation—are potentially much more efficient than threats, incarceration, or physical force. Consider this excerpt from a 1915 recording:

> Visitor called at 3:30 P.M. and found children sitting around a red-hot stove. Mrs. S. had just shaped four large loaves of dough which were ready for the oven. Two rabbits hung outside the window, and Mrs. S. said that they were to make a Christmas dinner for the family. A quantity of clothing which had been washed hung from the walls of the kitchen, the line on the roof being three flights up. The three rooms (on the first floor) in which the family live all open up on courts or alleyways which admit no sun and insufficient light. The tenement is not a decent place in which to live. Its general gloom is increased by the untidiness within the rooms.[25]

The distinctive feature of this recording is how every sentence, every phrase—regardless how equivocal they might at first appear—is treated as a resource to display the essential inadequacy of the family in question: "The red-hot stove at 3 p.m. following upon no fire throughout the morning sug-gests that Mrs. S. may be ignorant or careless about tending drafts and using coal so as to get the most heat out of it and at the same time to save the stove, to guard against fire, and to keep an even temperature for children. Also her having so hot an oven just as she was about to put in her bread shows that she does not know how to bake."[26] The general untidiness of the rooms, that wet clothes were hanging where they would get only minimal airing, "where moisture will enter any crack in the walls, and where the consequent damp-ness in the rooms will favor germs, not to say vermin, and would be propor-tionally bad for little children," were all mobilized as evidence supporting the general finding of "incompetent home-maker." [27] What I am highlighting, therefore, is the most obvious, yet least acknowledged feature of social work writing: that the details that were amassed in the case records were used to judge clients' moral status, to locate unconstructive and destructive behavior, social and familial irresponsibility, areas of instability and unwholesomeness.

After 1910, it was scarcely possible for a case record to be too concrete.[28] The amount of descriptive data increased because charity investigators were now utilizing questionnaires and techniques for case history writing oriented to making visible the smallest, most passing elements, to clarifying the subtlest relations and etiologies. Consider, for example, the sample questionnaires contained in Richmond's *Social Diagnosis*; in particular, how they targeted specific populations and classes of people:

> *Immigrant family*: "Are the people stolid or excitable? Warlike or submissive? Jealous? Hottempered? Given to intemperance? Superstitious? Suspicious?" [29]
>
> *Deserted wife*: "What are the wife's personal characteristics? Has she, for instance, a difficult or nagging disposition? Is she a good housekeeper? A good mother?" [30]
>
> *Widow with children*: "Are there relatives near at hand? Are they friendly? What plan for the widow's future do they advise? What material help can they give in carrying it out? What helps that are not material? What is their moral standing?" [31]
>
> *Unmarried mother*: "When did girl's or woman's sexual experience begin? Under what circumstances—was it with a relative, an employer, an older man, a school boy? Has she accepted money from any man or men for unchastity, or has she received only a good time—theaters, dinners, etc.—or board?" [32]
>
> *Homeless man*: "What are his ideas about education, about politics, about capital and labor, about social conditions? Does he believe in democracy, and under what form of government would he prefer to live?" [33]
>
> *Inebriate*: "Has he been unfortunate in business or family affairs? Has he suffered from any painful disease or been in ill health? Has he suffered any severe shock or loss which unsettled him and caused him to turn to drink? Is he happily married? Is his wife of a nagging disposition, or has she any bad habits that make trouble between them?" [34]
>
> *Insane*: "How does he carry his hands? Is his hair tidy or unkempt? Nails? Teeth? Untidy in eating and drinking? Any attempts at unusual dress or decoration? Is he fully dressed, half dressed, or naked?" [35]
>
> *Feeble-minded*: "Are there any variations from the normal in the size, shape, and relative position of the features? Is there any marked coarseness of features? Do the eyes roll? Shift? Are they wanting in changefulness? Is child cross-eyed? Are ears large, outstanding, or dissimilar? Is the lower jaw protruding? Is mouth usually open? Are there any abnormalities in the form, structure, and situation of the teeth?" [36]

Thanks to this new accumulation of evidence or, rather, to the new technology for gathering such evidence, two correlative possibilities were suddenly opened up: First, all those most in need of training and correction, of inclusion and normalization, could now be described, judged, measured, compared to others—not through the workings of a one-time-only census, but through a system of continual monitoring. Second, this system was faster, lighter, and more efficient than anything that came out of the courts or traditional investigative work. No search warrants were needed, no trials, no lawyers. Under this system, hearsay, rumors, the appearance of a person's home, its tidiness and cleanliness, the client's posture, facial expression, whether there is a "marked coarseness of features," whether the eyes "roll" or "shift," the client's "ideas about education, about politics, about capital and labor,"—every manner of circumstantial evidence became fully admissable in formulating such proof as social workers needed.

Clients' Consent

This is not to say that social workers were not concerned with securing consent. They were, of course. But social workers were also acutely aware of the many conditions that made securing consent completely impractical.[37] First, "in the cases of suspected mental trouble where the proof, as the social worker sees it, really must come from these other sources. . . . It would sometimes not be well to annoy the patient by trying to insist upon his consent." Second, "in cases of illegitimacy, the unmarried mother almost always refuses to have her family know of her condition, if they are a respectable family who will help her out of trouble. The motive in this instance is not only the client's desire to protect herself but her desire to shield her dear ones from pain and disgrace. Years of experience have proved that the love of parents and family makes it possible for them to bear such disappointments as come with a true knowledge of what has happened, and their helpfulness is so great in relieving the distress of the client that the distracted unmarried mother's refusal to have her family seen cannot be heeded—not to mention the definite rights of her near kindred, which supersede those of any outside agency." Third, "where the agency has good grounds for suspecting immoral conditions in the home which would lead to the neglect of children, morally and physically. For the protection of these children, who are unable to protect themselves, a worker would be justified in going against the wishes of his client."[38]

Also, as a general rule, if the social worker frankly knows that the client would not object to her interviewing someone if she were to ask permission, asking permission is unnecessary. Consent is unnecessary, too, when the client is knowingly deceitful. Lastly, if the social worker has any doubts, he need only remember that "if the results are good, the client is always reconciled to what has been done. If the results are bad, the worker can frankly admit that the client was right and he was wrong. . . . Almost invariably such a frank admission on the part of the worker secures not only the forgiveness on the part of the client but a certain sympathy as well." [39]

Consider, for example, "the perfectly true story of Mrs. J.," who in broken English implored a social worker to provide her some financial assistance: " 'My husband; he no citizen. My Josie she work, but me no canna work. Me sick here,' with an impressive hand on her heart and an upward turning of liquid brown eyes. 'My girl she marry and no helpa me now, and Angie she verra small. I tink she seek, she get no food.' " [40]

As the social worker attempted to piece together Mrs. J.'s story, two questions appeared to be of paramount importance. How old was Josie? She and her mother claimed she was sixteen, the legal working age, but perhaps she was younger and should be in school. And had Mr. J. even taken out his first citizenship papers? Only inspection of public records could definitely answer these two questions. Thus the social worker began her search.

> Letter after letter, ringing the changes on all possible spellings of the J.'s names, brought only "no record" from the Registry of Births. Letters to the offices of the Naturalization Service brought suggestions of further sources, but no light on the first papers. Then began a search of the records of various churches where Josie might have been baptized (the family had moved frequently, and broken English makes streets and other names difficult to understand). Finally the right church was discovered and the baptismal certificate established beyond a doubt that Josie's age was but fourteen. A few days later the records of the district court divulged the information that Mr. J. had taken out his first papers.

What this story illustrates is how the need for correct information could offset any hestitancy about pursuing the investigation without explicit consent. It was a simple matter of the "paramount importance" of determining whether Mr. J. had taken out his citizenship papers and whether Josie was, as she claimed, really sixteen. Only with this knowledge could the case worker help Mrs. J. get a cash allowance and persuade the reluctant Josie to return to school. Without the search for documentary evidence, Mrs. J.'s financial eligibility could not have been proven, "and Josie would undoubtedly have drifted on, without even the meager equipment of a full grammar school education." [41] The point is that the social worker knew, while Josie and her family did not, that knowledge of Josie's true age would ultimately benefit her and her family.

In short, given social work's obligation to form an all-around knowledge of the personality of clients and their situation, the social worker was justified in writing "letter after letter," in inquiring of public agencies, in

obtaining baptismal certificates, property transfers, and records of other
charity societies, hospitals, and courts. That the social worker in this instance
did not have permission to get vital statistics was irrelevant. She needed access to them to help the family. Also, she had license on the grounds that
Mrs. J. consciously obstructed by withholding information.

What gives the social worker the right to so unlimited a field of knowledge? "The same authority that gives parents and teachers the right to mold
children into all kinds of shapes, beautiful and ugly, the authority of necessity and inevitability. Like parent and teacher, the case worker, if she acts at
all, is bound to affect individuals. She experiments with the life process because she cannot help it; anything she does is an experiment in human behavior. As long as she does this in ignorance or in terms of doing good to humanity, she manages to escape full responsibility for everything but her
intentions." [42]

The Biographical Technique

On 5 December 1913, a St. Louis tea merchant named D. Simms notified
city officials that Mrs. May Brown and her four children were without food
and clothing. She had just returned from City Hospital after giving birth and
appeared to have no means of support. A social work investigation was initiated that same day. We see in this example that social work dealt with a question far more complex than whether or not the litigant commited a particular violation. [43] Social work decided on lives. It was the technique, or series of
techniques, to fill in all the sordid details of the client's biography through
any mode of inspection or interviewing as might be needed.

> 12-5-13.   Called on applicant; lives in one room in rooming-house at
> 900 Franklin; prior to giving birth to Erwin (at City Hospital, 11-15-13),
> she worked in the kitchen of the restaurant run by C. A. Appel, 800
> Franklin; earned $6.50 per week and was allowed to take some of the un-
> used food home to her children. Owing to mother's weakened condition
> she has not worked for three weeks and children are without food and
> clothing. The landlady, Mrs. Henry, and the neighborhood merchants
> have given her assistance. The applicant states that her husband deserted
> her July 1912 at Dow Run, Mo.; that she did not see him or hear from him
> until April 1913 when she was with him one day. She stated that he fre-
> quently got into trouble through drinking and gambling; that he got all his
> money by gambling; that he sometimes abused and mistreated her, but
> that she loves him nonetheless. Applicant spoke feelingly of her love for
> her children and her desire to do well for them and cried at the thought of
> having to part with them. She gave the names and addresses of previous
> employers, Provident Association, Attendance Department, etc., as her
> History Sheet.

Over the next two days, the social worker interviewed Mrs. Brown's former employer, a local merchant who knew her, an attendance officer with the Board of Education, two of her former landlords, a nurse from City Hospital, where Mrs. Brown had given birth, and a police officer. A total of seventeen entries were made in her record during this brief interval.

Some of this information was quite positive. For example, Mrs. C. A. Appel, who employed Mrs. Brown in her restaurant, said she knew her for about six months "and that she was a hard working and a good woman, and seemed devoted to her children, and that she would heartily recommend her for assistance."

However, the bulk the of the recordings identified areas of impropriety and instability. In particular, Mrs. Naunheim, attendance officer with the Board of Education, described Mrs. Brown as very negligent. When Mrs. Naunheim investigated to see why the Brown children were so often missing from school, she found that their mother was working in a laundry "and was away from the children practically all day; that Loretta took care of Grace and Charles, but that she was a very forward and worldly-wise child and was fast developing into a delinquent." The social worker noted in the record that "Mrs. Naunhein was amazed to learn that there was a son Erwin, three weeks old, because applicant had told her she was a widow."

The interviews with Mrs. Brown's landlords were also quite negative. One stated that she had to ask Mrs. Brown to leave after two weeks because her children were so noisy, and "because the applicant tried to 'make-up' with the solicitors who came for orders." The other landlord said that Mrs. Brown "was a smooth talker, had a ready-tongue and 'wouldn't know the truth if she saw it coming down the street.' Said that applicant frequently had men callers but that she had never heard her speak of her husband and understood that he was dead. She would not recommend applicant for relief, but thought the children should be put into an institution as they stole everything they got their hands on."

After phoning the City Hospital maternity ward and speaking with the nurse in charge, the social worker entered into the record that, as a hospital patient, "Mrs. Brown was exceedingly hard to manage; that she had a shifting eye, and in [the nurse's] judgment was not telling the truth." Then the social worker interviewed a local police officer, who reported that "the children were terribly neglected"; he wanted the children "placed into some institution where they would be taken care of" and "could bring the necessary witnesses to make a case."

Finally the social worker called on Mrs. Brown and shared these findings with her. She noted that Mrs. Brown became defensive, asserting that "her husband was the father of her child Erwin, that she never went out and always stayed home with her children." The social worker also noted that Mrs. Brown "seemed quite excited at questions put to her and talked rapidly; finally said she was through with St. Louis and was going to her folks in the country. That she did not want anything done for her and 'would they please drop the matter.'" Here are the last two entries in Mrs. Brown's record:

> 1-5-14.   Hearing before Judge Hennings, Juvenile Court, where children were declared neglected and commited to the Board of Children's Guardians, and mother was ordered to pay $8.00 per month on the first of each month.
>
> 1-6-14.   Children were delivered to Home Department of the Industrial School for placement by the Board of Children's Guardians.

What needs to be recognized now is that Mrs. May Brown's presenting problem was quite specific—she and her four children were completely without resources—but once the social work investigation began, there was a silent understanding that it was permissable, required even, to judge Mrs. Brown's truthfulness (she was "a smooth talker"), her child care practices (her children were "terribly neglected"), her sexual behavior (she "frequently had men callers"), her children's behavior (Loretta "was fast developing into a delinquent"). The critical point is that without any overt or explicit agreement, the issue at hand was treated as if it were entirely diffuse. Thus, it was not that observation was exhaustive or omnipresent; it was not, as Foucault wrote, "thousands of eyes posted everywhere."[44] The distinguishing features of this investigative approach were breadth of focus, mobility, and unpredictabilty.

This implies that the social work investigation, with the whole technological apparatus of visiting, interviewing, recordkeeping, and record sharing, brings about a curious transformation: the presenting problem indicates that there certainly is a specific need; but social work applies itself not to the need but to the person instead. And because it is focused on the person, not the need, there is no clear-cut, self-evident way to measure "success" or termination.

The most obvious consequence of this indeterminacy is that social work can go anywhere and use anything: personal items, opinions, impressions, word of mouth, facts of the smallest probative value, testimony that might otherwise appear trifling or irrelevant. What it lacks in precision and accountability it gains in flexibility and freedom. Accordingly, in the case of Mrs. Brown, we see that each entry in the record was accompanied by a wide range of written documentation describing small occurances having to do with behaviors, attitudes, possibilities, suspicions, whether Mrs. Brown was "worthy" or not, whether something did or did not take place, whether what took place was good or bad or might be good or bad. Although it was impossible to say what purpose all these observations served, it was clear that they formed a resource that could be called upon to document any number of proofs regarding Mrs. Brown. And, as it turned out, her family was entirely redefined and reorganized on the basis of the data that was supplied.

Now, the Brown investigation, involving the dissolution of a family in a matter of weeks, may very well be too dramatic and decisive to be called typical. It may also represent the very type of social work horror story I promised I would not call upon to make my arguments. Still, there is something about this case that deserves attention: specifically, even if we call it a "horror" story, we cannot help but notice how incredibly mundane it is. If there is horror here, it is entirely obscured by the language of social work, by a prose style that is completely passionless and stale. For example, the story concerns the involuntary separation of young children from their mother, yet this separation is described by an impersonal statement—"Children were delivered to Home Department of the Industrial School for placement." The closest the social worker came to acknowledging her clients' pain was to write "Applicant seemed quite excited at questions put to her and talked rapidly; finally said she was through with St. Louis and was going to her folks in the country. That she did not want anything done for her and 'would they please drop the matter.'" As for the social worker's own feelings, she stubbornly refused to identify herself in any way in the writing, even to the point of beginning sentences with "visited" or "called" in place of "I visited" or "I called." What was behind this stylized renunciation of selfhood, feelings, personness? Part of the answer, certainly, is that describing people as objects makes it easier to manipulate them. But there is another meaning behind the banality of the prose: the social worker is broadcasting that her ideas are banal, that she completely renounces individuality, originality, risk taking.[45] Her prose style proclaims complete conformity to the existing power structures, rules, and ideologies. She is not merely justifying taking children from their mother; unbeknownst to herself, her writing is a ritual enactment of her own submission.

The Mundanity of Social Work

What this horror-story-that-is-not-a-horror-story captures best is the fundamental mundanity of social work: that social work fits in, is expected to fit in, and likewise expects clients' accounts and experiences, both individually and socially, to fit in. The tacit assumption of social work is that clients' actions, and social workers' reactions to them, are determinate, coherent, and noncontradictory, that every instant of their behavior and experience can be coordinated with that of the previous instant and is fully apprehendible and knowable by social workers, the clients themselves, or anyone else who might care to understand them.[46] Social work is characterized by the non-exceptional—it is a practice in which either nothing of any consequence happens or when something momentous does happen, it is redefined as a matter of routine, as lawful, expected. So even though Mrs. Brown had her children removed from her against her will, this was displayed as dryly as if they were taken to the movies for an afternoon—it was a nonevent.

Let us consider a case record from the Family Agency of Chicago in which a mother of three, Mrs. Jendrick Novotny, was referred to a social work agency after her husband was commited to a psychiatric hospital.[47] As in the case of Mrs. Brown, the presenting problem was quite specific: Mrs. Novotny and her children had no sources of financial support. While the Novotny investigation had none of the speed and decisiveness of the Brown case, we see the same breadth of focus: how anyone could be talked to, how every observation was relevant. In particular, we see that the investigation was not limited to resolving Mrs. Novotny's financial need but, rather, extended to more global concerns: her housekeeping, her cleanliness, her mothering, her cooking, her children's behavior. It was as if the pettiness of social work observation served a purpose all its own, which was to demonstrate that arbitrary power could be exercised, that no topic was exempt, and that anyone could be interviewed at any time. These are the first three case entries:

> 4-26-18. Visited. Family, Mrs. Novotny, Anna (born September 24, 1911), Andrew (born May 2, 1915), and Joseph (born February 25, 1917), live in two clean and fairly good rooms. The rent is $7.00. Mrs. Novotny seemed dull of comprehension and a trifle erratic. Said Mr. Novotny was never a steady worker. Was last at Schmidt's in the Stockyards for two weeks. She knows no check number nor any other name of firm. Has done very little work during the entire year. He drank to excess, and finally she was obliged to have him sent away.
>
> Mr. Novotny came to this country six years ago from Moravia, Mrs. Novotny following two years later with Anna. Said they have no relatives at all in this country. She had one brother in Europe; doubts if he is living, on account of the war. She receives county supplies. There is little food in the house. Gave $2.00 grocery order.
>
> 4-27-18. Talked with Visiting Nurse. Anna had an operation one year ago at Zion Hospital. The wound is still draining. The doctor at the hospital said that nursing care in the home will not cure her trouble and wishes child to come to the hospital. Mrs. Novotny is unwilling. Nurse asks our help in getting consent.
>
> 4-30-18. Visited. Mrs. Novotny was washing at the home of Mrs. Marek, who interpreted. She said that Mrs. Novotny is Bohemian and that she does not attend any church. Mrs. Novotny promised to take Anna to the hospital tomorrow. She had no coal or milk.

Mrs. Marek said she has known Mrs. Novotny for four years. She lived two years at present address. Previous to that she lived one block north. She is sure that Mrs. Novotny has no relatives in this country. Mrs. Novotny does two days' washing a week in the neighborhood, earning $1.25 a day.

Visited landlady, who said she feels very sorry for Mrs. Novotny. She knows of no relatives.

Over the next two months, the social worker continued data gathering: talking to other social workers, reading past records, interviewing neighbors and employers. She also made four visits to Mrs. Novotny, none of which appeared to have been planned in advance with the client. In early May, she met Mrs. Novotny with her two children on the streetcar "while in the neighborhood," noting that "all were very clean." Five days later she "dropped by" the Novotny apartment, again "while in the neighborhood," noting that Mrs. Novotny "washes and irons beautifully" but "has absolutely no control over the children." There were two more unplanned home visits in June, after each of which the social worker made entries on the cleanliness and neatness of the Novotny apartment. The point here is that although these visits appeared spontaneous and off-the-record, the findings from them had all the weight of inspections and were filed away with the same formality as any other data-gathering technique.

On 1 July 1918, the social worker called on Mrs. Novotny again. Not finding anyone home, she waited in the hall. When Mrs. Novotny's eldest child, Anna, came in from playing in the street, the social worker asked her to let her in. The social worker then looked around, noticing that "Mrs. Novotny did not leave food for children, nor did she leave the children in the care of a neighbor." After the inspection, the social worker interviewed Anna herself, who talked freely about her mother and relatives. When the social worker finished with the little girl, she talked with a neighbor who "corroborated Anna's statements regarding Mrs. Novotny. . . . She also said Mrs. Novotny frequently leaves the children alone and is responsible for their bad behavior, as they are dependent on themselves the greater part of the time." The visitor had to leave shortly thereafter and so was unable to interview Mrs. Novotny that day.

Between July 1918 and November 1919 the ordinary pattern of visitations was interrupted by two events: Mr. Novotny died in the psychiatric hospital, and it was discovered that Mrs. Novotny had a secret bank account amounting to several hundred dollars:

11-29-19. Mrs. Novotny in office . . . insisted that she had no money and did not take any out of the bank on November 26. Showed her the report from the bank—then [she] stated the money was her husband's, which he had saved before they were married: Superintendent asked what she was going to do with money, and explained that she could not get a mother's pension while she had it. Told her to put money back in the bank and draw out a certain amount weekly. Mrs. Novotny said that the reason she did not tell Welfare Agency about the money was because she knew other women who had money and were getting help. When questioned further she said she did not know a specific instance of this.

The most interesting feature of the revelation of Mrs. Novotny's dishonesty is that it was not treated as a revelation at all but was defined as entirely mundane. Accordingly, she "was told to put money back in the bank and draw out a certain amount weekly," so her savings could last as long as possible. Mrs. Novotny, as part of this self-same mundanity, said that other welfare clients were no different from herself—they too were cheating. Granted, she was dropped from the welfare agency roles because she had her own money, but it was not a punishment; it was not a recognition of betrayal or dissimulation. It was simply that agency rules forbade carrying clients who had savings accounts. As it turned out, Mrs. Novotny was immediately reinstated when her savings ran out in October 1920. At that point, home visits resumed as before, the only difference being that more attention was devoted to her budget and expenditures.

The point here is that whatever else social work accomplished during the first part of the twentieth century, it penetrated the private space of the family. More remarkable is the casualness with which this penetration was enacted.[48] Without any trace of embarrassment or apology, social workers asked the most personal questions of clients' landlords, past and present employers, neighbors, relatives. If there was resistance, as in the case of Mrs. Novotny's lying, this was not seen as a foundational threat or as something that called into question the basic premises of social work practice; instead, it was perceived as being simply another problem—irksome, yes, but available to the same recipes and procedures by which social work typically performed its duties.

Social work rendered the most banal tasks and choices—housekeeping, child care, what to do about a mother who is not home, what to do about a husband who does not work—into domains of professional expertise. In this regard, social work knowledge (or expertise) appears not so much as a personal possession but as a mark of sociality, an emblem of normal or typical involvment in the social world. The point here is not that social work rightly or wrongly projected its concept of normality onto people's ordinary affairs but, rather, that it managed to carry off this involvment in an entirely professional way, as if one party had knowledge and authority and the other did not. To what did social workers owe this capacity? Ironically, it came from setting aside the philosophical and conceptual problems underlying their statements, decisions, plans. The most solid and evident fact about social work is simply the ongoing givenness of its world, and the activities performed within it. Meeting and speaking with clients, sharing with them a common area of action, devising and pursuing real and imaginary schemes and ideals—all these things are simply and cardinally taken for granted.

Intensification and Dispersal

As the social work investigation spread throughout the nation during the early decades of the twentieth century, there was the general recognition that this mode of inquiry could increase the influence and overall effectiveness of any social agency, institution, or function. It was simply that social work made it possible to penetrate people's daily lives, to pursue them into the physical spaces in which they lived and worked: "Only the case worker leaves hospital, clinic, office, and laboratory behind and observes the individual in action—at home, at work, in school; playing, loving, toiling, hating, fearing, striving, succeeding, failing." [49] What made the penetration so effective was that it was not imposed on the general population from the outside by some ruling elite but was supported from the inside, by those over whom it was exercised. [50] "It almost seemed as though the general public appreciated for the first time that poverty, sickness, and stifled life were not burdens to be borne helplessly but were evils which could to a large extent be corrected and prevented." [51]

Accordingly, without losing any of its essential properties, social work was adapted to medical treatment, education, child welfare, industry, courts, corrections, psychiatry. Now, of course, medicine, education, and child welfare are not social work—they used social work. The hospital social worker supplemented the work of the physician; the school visitor the work of the teacher; the family visitor the work of the welfare agency; the probation officer the work of the court or police officer; and so forth. What social work offered, specifically, was the capacity to blur the boundaries that separated schools, hospitals, and other institutions from the surrounding community. It enabled them to emerge from their fortresslike structures, from confining rules and formalities, and to circulate freely.

Beyond all the complex empirical and theoretical questions concerning what social work "really" did and what it meant, we have the evidence of its phenomenal expansion during the first part of the twentieth century. We know, for example, that by 1923, there were almost 400 social work departments in hospitals and dispensaries throughout the United States. [52] By 1931, that number had grown to 1,044 departments of social work in hospitals. [53] There were 25,000 professional social workers in the United States in 1929; [54] by 1933, that number had increased to 36,000. [55]

Apart from the growth in the sheer numbers of social workers and departments of social service, we have all this evidence of social work's frenzied activity, all this bustling, all this moving about, endless telephone calls, consultations, letters, visits, interviews. There was this silent understanding that if social workers did not make decisions for clients or, at the very least, urge them to make the correct decisions for themselves, clients' lives would quickly slip into the most extraordinary chaos. Hence, social workers operated under the continual imperative to do as much for as many people as possible. The following log from the first four hours of a family case worker's day illustrates the worker's frenzied schedule.[56]

> 9:00 A.M.   At Family Court. Spoke to worker regarding the C. family. Mr. C., a tailor by trade, has not been contributing regularly toward the support of his family. His work is highly seasonal and, in addition, a greater part of his earnings is spent on drink. In view of the fact that Mr. C. is in good physical condition, there seems to be no reason why he should not do some other work when there is no work in his own line. As he refuses to do so, however, his wife and two children are left without any support. It was agreed that the best plan would be to have Mr. C. report at the Court and put him under probation and strict supervision. Arrangements were made to have Mrs. C. call at the office to lodge a complaint against her husband.
>
> 9:30   En route from the Family Court to the main office.
>
> 9:40   Called at the main office. Discussed with Mr. L. of the Self-Support Department plan for the K. family, who came to our attention because of lack of funds to conduct their business. Gave Mr. L. social facts as known to us and discussed the advisability of considering family for assistance in conducting the business. Mr. L. agreed to send worker to look into the business aspect of the case, after which another conference will be held.
>
> 10:00   Called to see worker in the Home Economics Department to discuss possibility of sending a child to Camp Rose for the entire summer. Went over the child's record. Found that while the child was suffering from chorea and was pale and undersized, her nutrition was good and she was not anemic. Worker in the Home Economics Department felt she was not the proper child for this particular camp, but promised to put her on the waiting list so that if another child should drop out, it would be possible to send her.
>
> 10:30   En route from main office to Broadway near City Hall.
>
> 10:45   Visited a lawyer who offered to help us in some of our cases involving legal procedure. Discussed case of D. family where Mr. D., a laundry driver, was injured while at work. He had placed the case in the hands of a private lawyer. In view of the fact that this lawyer's handling of the case did not seem to protect of client's interest sufficiently, asked this

lawyer to investigate the case. Gave him detailed account of our contact with the family and social facts as we had them. The lawyer promised to find out what the status was and to enter into communication with the lawyer representing our client. He promised to send us a detailed report of his findings and recommendations.

12:00 M.   Lunch

12:45 P.M.   En route to East 96th Street.
Spoke to Mrs. C. Discussed advisability of putting in a complaint against her husband. She felt reluctant at first but when it was pointed out to her that Mr. C., who is an able-bodied man, should be made to meet his responsibilities, she finally agreed to call at the Family Court the next day to lodge a complaint.

Social work provided the means by which power could be extended and intensified (1) by encountering resistances actively, wherever they appeared;[57] (2) by making available new types of knowledge, in particular, the details of people's family interactions; (3) by getting information directly, as it unfolded; (4) by increasing the number of persons brought into the system (by extending services not only to clients but to their spouses, children, parents, siblings); (5) by introducing new modalities of influence, especially appeals to family loyalties and community norms; (6) by increasing the number and types of people who could be used to exert influence (in particular, enlisting family members to explain, persuade, confront, plead); (7) by creating, identifying, and coordinating connections with other social agencies—schools, hospitals, philanthropic organizations, clinics, nursing homes, and so forth—so that knowledge and influence could be shared and brought to bear in the most discreet, intense, and efficient ways.

But social agencies did not merely use social work; social work used them, too. We need to recognize that social work's effectiveness as a mechanism of persuasion was not merely added on to hospitals, schools, and child welfare but was amplified by its relation to them. In other words, because of social work's relations to these agencies and institutions, it did not have to rely solely on sincerity, enthusiasm, and friendliness to get into people's homes and make them talk of intimate circumstances and events. Through social work's association with a network of established institutional structures, social workers assimilated a vast armamentarium of reasons by which they were able to convey that it is not only right but necessary that poor people admit social workers into their homes for the purpose of gathering highly personal information.

On the most obvious level, we know that poor people seeking financial aid overcome whatever dislike they have of being investigated because they are desperate: "The line between these families on whom we have a hold that personal influence and real helpfulness as recognized by them, can give us, is the poverty line."[58] Quite simply, poor people have to put up with whatever is done to them for fear they might get nothing. The following selections from Strode and Strode's *Social Skills in Case Work* show how people's material need was not a problem to be solved so much as a wedge to be used. The last passage is especially interesting, revealing the need for social workers to deny to themselves that anything akin to "bribery" is going on; these are all simply "material inducements":

> A set of new dishes was the inducement which moved Mrs. O'Hara to co-operate in a plan for regular meals for her children. Bright curtains, a new stove, a rug, a bureau, or other piece of needed furniture often wins a client's interest and co-operation in better housekeeping.
> A client's nine-year-old son needed the inducement of a new catcher's mitt to get him to play ball with the neighbor's boys. He was not a very good player but the catcher's mitt was the inducement which kept him playing and helped him win a place on the neighborhood team.
> After a certain welfare client was given the opportunity to visit a hospital for the mentally ill, driving up to the institution with the case worker, she was willing to co-operate in a plan to commit her ailing husband.
> Material inducements are proper incentives to co-operate, not as bribes but as factors which help to compensate for extreme deprivation.[59]

Just as poor people have difficulty rejecting "material inducements" and the conditions that go with them, hospital patients must think very carefully before refusing to see a hospital social worker. To do so risks the judgment and reprisal of the entire medical staff including the physicians. As Richard Cabot phrased it, "When the social worker begins the difficult task of acquiring influence in a family, she starts with a great deal in her favor if she appears in the home as the agent of the physician. He has prestige. By reason of his profession, by reason of the institution which he represents, by reason of confidence already established by him in the patients' friends and neighbors, the new family is ready to have confidence in him."[60]

In child welfare investigations, the consequence of failure to cooperate with social workers could be far worse than the denial of relief funds or even medical care. For the single mother receiving a pension from the state, the ultimate threat was loss of her children—the breaking up of the family:

> *March 26, 1931.*—The Juvenile Court asked for placement by the Children's Agency for three Negro Children, Chester, Mabel, and Edith Harris, the dependent children of Chester and Jennie Harris. The father died on October 21, 1929. The mother was granted a pension $53 on November 21, 1930, with the provision that she give up drinking and remain in her mother-in-law's home, under the latter's supervision. When, in January, 1931, the mother moved to a furnished room, taking the two girls with

her, she resumed her drinking and began to live with men. On March 31, 1931, the pension was stayed by the Juvenile Court because of the mother's moral unfitness.[61]

When school visitors knocked on people's doors, they were not turned away either. There was simply so much more to be gained from relating to them in a friendly way. School visitors were in regular communication with the child's teacher and principal, as well as relief agencies, courts, the Society for the Prevention of Cruelty to Children, health authorities, police. On the one hand, the school visitor was able to reward cooperation by securing scholarships, by getting students into better schools and classes, by providing financial assistance and housing; on the other hand, the visitor had the capacity to report any suspicion of immoral, unhealthful, or criminal conduct.

On the whole, therefore, one can speak of the formation of a social work investigation that is not added onto other institutional structures like a rigid, heavy weight, but is so subtly mixed with them as to increase their efficiency at the same time that its own efficiency, as an investigative function, is increased. Not because the social work investigation replaced something in the hospital, school, or child welfare structure but because it was able to infiltrate them without undermining them, linking their various functions together, extending them, making it possible to bring the effects of power to the most minute and distant elements at the lowest possible cost—"in short, to increase both the docility and utility of all the elements of the system."[62]

CHAPTER 4

Self-Mystification

It is nonsense to say that great social work can be done without great
emotion. Our emotion is composed of the feeling that what happens
to flesh and spirit is important, plus courage, joy, satisfaction, and love
of our calling. . . . The union of great emotion and idea is the beginning
of great social work.

Miriam Van Waters, "Philosophical Trends in Modern Social Work" (1931)

To understand how social work language expresses power, we need to
recognize that it is a double-entry system. Power goes in two directions at once. Social workers mystify themselves at the same time they mystify clients.

Because social workers cannot carry out investigations if they perceive
themselves as deceptive and manipulative, they have to continually shield
themselves from any evidence that they are engaged in deception or manipulation: "Of all the mistakes that the case worker may make . . . , one of
the worst . . . is lack of spontaneity, of genuineness of attitude. This attribute
of sincerity is not one that can be assumed at will, for it must be unfeigned;
the lack of it is almost surely fatal to the establishment of a natural relationship between worker and client."[1] Because awareness of manipulation, self-
interest, or hierarchical domination represents for social workers an "onto-
logically fatal insight" into their activities, social work survives only insofar
as it hides from itself any awareness of what it is actually doing.[2]

What concerns me now is not merely denial—that social workers fail to
see what they are up to—but also how the closing of the doors and windows
of consciousness is accomplished in the first place. We can begin to understand the complexity of this forgetting by recognizing that it never has any
closure or finality. It is always in process. Because there is no true or complete forgetting so long as actors are aware of what they are doing, they must
not only cover their tracks but must find ways to keep themselves from finding out that they are covering their tracks. Above all, the processes of forgetting must be forgotten.

How, then, do social workers carry out their investigations? They do so
through a process of dissociation, through systematic denial, through the

practice of misunderstanding themselves, intoxicated and fired by ostentatious humaneness toward the poor and enthusiasm for their duties.³ Specifically, social workers keep themselves in a frenzy of enthusiasm in order to forget that they are engaged either in investigation or the concealment of investigation. They can acknowledge to themselves only that they are giving aid, charity, friendship: "We want to do social work because we have got something that we must share, something that is too hot to hold. . . . We are sharing that which we share because in view of all the bounty which we have received, in view of the beauty which has struck us dumb, in view of the flood of affection that we never have answered, we know what to do next."⁴

According to the rhetoric of mystification, what social workers need "is faith in their poor, humility of spirit, jolly comradeship, sheer psychic power to carry conviction for the right and sensible action against every argument springing from discouragement or bitterness or suspicion."⁵ Going further, the visitor "who would receive the confession of another man must see honesty in the thief without being blind to his thievery. He must feel neither surprise nor horror at any revelation that may be made to him, no matter how unusual. It is not enough to be silent and to refrain from expressing these emotions. They must not even exist."⁶

Within this self-hypnosis, whatever a client says, no matter how strange or absurd or wrong it may seem, is welcomed by the social worker: "She knows nothing but respect for any contribution of a client. She does not evince surprise, disapproval, distaste, no matter what takes place in a situation. . . . In many instances the case worker's belief in the client transcends the client's belief in himself."⁷

What is gained by such expectations and enthusiasms? Curiously, social workers are not held to greater accountability in their actions toward the poor. The very reverse is true. This frenzy of benevolence diverts everyone's attention from historical and cultural knowledge, from the types of analysis that can shed light on unequal benefits and sufferings, and raises questions about social work practices and ideologies. As social workers' discourse moves from friendliness and kindliness into reverence and awe—into unconditional acceptance and "unfailing patience and sympathy"⁸—intrusions are no longer seen as intrusions; the difference between patronizing and sympathizing, manipulation and guidance, becomes nondefinable.

Sincerity

We begin by considering how social workers' "sincerity" relieved them of responsibility for what might otherwise have appeared as uninvited familiarities, overzealousness, untoward judgments and advice. For example, in the following account of a home visit from the 1920s, we note how the social worker used her sincerity as both an excuse and justification—how she went about the task of seeing and describing her sincerity in order to make behavior that might appear impertinent or untimely seem (to herself and other social workers) entirely benign and expected.

The story begins with the social worker rapping at the door, and the client, Mrs. M., opening it a few inches, looking at the social worker through the crack.[9] "Good morning," said the social worker. A momentary hesitation; no reply. The social worker proceeded: "You have no idea how lovely your plants look through the window with the sunlight on them. Is the bright one a fuchsia?"

Mrs. M. opened the door bit wider and, seeming to brighten, said, "Yes, that came from my mother's grave. Most folks do not like old-fashioned flowers." "Oh, I do," said the social worker. "And you have so many. What are the others?" Now the door opened wide in invitation. The visitor followed Mrs. M. into the house, and there followed a discussion of potted plants: how frequently plants should be repotted, and whether it was a good idea to put them on the porch in the sunshine so early in the season. The social worker offered Mrs. M. some pots she had in her attic; she suggested that the drainage would be better than in the tin cans. She also offered her a sample can of paint that had been left at the office, enough to paint two of the larger pails in which Mrs. M.'s plants were growing. By this time, Mrs. M. was talking quite openly and finally said with obvious pride,

> "I don't know why, but plants just seem to grow for me."
> "How lovely," said the visitor, "I think plants do not grow for people who do not appreciate beauty. Flowers always make me feel that I ought to keep my house looking its best for them. Do you feel that way, too?"
> "I never thought about it. But I do like to sit and look at the flowers. I do not think of the house much. I can just turn my back on it and forget it."
> "Oh, but wouldn't it be dreadful if the flowers turned their backs on the house and on us when we look badly?" (*laughingly*).
> Mrs. M. laughed, too, but said practically, "They haven't any backs."
> They both laughed at what to Mrs. M was an absurd idea.

We can see that for the social worker in this home visit, there really was "faith in the poor," "humility of spirit," "jolly comradeship," and "conviction for the right and sensible action against every argument springing from discouragement or bitterness or suspicion." As proof, she had the documentation of shared laughter and positive feeling, of ceaseless optimism, her common touch, the compliments directed at Mrs. M. ("I think plants do not grow for people who do not appreciate beauty"), the continual demonstration of belief in the possibility of improvement ("Oh, but would not it be dreadful if flowers turned their backs on the house and on us when we look so badly?"). Only to outsiders and critics, and perhaps to Mrs. M. and her husband, was there any suggestion of manipulation. Only to them could the discourse on the beauty of Mrs. M.'s potted plants ("You have no idea how lovely your plants look through the window with the sunlight on them") be analyzable in terms of deception and power.

We know, of course, that the social worker did not make this visit just to discuss potted plants. Indeed, as soon as Mrs. M. was comfortable, the visitor suggested they go over the M. family budget, item by item, "all in the confidential manner of visitor and worker understanding each other and planning together to make it clear that Mr. M. couldn't help but get *their* points and see that his allowance was inadequate" (italics added). The social worker suggested that Mrs. M. would have a better chance of getting her husband to give more money for the house if she rehearsed her arguments. Thus they did a role-play together. Mrs. M. did her best to pretend that the visitor was her husband, and the visitor responded as if she were Mr. M., imagining all his objections and arguments. At the end of this, the social worker reassured her client, "Now, Mrs. M., we'll stand by you and I'm sure we can win out if you'll just have the house cleaned up and give Mr. M. a good dinner before you start talking to him."

In order not to overwhelm Mrs. M. "with too long concentration on one subject," the social worker suggested that they go out and sit on the front step in the sun. After the difficult budget discussion, it was important to clear the air with something refreshing and bright:

> "Mrs. M., I don't believe you know what lovely skin you have. You must have been a good-looking girl."
> Then followed a discussion on how hard it was to keep one's good looks having children so close together . . . , how expensive good looks were—that, for instance a good dentist would charge $100 or more for a "set" of teeth; that it was too bad that Mrs. M. could not afford to have them, she was so young, and she would look so much better with her face filled in, and of course she'd feel better if she could chew her food properly.

The interview ended with Mrs. M. wondering how she could get the money for the new set of teeth: "Well, I know Mr. M. ought to give us more money, . . . but he does not and when I ask for money he says its gone and what can I do? I do not *like* to go to you people and ask for things." As her closing comment, the social worker offered, "I'm sure we'll be able to win Mr. M. around working together."

The crucial sociological question, for this chapter at least, is not how the client came to trust the social worker but how the social worker came to trust herself. How did she manage to keep herself from being discredited in her own eyes? For example, how did it come about that the social worker did not question her motives after using flattery as a wedge for gaining influence ("Mrs. M., I don't believe you know what lovely skin you have")? And how did she dispel the possibility that she was interfering in the M.'s marriage after so carefully coaching and rehearsing Mrs. M. on how to get her husband to alter his budgetary practices?

The answer is that these doubts were refuted by "sincerity." Now whether or not this social worker was truly or sincerely sincere is irrelevant. What matters is that she sincerely believed she was sincere.[10] To establish this belief, she meticulously showcased her "frame of mind" on the day of the home visit: "That particular morning I found the Ford was not running and I groaned inwardly at the thought of those ten blocks to walk from the car line. But when I left the street car the sun was shining, there was a lovely breeze, everything was so fresh and green and springlike, the birds were singing and suddenly I felt a new and joyous hopefulness. It seemed to me that there must be some spring which, if touched, would make them respond to beauty, express more activity and joy, and that it was my job to find that spring." [11]

For this social worker on this morning, "sincerity" was much more than a mere hypothesis. She backed it up by detailed accounts of how she was transported by the splendor of the day—"the sun was shining," "the lovely breeze," that "everything was so fresh and green." She took particular pains to document that there were no preconceived or rationalistic motives behind her actions: "the birds were singing and suddenly I felt a new and joyous hopefulness. . . . You see, it was not any plan about how to approach Mrs. M.—just a greater desire for understanding."

What needs to be recognized, then, is that gaps or failures of consciousness in this social worker and others—specifically, their failure to see themselves as manipulative—do not result from some incredible shallowness or naïveté. Rather, their "failure of consciousness" is an artful failure. In particular, social workers exercised continual, yet unwitting, ingenuity in their capacity to obscure any appearance of insincerity by always finding ways to locate and highlight evidences of genuineness and spontaneity in their actions. Thus, when Richard Cabot described social workers "as people who find the world so glorious, so overflowing, in what it has done for us, that we want to even up, to pay out . . . to share our *enthusiasms*," [12] he was not displaying the motives for social work so much as the "vocabularies of motive" that make it possible to conduct social work in the first place.[13] Put somewhat differently, rather than "sincerity" being a fixed element located within social workers, it is a professional resource that social workers use to manage the interpretation of their actions.

The crucial benefit from these displays of "unfeigned genuineness" is that they make clients give information willingly; they "release him to the point where he talks because he wants to, and not because we want him to." [14] Genuineness and sincerity thus make it possible to find out how much coal is in the cellar and how much food is in the cupboards, without actually requiring the social worker to peep into the cellar or pump information out of children. In the words of Gertrude Springer, "The first visit should demonstrate to a family, not that we have them under suspicion, but that we'll trust them if they'll trust us. If we can get off on that foot the truth will ultimately come out much more clearly than if we look for it under the beds or in the closet." [15]

In summary, the fullest realization of the social work technique requires that the investigator must, in some part of the self, be convinced of the superfluousness of investigation. To be effective, social workers must actually feel that the investigation is little more than a formality: "If you [as a social worker] begin by believing that there must be something in him to respect or admire, you will find it, and can meantime win him to respect you. You cannot persuade him to give you his confidence and ask your counsel if you despise his." [16]

Doing Good

Social workers need to think of themselves as "doing good." They must believe they are responding to real needs and actually helping clients. As we have seen, this mode of self-recognition is not achieved automatically; social workers have to be convinced. They have to refute any doubt that their well-intentioned acts are in fact beneficial to individuals and their families.

There is one arena in which we can easily see this self-persuasion at work: in the stories social workers tell about themselves. I am not referring to stories told during conversations, which involve turn taking and negotiation and thus readily lend themselves to challenge, but rather to the case descriptions printed in social work textbooks and journals that illustrate typical and expected social work encounters—that illustrate what social work can and should be.

The most distinctive features of these stories is their simplicity, the starkness of the images, the economy of plot and movement. This means that social work stories aim at causing an immediate impression. No matter how attentively they are examined, the reading is essentially exhausted at one stroke. Like professional wrestling, where nothing unexpected is allowed, where the participants scrupulously adhere to the assigned scripts, social work stories offer no surprises or subtleties. At the same time, the messages are almost always excessive, exploited to the limit of their meaning. In real experience, successes and failures may be mostly fleeting and elusive, but in social work stories they are exaggerated, endowed with absolute clarity. [17]

Here are three examples from early social work texts. The first involves a small Italian boy who was always in trouble at school for being tardy. As soon as the social worker was assigned the case, she visited the family at suppertime (to ensure that all members were present) and, adopting a sympathetic tone, asked what the problem was. She found there were seven children and the mother was dying of cancer. Although a married daughter lived next door and came in every morning to help out, the social worker learned that the boy who was so often tardy was needed to help with the other children:

> He took the youngest child to school across the car tracks, which prevented his getting on time to his own school. The punishments, of course, have ceased, and a satisfactory adjustment has been made. Any of us would have known enough to do that part of it, once the diagnosis had been furnished. The crucial thing was the making of the diagnosis—getting at the facts. The point to observe is that it was the trained social worker, with her ingrained principle of investigation—the instinct for the bottom fact—who performed that essential service.[18]

The second example also involves a boy who was labeled a truant. Again, a home visit was made to determine what was behind the apparent problem. In this instance, the social worker learned that the boy had lived with various family members since the death of his mother six years previously, that no one wanted him, and that there was an ongoing battle to control a small allowance coming from an estate administered by one lawyer and one guardian:

> Found that this boy should receive $16 a month from the Government as a minor child of a Spanish War Veteran, but that the guardian and the lawyer divided $9 of this between them and some member of the family received the remainder. Case brought into court, a sister made the guardian, the lawyer called in for an accounting of the way case had been handled, and arrangements made whereby the boy should be given a decent home, and the full amount of pension to which he is entitled. Also physical defects were corrected and the boy was helped in such a way that he no longer felt he was uncared for, and became happily adjusted in school.[19]

The third story involves a sixteen-year-old boy who had become quite helpless after an attack of polio. The only thing the doctors could do for him, it seemed, was to prescribe braces, making it possible for him to walk with crutches. But the social worker quickly discovered that his physical disability was only half of the problem:

> Two or three years of sickness and idleness and an indulgent family had left him with little ambition. The social worker had not only to teach the boy patiently and persistently to keep at the job she procured for him, but also to strengthen the morale of his family so as to prevent them from giving him entire support. She taught both patient and family that happiness was to be found in work, not in idleness, and that the best protection for this boy was to care for himself.[20]

We need not pause to consider the degree of truth or falsehood in these stories. What is of more immediate concern is that they possess a definite style and structure. In the first place, they always presume a real world inhabited by real people, in which events unfold in logical, temporal sequences (beginning, middle, end). In these narratives, everything is sensible, everything is describable, nothing goes unexplained. Their most striking feature is the portrayal of social work efficacy: Social workers always appear able to diagnose people's problems immediately, regardless of how complex or deep-seated these problems might at first appear. They describe themselves as having direct access to solutions and always appear ready and willing to put the solutions into action. The social work "intervention" is the action taken for the purpose of solving the client's problem, and the last lines of these stories always describe the happy state of affairs that prevail after the intervention is complete: "He has learned to acknowledge his mistakes and atone for them like a man," or "Today she is married and living in a pleasant and well-kept home of her own," or "With that source of embarrassment eliminated, Peter's whole attitude toward school changed and he ceased to be a truant."[21]

In the following example, from *The Field of Social Service*, we see how social work completely reversed a family's life from negative to positive by providing a budget and loaning money. The intervention begins with the social worker making a typewritten list of the family's debts, "which showed by actual figuring that certain payments made upon certain debts each month would in less than a year bring them to the point of solvency."[22] Copies were given to Mr. and Mrs. X, who were then persuaded that the plan would be a success if followed in all its details. "The result of this arrangement was that the man and woman actually entered upon a new era in their married life. Mr. X gave to his wife his weekly earnings with the exception of a small amount reserved for his personal needs. She knew she could count upon this sum weekly, and she had before her a full understanding of the demands and how to meet them." The new budgetary practices not only resolved the Xs' financial problems; it solved *all* their problems.

> The doctor and the social worker at the hospital were now given their first real chance of curing their patient, for we had a direct attack upon the source of her worry. As time passed the children said they hardly knew their parents as they now appeared in the home, and the steady improvement of X dated from the moment the new plan was placed in her hands in tangible form. She will not be a well woman for some time, but the year has passed and all the debts are paid, including the advances made by this Association; the family is restored to solvency and happiness, evidence of which is given in Mr. X's statement to us when he made the final payment on our loans; "I truly believe," he said, "that but for this help of yours, my wife would have been dead and our home lost. We now have

courage to send Henry to the Agricultural College and our winter's coal is in and paid for."

Whether or not Mr. and Mrs. X "actually entered upon a new era in their married life" as a result of the social work intervention is not the issue. What matters is that we have written testimony that they did. Because social work controls its own historiography, we have no way to discredit its version of its own efficacy. Because we have no alternative histories of social work—say, histories written by clients—there are no stories showing how the excellent budgets contrived by social workers failed to perform in the expected way. It is for this reason that social work's capacity to render and preserve stories about itself is so important. Like Plato's "noble lie," such stories not only impose a certain reality on the audience but also reinforce the unequal capacity to impose reality. By continually displaying social work integrity and skill, these stories proclaim social workers to be good and truthful storytellers. What that means, and what it means when social work makes itself look good (by "doing good"), is that those who control language are in the position to justify (and continue) their control of it. The control of language is not a zero-sum resource; it is not something that gets used up by one party and is then taken over by a second; it is self-perpetuating, conservative, endlessly recyclable.[23]

Another, slightly more elaborate vignette from *The Visiting Teacher in New York City* concerns an adolescent named Miriam, whose school principal described her as "incorrigible with a tendency toward immorality, unruly in the classroom, untruthful, and untidy in appearance." He asked the social worker (or "visiting teacher" as they were called in those days) to take her out of school and send her to work. Characteristically, when the social worker called at the home, she did not find an "incorrigible" or "immoral" child but rather one who was overburdened, poorly nourished, neglected. She found that Miriam's mother had died a short time earlier, leaving Miriam responsible for a household consisting of an unemployed father and two brothers. She prepared the meals, washed the clothes, and performed all the chores her mother had done when alive:

> Of a highly sensitive nature, very retiring and backward, she made few girl friends. She craved love and affection, was very sympathetic, but there was no outlet for these emotions. She was untruthful, but she told tales to win sympathy. She was on the street at night, and while she did not seek companions of the lower type, they came to her, using her as a shield to cover some of their wrong-doings.
>
> The visiting teacher became very friendly with Miriam and found new friends for her, and the old ones were given up. Through the assistance of the relief organization the family was moved to better quarters. Work was secured for the father, and the younger brother was placed in a Hebrew class in a neighborhood organization.

When Miriam was promoted to the seventh grade the visiting teacher watched her very closely. She asked that the child be given to an especially sympathetic teacher to whom she told the story of her home life.

Throughout two years, the visiting teacher followed her progress. The child came back to her with all sorts of problems, now a discouraging mark in school, now household cares that needed school help for her adjustment and again financial difficulties caused by the unemployment of her father or brother. Tutoring was provided, arrangements were made to excuse her a little early so that she could prepare the evening meal for the Jewish Sabbath; and plans for tiding the family over a period of stress were worked out with the agency of relief.

Gradually Miriam showed the result of this friendly supervision. The dime novels which had been her choice and rough friends ceased to satisfy her, and when she graduated she had won the affection of all the finest girls in her class and the genuine respect of her teachers. All trace of immoral tendency disappeared.[24]

In the first place, the style of such passages should be noted. It is a period style, of course, replete with all the images one would expect to find in stories of orphaned girls, those imperishable symbols of the human spirit. What is new here is that social work is given responsibility for uncovering and harvesting all this virtue. Because of the social work intervention, Miriam not only gave up having rough friends and ceased reading dime novels; she also won the affection of the "all finest girls in her class," and "all trace of immoral tendency disappeared."

How did social work accomplish these transformations? We do not know, and the truth is, no one really cares. Readers are completely uninterested in knowing how Miriam became morally upright, and rightly so; to require a precise explanation for Miriam's progress would amount to denying the story's real theme: the spectacle of social work healing and redemption. The point of the story is not to reveal some algebra of intervention by which specific acts logically yield specific consequences. What matters is that everyone is reassured, installed in the quiet certainty of a universe where social workers are social workers, and clients are clients. In this most legible of bifurcations, social workers act, and clients are acted upon; social workers heal, clients suffer; social workers are powerful, clients are helpless. What matters is that the whole client–social worker drama is ordered with reference to one group's efficacy and superiority.[25]

It's a Wonderful Life

Now we examine a slightly different social work story line in which the social worker is portrayed as successfully intervening to quell political action and social protest. In this example, originally published in *The Family* in 1939

under the title "Client Co-operation," an unnamed social worker in an unnamed community shows how it is possible to convert angry and frightened
relief demonstrators into an unashamedly optimistic and cooperative bunch
of neighbors. This story portrays a social worker's almost magical capacity to
redirect and motivate people into "healthy" relations at the same time as it
highlights and reinforces the belief that political change should not be handled through broad-based institutional reform. What matters, according to
this mythology, is that social problems be traced to individual failure.

The story begins with a description of relief clients "in patched overalls
and ragged sweaters" marching down Main Street to the old pavilion at the
edge of town. Their wives and whimpering children follow, anxious and
afraid: they were afraid of arrest and of losing the relief they had been getting, but "the men said they'd nothing to lose!" After six years of drought
and crop failures, and all the humiliation of relief, the tension had become
unbearable. Something had to be done.[26]

When they arrived at the barnlike pavilion, the men sat down front and in
the center, with the women and children forming a restive fringe around the
edges. Uncertain how to begin, "the silence . . . more choking than the dust-
laden air," someone finally spoke:

> Me and Jeff here aint much for talkin', but we did not come to talk.
> We come to do something. The government says there is to be work and
> relief aplenty for all that needs it. We aint gettin' enough though, and
> we're meetin' tonight to talk over why we aint. We've gone to the Com-
> missioners. We've spoke with the mayor. Some has written the President.
> And all of us has set and set in the relief office. But what's come of it?
> Nothin's come of it, that's what! Something's got to be done. We're tired
> of hearin' what's goin' to be done. We want something done now. We
> mean business tonight. So, speak up fellows, and let's hear what you think
> to do. . . .
>
> Some are afraid they'll be taken off relief if they talk. We're half the
> town though, and they cannot let us all starve, leastways not the women
> and kids. But while you're thinking about what to say, maybe the social
> worker can tell us why we do not get enough. We asked her to come, and
> I notice she's here. She's so new in the county, she cannot rightly know
> how bad things are, but we'll be glad to have her say something. Maybe
> she can answer some questions.

If poverty stems from an economy that fails or from an exploitive or in-
different government, then social workers have no claim to authority—they
are not the ones who can answer questions and provide direction. Authority
belongs to the politician, the economist, or the radical. But if it can be shown
that joblessness stems from the townspeople's own inadequacies, from their
childishness, their naïveté and ignorance, then authority is vested in the social worker's specific area of competence. That is why it is so important to es-

tablish that the townspeople are ignorant, childlike, disposed to act, not think ("Me and Jeff aint much for talkin'"). It establishes their need for a leader, someone mature and educated. This is precisely why we now welcome the social worker's entrance into the story. We trust that she will measure up—that she will carry out intelligently and to the last detail all that the townspeople cannot do on their own. What this vignette provides, then, is the moral drama of suffering, defeat, and redemption; we see not only why the townspeople suffer (they are children) but how the social worker redeems (she is good). Here is her entrance:

> The social worker, the fifth in the county in two years, came forward slowly. She felt the tension; felt rather than saw the anxiety, the spirit of hopelessness, frustration, and defeat. She told them how glad she was getting together to talk things over. There was so much they could do by all working together.
>
> Like quick rain on a dusty field, this simple reassurance cleared the air of fear. A babble of voices responded: How could Widow Kane care for eight children and her aged mother on her slim relief order? Why was Lief Peters taken off the work—because he had only one arm? Everybody knew Lief was worth any three two-armed men in the county! Why did folks get relief who did not need it? Why were farmers on relief, when they had milk, eggs, and vegetables for sellin'? Men who did not have a roof over their heads, why couldn't they get help?
>
> The social worker answered their questions as best she could. Rules and regulations were explained; a brief sketch of the history of government relief was given; state grants were interpreted. She admitted relief was far from adequate, and that there might be many receiving help who did not need it. She talked to them about their value as a group, and how they could accomplish things by working together. It was true that Widow Kane needed much more than the amount of relief granted her. The roof to her house was leaking badly, and other repairs were needed. Could any members of the group do anything to help? Were there any carpenters present who would volunteer their services? Were there some who would help work a plot in the community gardens for Widow Kane until her boys were old enough to do it? Would some of them speak to the people who had not told the truth about their resources? Such people probably did not realize they were robbing their own needy neighbors; they might be thinking they were just getting their share of government "graft." No need to report the names of such people to the relief office; let the ones who knew such speak to them as neighbor to neighbor. Without doubt there would be more relief, if only those received help who honestly needed it.

Thus the meeting progressed, with the social worker opening the way for the townspeople to tackle a number of their own problems. Somehow, because of the social worker's participation, "the air of sullen despair" gave way to "a spirit of resolution and determination"; there was also a new spirit of cooperation, of neighborliness: "Grandpa Searles declared they'd been told aplenty what each could do for himself, and they'd hear a lot about what the government was a-goin' to do for them, but they sure had not given enough thought to what they could do together to help each other."

Subsequent meetings proved this was not simply hot air. A number of relief clients asked to be dropped from the rolls, making it possible to increase the assistance where it was most needed, and when it became apparent that money had to be raised to finance future activities, "it was decided to raise the money by an old-time square dance, instead of by dues. Fiddlers and callers were available from their own number. So successful was the gathering that it was decided to 'make good times' a regular part of their meetings." While these activities raised money, "the greatest benefits were in the emotional release, the feelings of reassurance, of adequacy, of 'belongingness,' which came to their relief clients through their group activities. Within a remarkably short time, from a sullen, frustrated, rebellious crowd of unhappy clients, they became a happy, well-integrated, cooperative group."

Having read this, one wants to make some kind of wholesale reference to social work's political role. This is the kind of story, one wants to say, in which social work's political agenda breaks through to the surface, in which social workers cannot help but recognize themselves quelling political insurgency. But if we read this story within the context of other social work vignettes, we get a renewed and increased appreciation of how this genre masks such recognitions. Note that the social worker does not attempt to overtly suppress or combat the townspeople's political action. Poor people may be massing and marching, angrily denouncing a system that oppresses them, but the social worker does not see things that way. She reframes everything that smacks of the political into something interpersonal and individual: "She talked to them about their value as a group, and how they could accomplish things by working together. It was true that Widow Kane needed much more than the amount of relief granted her. The roof of her house was leaking badly, and other repairs were needed. Could any members of the group do anything to help? Were there any carpenters present who would volunteer their services?"

Because social work frames its intervention in the language of helping, it is freed from the responsibility of taking a political position or performing political action. The central issue, according to the narrative, is humanist: how to replace "sullen despair" with a "spirit of resolution and determination," how to make a "frustrated, rebellious crowd" become "a happy, well-integrated, cooperative group." But underneath is a moral that is purely partisan: only by becoming rule-abiding citizens and good neighbors can the townspeople gain happiness and autonomy; only by giving up political protest can they gain self-respect and independence. In other words, the social worker induces clients' submission to governmental authority, not by threats or warnings but, in the style of a Frank Capra movie, by earnestly cheering them on, by motivating them to see things differently, by asking them to change their attitudes. It is the difference between *The Grapes of Wrath* and *It's a Wonderful Life*: according to the former, the problem is in the bad system; according to the latter, the problem is people's bad attitude. The vignette concludes: "Today, the majority of social workers realize that the most serious problems confronting them are linked with mental and emotional breakdowns in their clients. Feelings of inadequacy and defeat, loss of ambition, apathy, are problems more tragic than material privation. No matter how defeated a relief client may feel, however, he seldom fails to respond to the stimulation he receives in being part of a functioning group. He gets a holiday from himself and his troubles." [27]

Like Marie Antoinette's mythic pronouncement, "Let them eat cake," the social worker declares, "Let them have emotional support." True, the towns-people are hungry, but "feelings of inadequacy and defeat, loss of ambition, apathy, are problems more tragic than material privation." This is not to say that the social worker's remarks are the equivalent of Marie Antoinette's. There is a critical difference: Marie Antoinette's words take power to its point of maximum obviousness; they are overwhelming evidence of cold-ness, distance, arrogance, while the social worker's words take power to its point of maximum subtlety; instead of coldness, her words represent em-pathy, caring. It is the difference between power that fails and power that succeeds.

What makes social work so effective is simply that it relies on images that simultaneously mask and justify it. For example, clients' gratitude, which comes at the end of these case examples, affirms clients' helplessness and in-feriority at the same time that it proclaims the benefits social work provides. This is a generous, bountiful dominance and thus not identifiable as a domi-nance at all.

Clients' Problems

Let us consider the role of the "presenting problem" in these vignettes. Every case example begins with a pressing problem or series of problems and maladjustments that justifies social work's involvement at the very same moment that it diminishes and stigmatizes the client. In fact, it is by describ-ing clients in terms of their problems that the social work invitation is ac-complished in the first place. The language that constructs clients' helpless-ness and dependency is also a rationale for vesting authority in social workers. The language that creates the relation of dominance is the language that makes that relation appear necessary, ethical, benevolent. For example, note in the following vignette that every statement that describes the client and his family in negative terms serves also to explain why the social worker needs to become involved:

> Donato was a violinist of fair ability, but a fondness for liquor, unwisely indulgent parents, and a wife whose standards of home-making were below his own, had contributed to his deterioration. For fifteen years he had slipped from one failure to another until at last he was going about the streets seeking alms in return for music. Even in this he was unsuccessful, and at length his wife and his five children and he were reduced to living in these miserable rooms. They faced a winter without money for fuel and with no apparent means of paying the rent now overdue or of providing the next day's food. Donato's parents had come to the rescue on so many occasions that they were unwilling to help, and Mrs. Donato appealed to a social agency.
>
> A social case worker called upon the family in the late afternoon and found Mr. and Mrs. Donato and their children sitting in semi-darkness. . . .
>
> "If I am to be of any help to you," she began, "I shall need certain information." [28]

Describing Mr. Donato and his "presenting problem" in this way generates the conviction that social work has no choice but to be involved. It does what it does because it must. And if these case descriptions appear to focus almost exclusively on the poor, this is not a matter of design but of accommodation. The inferiority of the poor is treated as something discovered, not created, as something that entirely predates social workers' activities and intentions. Social work acknowledges, of course, that "people who are physically, mentally or morally unfit to take their proper places in society are distributed in all classes of people." [29] However, social work also acknowledges that "those who are shielded by wealthy relatives or friends are not as likely to become public charges as those from poor families. Their relatives and friends make the necessary adjustments to offset their failures instead of calling upon public servants to do it." [30] In other words, social work treats social class inequality not as an essential feature of its existence but as a practical, post hoc adaptation: first there was inequality, then there was the inability to cope with it, next came social work.

Obviously, then, it is not simply a matter of social workers fooling clients (or the middle class fooling the poor)—social workers enact the ruse on themselves before they enact it on anyone else. They thoroughly convince themselves of the irrelevance of their own class interests. They convince themselves that their actions are motivated by compassion and fairness, and not by their professional and political affiliations.

The critical point is that the neutrality of social work stories is preserved just so long as we think of them as literal transcriptions of dialogue and action. The moment we suspend the presumption of literalness, we see that what at first sight presents itself as apolitical appears to function socially as a method of structuring perceptions of authority, status, worth, deviance, and the causes of social problems.[31] Instead of turning to social work case studies as already classified and defined entities, as inherently nonproblematic and nonpartisan, we may examine them as signals for political and cultural analysis much as we do fiction writing, advertising, or speech making. Therefore, in reading the following story, published in *The Family* in 1922, readers should not consider truth or falsehood but, rather, function and fit—the story's rightness as a support for particular values and role divisions. Whom does this version of reality benefit? Whom does it disadvantage?

The Bad Penny

"Tell yer wot," said Mrs. Whidden with the large sigh of one finally grasping the situation. "You g'wan over to th' Sassity and they'll fix yer up. . . . Now do not be a silly little fool, Lizzie," as her companion demurred, conscious, as only nineteen can be conscious, that the disasters of nineteen are beyond all human help. "Now do not be a fool—you just g'wan to the Sassity—why I'll be bound if I do not take yer myself," said Mrs. Whidden to Lizzie.

By a route long familiar to Mrs. Whidden, the two journeyed to the district office. Many times during the last chaotic ten years had Mrs. Whidden gone to the Society and the Society to her. Many a crisis had they weathered together—the crisis of unemployment, the crisis of babies born and lost, the crisis of a husband often sick and jobless—and through these ten years was woven the binding chain of a hearty and consistent intemperance on the part of Mrs. Whidden. No, not ten, for the last three years had seen an astonishing change in Mrs. Whidden.

After twice taking the cure and half a dozen times the pledge; after the dreary succession of drink-soaked furnished rooms that could never be a home; after repeatedly touching the bottom and nearly establishing a legal residence there, Mrs. Whidden had been precariously climbing toward sobriety and decency. . . .

"I guess we need some help," began Mrs. Whidden, and the secretary, wise in the dark precipitous places of family case work, braced herself to watch the fabric of the seven years' patient work and the bright pattern of the last tenuous three falling into dust again. She did not notice the misery-haunted girl in the corner until Mrs. Whidden went on. "You see Lizzie here, her husband's left her and the baby and no money. And first she ses she's going to live with a fancy feller in blue cloth gaiters on Eleventh Avenoo and then ses she's going to drown herself in the River and her husband gone on her an' all—You know how it is yerself," thus Mrs. Whidden tactfully softening the plight of her friend; "and I ses to her I ses 'do not be a silly fool, Lizzie,' I ses. C'm on over to the Sassity' and now," Mrs. Whidden leaned comfortably back in her chair, "you fix Lizzie up."

About an hour later, having talked over the situation which was not so desperate after all; and having suggested to Lizzie the plan which was so much simpler and more sensible than living with the blue-gaitered gentleman or throwing herself in the River that runs occasionally so close to Eleventh Avenue, the secretary, her brief-case full of still unfinished reports, went out to the subway; and as she bought her ticket, for some unaccountable reason she felt like whistling.

"I told yer they'd fix yer up," said Mrs. Whidden handing the girl a cup of soup. "Me an' the Sassity knows a thing or two. It do not pay to be wicked or foolish, that wot we ses. Gawd, wot with runnin' around wit' yer worryin' after yer and fixin' yer up at the Sassity, I'm pretty near wore out, I am," said Mrs. Whidden to Lizzie.[32]

The function of such tales is not to tell the truth; it is to portray a world that reassures; it is to render the audience's moral universe orderly and intelligible. It is the same function as Japanese theater or French mime or a Punch-and-Judy show, whose principle is to make every status and relationship maximally visible. Each success and failure is emphasized, overstated, confirming by excess the part that has been assigned to each figure. The purpose of this clarity, therefore, is not to teach viewers something new about their world. It is, rather, the pleasure of confirming and reconfirming and reconfirming again what they already believe.

There is no more a problem of truth in a story such as "The Bad Penny" than in a puppet show. The difference is that a puppet show announces itself as spectacle, as theater, and social work does not. Also, the moral situation that puppets represent more often revolves around the personal and private, while the social work story revolves around social class. That is why the dialogue in "The Bad Penny" is so important. Mrs. Whidden's line, "Tell yer wot," which opens the story, announces the future contents of her role just as clearly as the physical appearance of puppets display their essential moral status. Social work offers a human comedy, in other words, where the stereotypes of class show at an instant who has problems and who does not, who needs help and who can provide it. So Mrs. Whidden's language—her "You g'wan over to th' Sassity"—by locating her class position, signals in advance that she can never be anything but childlike, dependent, grateful. Thus her closing lines ("I told yer they'd fix yer up. . . . Me an' the Sassity knows a thing or two") do not offer an outcome or resolution; they are part of a ritual, a repetition.

However true or false these social worker–to–the–rescue stories may be, they teach us to see social work interventions as momentously dichotomous. They represent a mythology in which one group is always the subject and the other the object. These divisions appear not only in the narrative but also in the "ordered procedures for the production, regulation, distribution, circulation and operation of statements."[33] In other words, those who dominate within the imagery of the social work story are in exclusive control of the writing and reading. Those who dominate the action dominate the printed word. We can now begin to see how closely related the world that social work stories create is to the world that social workers and clients actually inhabit. At all points they touch each other, with myth affecting reality and reality affecting myth.

The Logic of the Social Work Narrative

What social work stories show is that people come to be poor not because they are provided with fewer advantages than others, not because of conditions over which they have no control. Rather, it is that the poor behave less rationally, make worse choices and fewer sacrifices, prefer leisure to hard work. They have the wrong attitude. As L. A. Halbert phrased it in *What Is Professional Social Work?* "Pauperism is a state of mind. We want none of it. We want the victims of misfortune to be determined to win in this present world in which they live no matter whether it is good or bad or what kind of world it is. They cannot find their salvation in some special reform or future millennium for the simple reason that they are liable to die before that kind of relief gets here, or at least they will lose a lot of good valuable time waiting when they might just as well enjoy life and solve their problems themselves."[34]

Now if we ask why social work assumes this point of view, the answer seems obvious. It completely dovetails with the American belief in an open class system, "that the royal road from the log cabin to the White House was open to all."[35] It goes along with the culture of capitalism, which "measures persons, as well as everything else, by their ability to produce wealth and by their success in earning it; it therefore leads naturally to the moral condemnation of those who, for whatever reason, fail to contribute and prosper."[36] This mode of analysis also benefits social workers themselves. As members of the middle class, they can interpret their superior status as deserved: They made the correct choices and sacrifices. They worked hard. The poor did not.[37]

From the beginning of "scientific" charity in the United States, the investigation of individual capacities, choices, and motives was treated as central to understanding the origins of poverty. As early as 1886, the National Conference of Charities and Correction was told that "Charitable work, in the best sense must be done by the individual . . . for the individual. . . . Each case is a special case, demanding special diagnosis, keenest differentiation of features and most intense concentration of thought and effort."[38] Not only was poverty seen as individual failure, but there was complete denial of social class interests and experience: "The poor, and those in trouble worse than poverty, have not in common any type of physical, intellectual or moral development which would warrant an attempt to group them as a class."[39] Although the individualized ("scientific") approach was seen as a radical advance from earlier charity discourse in which the poor were lumped together and portrayed as constitutionally inferior,[40] no one recognized that the seemingly new approach was in fact another way of articulating the old moralism: that the conditions under which the poor live are ultimately traceable to failures in the poor themselves. If we are to understand the logic by which the new scientific charity explained poverty, then we need to recognize that its main feature is not the rejection of moralistic judgment but, rather, a particular manner of expressing judgment—through an ethic of personal responsibility, private initiative, and individual achievement.

We should also be clear that viewing poverty in concrete terms—as it existed for this man, this woman, this family—is not a problem in itself. The problem is that the individualization and personalization of poverty results in individualized and personalized blame. It results in a discourse focused on clients' defects—their false pride, their covetousness, their dependency and weakness.

Accordingly, social workers anticipate meeting every financial need, using every available resource, exerting every effort to rescue clients—only to discover that something within them resists rescue and continuously undermines its accomplishment: "Is not the reliance on relief merely another symptom of that emotional dependency which is present in every client and in which he threatens to be engulfed unless casework can come to the rescue? Is not the fundamental question in some of these cases a question as to whether there is anything left to rescue in clients reduced to abject emotional dependency by their previous experience?"[41]

Even during the Great Depression, the central problem for social work was not that of helping the unemployed find jobs but, rather, explaining the psychological problems that result from job loss and prevent clients from finding new ones. Thus, in 1930, Miriam Van Waters, who was then president of the National Conference of Social Work, declared, "The true springs of action are in the internal nature of man. Hence the uselessness of programs, particularly those dependent on state action, or force."[42]

True, social workers study the community in ways that psychologists and psychiatrists do not. As noted in the previous chapter, they interview clients' neighbors, shopkeepers, fellow workers, employers. They are out and about. This has sometimes been called the "sociological" approach to social work. However, even a cursory analysis of these "community investigations" shows that they were not utilized to make assessments of the community itself but were instead used to form judgments on the character and normality of the individual client. If an employer is interviewed, the first and foremost reason is to learn how the client functioned on the job, why he quit, how he got along with peers, and so forth. Consider, for example, the use that a social worker made of information provided by a former employer—the proprietor of a garage—about a father who was being investigated for not supporting his children: "No signs of liquor during the eight weeks that the man worked for him, but he often failed to come to work. Shiftless and lazy. Was warned that if he did not do the work properly he would be discharged. But for his carelessness might have had the work indefinitely." [43] The point is very simple: community information is not used to tell the community story; it is used to tell the client's personal story. The client's discharge is thus traced to *his* "shiftlessness" and "laziness" and not to the social origins of these problems.

We have already discussed why social workers saw clients so negatively. By attributing their meager life to psychological and moral deficiencies and not to political and social conditions, social workers could readily infer that their own success, and that of their fellow bourgeoisie, was due to such factors as diligence, thrift, character—to something located within them: their essential nature. The unseen, unanticipated, yet deeply satisfying, result was that such analyses proved that the social structure social workers encountered was fundamentally just, and their own position in it, deserved and legitimate.

But the logic of this narrative went one step further. Not only were clients' problems attributed to them, but credit for solving their problems was given to members of the middle and upper classes—specifically, to social workers who provided direction, inspiration, leadership. Again and again, the case studies that filled the articles, books, and pamphlets written by and for social workers described rescue operations organized and conducted by social workers. Even when the social worker did not single-handedly straighten out people's problems for them, she was still their guide and interpreter: "She sees her task in terms of helping people to understand themselves, of arousing in them an appreciation of the handicaps, struggles and achievements of others and of giving them insight into the way they are affecting each other. She is dealing with attitudes, with breaking down those that are destructive to themselves and to others, and with building up socially useful ones in their places. The family case worker is a motivator and teacher. She is teaching husband and wife how to live together more amicably; she is helping parents to understand their children; she is showing them where they are failing in their methods of training their children, and she is suggesting other ways more likely to prove successful." [44]

The central point is that within the social work narrative one group was always active and the other passive. One group led, the other followed. Social work was thus deeply committed to demarcating differences that revolved around activity-passivity, dominance-submission. According to this image making, clients failed when they resisted social work directives and were successful when they cooperated. These vignettes, taken from Ida Cannon's *Social Work in Hospitals*, illustrate:

> A weak-willed man with a fretful and despondent disposition was sent to a social service department with a diagnosis of incipient tuberculosis. After much effort, the patient's family was provided for so that he might go to a sanitarium where, the doctor said, the disease might be arrested. He stayed there two months, idle and resourceless after an active life, complaining and worrying the entire time; then left against advice and returned home, where he died a month later.
>
> Another patient, a colored porter, emaciated but with fire in his eye, was pronounced "advanced tuberculosis—not a hopeful case." He was too ill to be admitted to the sanitorium, for only incipient cases were accepted. He was, however, ready to make a fight. Admission being secured to a tuberculosis class, he followed explicitly all directions, slept out of doors even in the coldest weather, and accepted in a wholesome spirit the aid that was provided for his family. After a year and a half he was able to work. For fourteen years he has himself provided for his family.[45]

Two cautionary messages emerge. One is that those who do not cooperate have "bad character": The man who left the sanitorium against advice and went home was described as "weak-willed" and "despondent." By contrast, the man who "followed explicitly all directions" and "accepted in a wholesome spirit the aid that was provided for his family" had "fire in his eye." The second message is that clients who do as they are told are successful. The resistant client died almost immediately; the cooperative one lived more than fourteen years longer.

Clients are not always compliant in social work experience. Social work stories affirm this. However, with the most creative nonchalance, this is turned from evidence of social work failure into evidence of its success. This is because social work stories redefine client resistance into the explanation par excellence of clients' predicaments and maladjustments. Like the "weak-willed man with a fretful and despondent disposition" who died before his time, resistant clients—those who prefer to go their own way, either without or against social workers—appear in social work stories as human wreckage. Only clients who cooperate with social workers meet a favorable end.

So even though social work described its goals in terms of getting clients to "act autonomously," "talk more freely," "feel more important," "feel more effective and assured,"[46] these outcomes always have to be accomplished with a social worker or, at the very least, on social workers' terms. Social work may have explicitly sought the enhancement of clients' freedom and autonomy, but the "freedom" and "autonomy" social workers consider appropriate for clients cannot be their accomplishment—cannot be taken by themselves—but, rather, have to be given them by social workers.

Social work language and imagery, therefore, while often appearing friendly and compassionate, demands and legitimates the dominance of one population over another. Made to appear as passive objects, social work clients must sacrifice their will to that of the social worker if they are to successfully overcome their difficulties. Psychologically, morally, and economically vulnerable, poor people, as social work shows, need the protection of the bourgeoisie.

Part 2
Aggressive Social Work

CHAPTER 5

Reaching the Hard-to-Reach

The "hard-to-reach" person is a special kind of client—and his brothers are legion.

Few social workers fail to recognize him. At intake he presents problems of disorganization and, usually, financial need; in treatment he fails to keep appointments; is hostile or withdrawn, and sabotages most efforts to help him.

Having named him, how can social workers reach him? How can social workers break down barriers that stymie their work with him?

Evelyn A. Lance, "Intensive Work with a Deprived Family" (1969)

Social work is based on the notion of penetration: social problems are no longer cleansed from the public streets but from its most private cells. "Reaching out," "reaching the hard-to-reach"—these terms link social work to its mythic origins: settlements located in the midst of the foreign colony, explorations of "hidden hovels," "unseen burrows," "pitch-black coops," places "prolific of untold depravities." In this imagery, the home is the final layer of resistance: it is the target, the object of scrutiny and judgment, the target for renewal and transformation.

So if we mark off the 1950s and 1960s, it is because this is a time when discourse on penetration was more deliberate and explicit than ever before. Images of doors and doorknobs, bells and knockers, hallways and entrances, filled social work texts. To play the social worker in this age was to speak loudly and insistently of visitation, to hyperbolize its necessity, so that the client who was resistant became exaggeratedly so, and the social worker paying the visit filled the page with the spectacle of determination and persistence. This scene was published in *Casework Notebook* in 1957:

> There was no doorknob, but after repeated knocking, a fumbling was heard as a doorknob was inserted on the inside of the door. Mrs. D. poked her head around the door, her hair up in curlers. All the worker could see of her was down to the neck. Mrs. D. said, "I got your letter, I have no problems, if you're talking about my boys, that trouble is all over." Worker said she still had something of concern to talk to Mrs. D. about,

that they should talk about her relationship to the boys. She asked if they could make another appointment. Mrs. D. said she would call when the worker could come. Worker said how about tomorrow. Mrs. D. mumbled OK as she shut the door.[1]

According to the text, the social worker called at Mrs. D.'s home the next day. She knocked, but there was no answer. Someone must have been home because she could hear music playing, so she went to the drugstore at the corner to call Mrs. D. Still no answer. The next day the social worker sent Mrs. D. a letter in which she said she was sorry she had missed her, and said she would call again, specifying the date and time. However, when that day arrived, the social worker was again disappointed. No one answered the door.

> On Monday of the following week, worker telephoned Mrs. D. saying that she (the worker) probably made a mistake in appointment time the preceding week. Mrs. D. was very apologetic, said she had forgotten, had been taking care of her daughter's baby. Worker said she did not like to go into too much detail over the phone, but explained she had talked to the school and had information about the boys that she felt should be talked over with Mrs. D. Mrs. D. replied that she had already talked to Father X. at the school, that it was all settled. She had also talked to the police, and everything was all right with her boys. Worker said she had more recent information from the school, and wanted to talk it over in person. She suggested a date the next day, but Mrs. D. could not see her then. Worker went through every day of the week, but Mrs. D. had the same excuse. Finally the worker said what about next Monday. Mrs. D. replied that she would call if she could see the worker on Monday.
>
> The following Monday, Mrs. D. did not call. Worker called her on Tuesday, Mrs. D. answered saying "I cannot even talk today," and hung up.
>
> On Wednesday, worker called again to set up an appointment for the following day.

And so on, appointment after appointment, frustration after frustration, the social worker struggles to get inside her client's home, images which, if believed, turn the social worker into the most remarkable cultural artifact: the Platonic Ideal of persistence, a human being who is impervious to rejection. She keeps coming and coming and coming.

In the past, "if the family was not willing to be served, the case was closed."[2] Now, social workers "must go often enough, stay long enough, go despite rebuffs, discourtesy, frank hostility, and nonchalant denial of need or wish to use service."[3] In the past, social workers assumed that case closings were inevitable, and excused their contribution to them by blaming "client failure." Now, social workers affirmed the need to take the scalpel to their failures, to jar themselves out of their middle-class satisfaction, and to pursue clients aggressively: "What seems to be indicated is a fresh spurt of enthusiasm in casework, a zesty attack on casework's unsolved problems, and a reaffirmation of the earlier faith of social work in the plasticity of man and social work's ability to be the catalyst in social change." [4]

How Do We Account for the New Aggressiveness?

Clearly, the economic successes of the postwar years played a part. You have to be pretty sure of yourself to participate in such a Sisyphean effort. Yet, paradoxically, the new aggressiveness was also driven by suspicion and doubt. Consider that the years of America's greatest economic success were also the years when enrollment in material assistance programs grew at an unprecedented rate. For example, between 1945 and 1961, enrollment in the Aid to Dependent Children (ADC) program jumped from seven hundred thousand to well over three million.[5] Not only were taxpayers increasing their responsibility for the impoverished during years of general prosperity, but the impoverished appeared to be growing in numbers.

How did the white middle class respond? Surely not by blaming itself. According to the conventional wisdom, the poor were trying to get away with something. There was all this talk of assistance awards to unworthy applicants, expensive furniture in the homes of welfare recipients, and the need to "crack down" on fraud, overly tolerant investigations, "unclean rolls."[6] Several communities had drives to publicize the names of welfare recipients, and as a way of weeding out suspected "frauds," entire caseloads were shut down, with all welfare recipients required to undergo new application investigations.[7] For the first time since the Great Depression, public welfare became front-page news, with lurid stories of "chiseling" and "hotel" cases, creating the impression that relief had become a luxurious way of life.[8]

Criticism was especially pronounced regarding mothers on ADC. They were generally perceived as nonwhite women who had illegitimate children specifically to avoid work.[9] As Charles Stevenson phrased it in *Reader's Digest*, "We must curtail this burgeoning dependency, instead of creating more. We must stop coddling parents at the expense of children, insist that money given in the name of children be spent for them. We must send chiseling parents to jail, even if it means finding new homes for the children who, God knows, need a decent, moral climate in which to grow up healthfully." [10]

Interestingly, the representation of fraud in the popular press was completely unmatched by any evidence that such fraud was actually occurring. For example, only two clients were tried for welfare fraud in Detroit in 1948, and no one was convicted, yet the headlines and impressions created by the press were that between 30 and 50 percent of the welfare clientele were "chiselers." Similarly, the California Department of Public Welfare found that only 1.5 percent of the families on its caseload were receiving funds fraudulently, yet Charles Stevenson held that "the losses through chiseling [in California] are estimated as high as 15 percent of the ADC budget." [11]

Social work was not blamed for all this "chiseling." Quite the opposite. Government agencies were criticized for not doing enough social work—for not doing a better job of getting into welfare clients' homes, for failing to monitor their profligate spending and unwholesome domestic practices. The problem was that in their rush to correct "the welfare mess," there was a deployment of a type of social work that had more in common with crime detection than the methods Mary Richmond described some fifty years earlier. Instead of exchanging "confidence for confidence," as friendly visitors had taught, there were now surprise home visits and searches, "social work" investigations without the knowledge or consent of clients, more efforts to catch clients in unstaged situations, more criminal prosecutions, and, in general, more workers representing themselves as something other than what they actually were as they questioned employers, friends, and acquaintances of individuals under investigation.[12] To illustrate, one mother receiving ADC reported to her worker that her only income for herself and her three children was her welfare payments, and that there was no other adult living with or contributing to the support of the family. However, during a noontime visit, the worker found a man in the apartment who was fully clothed but wearing bedroom slippers. The discovery of the slippered man prompted a follow-up visit two days later at 2:30 A.M. in which the man was found in bed in the client's bedroom. The client then admitted that this man was in fact living with her and contributing money to the household. She was prosecuted and found guilty of grand theft.[13]

This form of coercion was fairly common in the late 1940s and early 1950s but quickly faded from use because it was not supported by the court system. Investigations into people's homes conducted against their consent and without a search warrant were repeatedly deemed unconstitutional. For example, in 1948, the Supreme Court considered a case (*Johnston* v. *United States*) that had many of the features of a nocturnal investigation. After a tip-off that guests were smoking opium in the Europe Hotel, the police and narcotics agents knocked on the suspects' door and demanded entry. Even though the suspects were indeed smoking opium, the Supreme Court held that this search violated the Fourth Amendment: "Crime even in the privacy of one's own quarters is, of course, of grave concern to society, and the law allows such crime to be reached on proper showing. The right of officers to thrust themselves into a home is also a grave concern, not only to the individual but to a society which chooses to dwell in reasonable security and freedom from surveillance. When the right of privacy must reasonably yield to the right of search is, as a rule, to be decided by a judicial officer, not by a policeman or government agent." [14]

The law appears unambiguous, yet we are left with an extraordinary dilemma: If people can legally retreat to their homes and there be free from unreasonable government intrusion, how can the community keep track of its most parasitic and pathological elements? If our laws forbid forced searches and surveillance, must we then submerge our need to monitor potential and actual threats?

This is where traditional social work came to the rescue. It showed how it is possible to maintain the most intensive and intimate surveillance without abridging the democratic principles that define us. According to social work, there is no need for government agents to appear as police, barging in at all hours, gaining entry through fear and intimidation. Its message is that friendliness, sincerity, and enthusiasm can be much more effective, that we can gain entrance by producing confidence, by writing letters requesting appointments, by addressing clients respectfully, listening thoughtfully, playing with their children, performing favors.

Democratic Surveillance

The following vignette, taken from a paper by Alice Overton titled "Aggressive Casework" illustrates how it is possible for surveillance to be aggressive yet noncoercive, persistent yet friendly.[15] The story begins with eleven-year-old Edward J. being referred to a child guidance clinic by his school because "he was restless, high-strung, disruptive." When Mr. and Mrs. J. refused the help, this led to a second referral—to the branch of the Department of Welfare that dealt with noncooperating families. Here is what happened when the social worker visited Mr. and Mrs. J. at home:

> It was the father who greeted the social worker in the hall with a stern order to take off her boots. He then walked into the apartment ahead of her while she remained standing for twenty minutes, listening to an outburst from both parents against the school. She was told that they were "sick and tired" of going to school about complaints. She replied that she wanted to help work things out so that there would be less difficulty. She was finally asked to sit down. The mother later yelled for Edward to come in so the lady who had come with more complaints about him could get a look at him. Edward was silent, sullen, and defiant; he made no response when worker gave him her name and restated her wish to help him and his parents so that the school experience could be a happier one. The father then renewed his tirade, while the worker made no attempt either to divert him or defend her position.

What she did instead was try to establish a regular time for future visits. The father, of course, ungraciously declined. He and his wife were busy every day and every evening, he said. The worker insisted. Even if he could arrange a convenient time, said the father, he still would not want to see her again. They went back and forth like this for some time. Then the worker said that she was just *concerned* about them and their son. This seemed to irritate the father more than anything else she had said. "In a very challenging way, the father asked if the worker thought their convenience was more important than their son's welfare, and when she restated the question he replied that someone being interested in them, and in their son, was more important than their inconvenience."

This was the turning point—at least for Mr. J.: "The father began to move toward the worker first, using in later interviews what had been said in order to reshape his own attitudes toward his son. It was painful for him to see that the discipline he had experienced as a boy had not been helpful to Edward, yet he struggled steadily to give more support to his son. As the father came to make a freer and more open use of the worker and as Edward improved, the mother began smoldering in a corner. She glowered at the worker and scarcely spoke during the next five months."

However, as time wore on, Mrs. J. also came around: "The mother, who had previously tried to trap the worker into lying just as she did with her children, was now able to say that at least the worker has always been honest and that she never takes sides but 'tries to see things as they are.' Through this transitional period, the mother presented the worker with a hand-made table scarf, saying she did not like the worker coming in the beginning but she was used to it now. The father and the school have told us about the marked improvement in Edward. He has caught up to his grade level in school. He is more comfortable in his relationships and he rarely wets himself now. . . . A surprising recent development came when the mother sought out the worker at her office and asked her to take over from the court the responsibility for the supervision of Mabel [a daughter who had been taken to court for running away]. Both the mother and Mabel are now coming in for office appointments."

The central message is that persistence works. As proof, we can see that Edward's school problem had almost completely disappeared; the family was coming in for office visits; instead of insults, the social worker was given a table scarf. This did not mean, however, that a sympathetic, persistent approach is all that is needed. Good intentions and a commitment to "reach out" to clients do not by themselves get the social worker very far. You cannot win clients over by simply appearing at their door, declaring, "I've come because I'm concerned about your problems." The client can easily respond, "Who asked you?" or "What problems?" You need to be able to explain why you have come with detailed factual evidence. To convert the hard-to-reach into consenting clients, social workers need an intimate awareness of clients' history.

Here is the catch: the hard-to-reach are not inclined to grant social workers permission to do anything at first, much less examine their files. So how are social workers to gain these vital historical data? The answer, quite simply, is they do what they must, even if this means obtaining resistant clients' files before clients grant them permission. And for those who might consider this sharing of information premature or unethical, social workers reasoned that there is at stake an ethical obligation more pressing than confidentiality: the obligation "to reach out to these families and make known to them clearly and unmistakably that the total community was concerned about them, and could not continue to let them hurt themselves, their children, and the community." [16]

Social workers argued that if the sharing of information is performed by professionals for the purpose of benefiting the client and the community, then any concern about protecting people's rights has already been resolved.[17] "The matter of confidentiality has been subject to much confusion. All of your families should know that social agencies share information about them for their benefit and in a responsible professional manner. Complete confidentiality is a myth. We could have no social service exchange; we could not dictate a line to anyone or keep any records. In fact, we would all have to be in private practice if we were to follow an absolute rule of confidentiality." [18]

The important question is not how information is obtained but how information is used. Ironically, we can only know how to use information when we have complete background on those with whom we are dealing. In some instances, the best approach is complete openness and directness: "One family denied the existence of any problem, until the worker brought and read to them a detailed account of their appearances in court." [19] In other cases, however, such directness is much too threatening. Instead of confrontation—with social workers immediately telling clients what they know, who they are, what needs to be done—they need to quietly and invisibly insinuate themselves into clients' lives.

Consider the case of Mrs. C. and her husband, who had rejected all efforts at help by welfare, probation, public health, public school, and other agencies. "Pooling of information indicated serious family problems": the husband was an alcoholic, the teenager was "an unapprehended delinquent," and the next two children had "behavior and learning problems." Obviously, social work could not just withdraw. But it needed an opening, a wedge of some sort.

> Eventually a contact with Mrs. C. was made through the one neighbor she talked with who brought her to a meeting of the Auxiliary, a group of mothers who met at the [community] center to provide refreshments, party decorations, and so forth for the children's groups. Mrs. C. attended several meetings at which the caseworker was present, and one time expressed interest in obtaining a recipe mentioned by her. The next day the caseworker dropped by to give it to her. After two more such visits, the caseworker was detained by Mrs. C., who introduced the subject of her

husband's abusiveness toward her and whether she should continue to tolerate it.[20]

Social workers knew that Mrs. C. needed help: "pooling of information" among themselves made that abundantly clear. Yet, she repeatedly rejected overtures from the welfare workers, probation officers, and public health workers who attempted to become involved with her. So social workers had to adopt a new tactic. Instead of reaching for her, they waited for her to reach for them. The critical element is persistence; social workers did not give up but quietly waited in the wings until the right moment presented itself. What defines this as aggressive social work, then, is not the overwhelming display of righteousness but the steady discipline that held that righteousness in abeyance until the client herself showed some readiness to open herself up. To this end, the social worker attended several meetings with Mrs. C. as a participant in a group of mothers interested in arranging parties for their children. Because the social worker managed to make herself appear more as a friend or neighbor than as a professional, Mrs. C. was not guarded or suspicious. Eventually Mrs. C. approached the social worker on her own, asking for a recipe: "The next day the caseworker dropped by to give it to her. After two more such visits, the caseworker was detained by Mrs. C., who introduced the subject of her husband's abusiveness." The tactic succeeded because the invitation was so quiet, the plan so spontaneous, the deception so sincere.

Not Intruding

Aggressive social work was not easy. It took enormous amounts of time and patience. Also, broken appointments, unreturned phone calls, slammed doors, threats and insults, made social workers feel bad: "It is the most natural thing in the world to shrink from going where you are not wanted. There is fear connected with the role of intruder—fear of hostility and rebuff."[21] To complicate matters, it is almost impossible to be friendly and sincere to a client who hates you. Yet friendliness and sincerity are the very approaches required to make the social work investigation successful in the first place. Thus, the challenge to social workers seeking to visit clients who did not wish them to visit was "to discipline our natural feelings . . . to maintain a compassionate reaching out to people who fear and dislike us, sight unseen."[22]

So before they could successfully reach out to unwilling clients, social workers needed to find ways to stay involved, enthusiastic, free from resentment and cynical thoughts. One way, as Ira Glasser noted in his essay "Prisoners of Benevolence," was to say to yourself, "I provide an essential and benevolent service. I am a helping professional. I teach, I heal, I rehabilitate, I provide shelter."[23] Another way was to simply tell yourself that regardless of how rough the going is initially, the hard-to-reach eventually come round to appreciating you: "Experience has proved that people do not resent a social worker who demonstrates genuine concern for the welfare of the family. . . . And if you are still uncomfortable with the aggressive or intruding role, please remember that your aggression is not against people but against their troubles. You go out to stand with people against their troubles."[24]

One of the key methods by which social workers reassured and emboldened themselves was to repeatedly imagine and articulate sets of images—narrative demonstrations—of the good effects of thrusting themselves into situations in which they are unwelcome. So, unlike earlier vignettes that almost always portrayed clients as immediately cooperative with and grateful for social work interventions, a new story line appeared in the 1950s that had clients energetically attempting to ward off social workers during the initial stages of visitation, only to dramatically shift into a welcoming and appreciative posture at a later stage.

What remained the same, however, is the grandiloquence of the final transformation. When the social worker eventually wins the client over, the signs and gestures accompanying the success are always exaggeratedly visible: the client gives the social worker a gift, the psychiatric symptoms disappear, the house becomes clean, the unemployed husband gets a job, the drunkard stops drinking. By the end of the story, those who originally appeared repugnant and resistive fill to the brim the image of the cooperative, grateful, motivated client.

Here is an example from an article titled "Serving Families Who 'Don't Want Help.'" Again, the family was referred because the eight-year-old son, Raymond, was disruptive in school. And as might be expected, on the first visit, the father, Mr. R., slammed the door in the worker's face. When she finally managed to get into the house, Mr. R. angrily denied his family had problems; he said that he had whipped the stealing out of Raymond, and that they had no need for a social agency. He proceeded to blame the school system and teachers for any difficulties in his children's school adjustment, saying the teachers were unable to discipline his children. Then, he accused social workers of prying into his affairs and of telling him how to run his family. "He said he would not stand for this. He had been pushed around enough, and he just wanted to be left alone. He wanted to be his own boss."[25]

In the visits that immediately followed, the father broke appointments, came in drunk, or would wander into the kitchen, where the worker was talking to the mother, only to put in a brief appearance. "As the worker continued to maintain an attitude of respect for him, Mr. R. gradually entered into more extended conversations. Later, the father's first reference to his own criminal record seemed to be a means of testing the worker's acceptance of him. . . . Gradually, Mr. R. explained why he felt bitter and hostile toward agencies, and why it had been necessary for him to fight them. He had not had an easy life. His father, a very strict man, had not fully supported the family. His four older brothers served long prison terms for robbery and assault. Mr. R. himself had been in the workhouse. Nobody had shown much trust in him and he could not trust anyone—so he told others as little as possible. And when he could not get what he wanted, he fought for it."

As Mr. R.'s confidence in his social worker grew, dramatic improvements in his functioning began to appear: "Mr. R. surprised his wife by completely redecorating the house. His drinking decreased and his appearance improved. His attitudes toward authority showed even further change. . . . He was able to make a number of visits to the new principal and he seemed pleased that he could talk at length without losing his temper."

Here is the moral of the story: backing away from clients at first, second, or third rebuff is not really respecting their wishes; rather, it amounts to acquiescing in denying them the chance for a good life. The proof lies in clients' very own statements, word-for-word testimonials describing the benefits of having a social worker come to their home and repeatedly challenge them to become involved. It is in these testimonials that the display of social work success attains its point of maximum sentimentality: "You gave us hope and courage and self-respect," one mother beamed. Another said, "You knew when we could help ourselves and the times we were not able." Still another said, "You came filled with confidence and enthusiasm that soon became contagious." [26] The following comments were attributed to a mother whose family had been on relief for almost nineteen years:

> I was tired of the ceaseless struggle to keep going on—to what? There was no future for us, nothing. That was the situation when the Family Center worker came to call. She must have thought I was a near hopeless case and hard as nails. I had no faith in anyone. She came time and again—not pushing, but little by little she drew my problems from me. She gave me the courage to help myself, first my physical condition and then to think straight again. Gave me faith and hope once more. She helped me solve my problems—as when my daughter was very ill and troublesome she came, and though she did not say much, I knew she was there, the staff I could lean on. I needed her strength, but as time passed I found I was restless, wanting to do things for myself. Then she gave me ideas of what I may do. I am now partly supporting my family and thinking of the future and all sorts of plans.[27]

Through testimony such as this, social workers avoided moral culpability—and thus avoided self-blame and the blame of others. Aggressive social work was about helping, not intruding or coercing. So if clients resisted at first, their "no" did not really mean no. They were only "testing" to see if social workers would do what they said they would:

> In such testing a parent might hang her head out a window during the entire interview, or let the television set blare as loudly as possible. (Fre-

quently, reducing the volume of the television set, or finally turning it off, was a barometer of a family's acceptance of the worker.) Often the parents left the room during the interview or even went out of doors, only to return later expecting to find the worker still there. On some occasions a mother would surround herself with friends or relatives. On other occasions she would be rude, and take pleasure in the children's overt aggression to the worker.

The worker's response to this behavior was central to the establishment of trust. Standing up to the terrific ordeal of testing, which sometimes lasted a year, and responding with flexibility, consistency, constancy, and lack of retaliation, provided the basic framework for the establishment of trust. This meant that the parents accepted the worker as someone who was reliable, predictable, and consistent, and involved in the family activities, and the worker accepted herself in that role.[28]

Clients' resistance—at least, social workers' descriptions of it—is based on a paradox: the more vigorously clients reject social workers, the more they really want them; the greater the hostility to social work, the greater the need of it. Resistance is really a representation of clients' underlying vulnerability: "Clients who most need, and often most desperately want, help, are least able to ask for it. Sometimes they just do not know where to seek it. More often they are people whose lives have given them little reason for trusting and seeking help."[29] According to this logic, refusing and rejecting clients only appear to be angry at social workers, "making them the objects of the anger of hurt children, displacing onto them the resentment that belonged to the depriving parents."[30] Why is the social worker the target of such primitive feelings? "Because the social worker holds the power to give or to withhold the wherewithal of life itself: The client's relationship to his own parents tends to be recreated with special force since the client's needs for food, for shelter, for acceptance of his acute feelings of panic are being met—or denied—by the social worker."[31]

Social workers need not fear forcing themselves on clients, nor fear a client really rejecting them, since this is a manifest impossibility anyway. How can a mother "decide" to terminate social work when that "mother really does not know us and cannot feel that we unselfishly desire to help her for she has not yet been able to experience the special kind of relationship with a social worker—a relationship that is different from other life experiences—that is the very heart of our professional service?"[32]

All possibilities prove resistant clients wrong: only by accepting and experiencing social work can clients reasonably decide to reject it; yet, if clients who actually experience social work should attempt to reject it, that act, by its very irrationality, amounts to proof positive of their desperate need of it.

The underlying assumption is that all clients, whether they acknowledge it or not, want to live in harmony with the dominant culture. Clients' and social workers' interests are fundamentally the same. Accordingly, there is no contradiction between safeguarding the client's autonomy and the imperative that "the social worker must unequivocally represent the demands of the dominant culture and strive to help the family live up to them."[33] Clients are not enemies who must be corrected or changed: all clients, despite their protests to the contrary, want to be normal. The challenge, then, is not for social workers to convert clients but to help them be who they truly are. As George Orwell put it, "The command of the old despotisms was 'Thou shalt not.' The command of the totalitarians was 'Thou shalt.' Our command is *'Thou art.'*"[34]

Obviously this logic imposes meanings not only onto clients but also onto social workers. To withdraw from resisting clients—to take their rejections literally—amounts to denying them a fair opportunity to realize their potential. It also denies to clients a fair and democratic opportunity to decide if they want help: "We need to extend and insure the individual's right to self-determination by adding the individual's right to know—the right to know of the community's positive concern, to know that there are resources available and how they can be used, to know what a helping service is, to know of the social worker's personal concern and interest, to know that he is seen as a human being in his own right rather than a community 'problem,' to know of the social worker's conviction and ability to be helpful, to know that the social worker is a giving person without being demanding."[35]

Confusion or uncertainty about aggressive social work only occurs when observers fail to consider social workers' good reasons for persistent visiting. As in any mystifying spectacle, these good reasons completely contradict the superficial impression, burying it in insignificance: client resistance is not a reason to discontinue visitation. To resist is to announce one's need for a visit. Resistance makes social work necessary.

CHAPTER 6

Framing the Poor

Conceptual or abstract thinking conveyed through words and phrases is beyond the capacities of this unsophisticated group, members of which are marginally educated, whose lives are a social and cultural wasteland, who act out anger and hostility, who have a low frustration tolerance and poor impulse control. Moreover, in the formative years of the parents and now of their children, words were and are used to manipulate and confuse others. These people do not comprehend the true meaning of words, have little faith in them, and are unable to carry out concepts defined by words alone.

Rachel A. Levine, "Treatment in the Home" (1964)

In earlier portions of this book, I argue that social work literature from the first half of the century blamed the poor for their own poverty: they were lazy, dependent, passive, pleasure seeking. During the 1950s and 1960s, however, victim blaming reached an entirely new pitch. Consider these excerpts from a paper by Joshua Perman titled, "Role of Transference in Casework with Public Assistance Families," published in *Social Work* in 1963:

> Rarely are both parents in the home. Generally the mothers have lived in a common-law relationship with a number of men who became the putative or acknowledged fathers of their children. The families often multiply rapidly. Many of the family members are illiterate because of low intelligence or emotional reasons. The mothers (usually the only parent) are, for the most part, psychologically too self-centered and impulsive to have sufficient interest in and responsibility for their children. A number of them, because of their unconscious needs, frequently become pregnant. They are also relatively disinterested in their children after they are born, or even turn against them. . . .
>
> In most cases the children are intellectually retarded or emotionally deprived and have learning and behavior problems in school. They are frequently involved in acts of delinquency. Incest, narcotic addiction, prostitution, homosexuality, and criminal acts have been part of their family background. . . .

9 7

> There have been men coming and going in their lives, each developing short- and long-lasting sadomasochistic relationships with their mothers. The children have been exposed to all the polymorphic perverse activities of these adults and soon begin to imitate them. . . .
> The psychiatric diagnoses of the parent or parents have ranged from psychosis to borderline character disorders.[1]

There is a peculiar cycle here: Social work investigates suspicious populations, but its investigations, or at least the findings derived from them, make the investigated appear even more suspicious. Investigations provide the warrant for future investigations. Perhaps the additional stigma is necessary because if social workers are to peer into the homes of people who want no part of them, if they are expected to visit the poor despite the latter's articulated desire to be left alone, they need good reasons. Accordingly, the more foreign and perverted clients can be made to appear, the more authority social workers have to visit and keep visiting. Aggressive social work, a social work at war, is so much easier with families defined as psychotic, sadomasochistic, rapidly multiplying, polymorphic perverse.

If it can be shown that clients are infantile and primitive, then social workers are licensed to treat them as infantile and primitive: "Since the client cannot, in the beginning, formulate his problem, the caseworker must do it for him in a 'these are the facts as I understand them' manner."[2] Since "children and families in lower socio-economic groups seem totally unaware of the nature of the society in which they live, what it expects of them, and what they can realistically expect of it,"[3] social work must supply the knowledge and skills that they lack. If the client is apathetic, social work must inspire. If the client is disorganized, social work must provide order. If the client is nonverbal, social work must demonstrate how to speak and what to say. And if clients are passive and will not come to social work, social work must be aggressive and go to them.

Degrading the poor vested social workers with the authority needed to monitor and control them: "The parents must be taught how to rear children; the children have to be taught how to think and then how to think in social terms, how to behave in accordance with the basic rules of deportment in social situations, and how to differentiate people in terms of social role and as individuals." Like animals, "these people have no concept of a family as a group of individuals related by kinship, marriage, or some systematic, regular association, no awareness that parents and children have distinct roles to play, and no sense of the family as an intimate group with immediate and long-range individual and group goals that require thought and planning."[4] This is especially true of Negroes and Puerto Ricans whose "self images are derogatory, a reflection of the stereotypes rampant in our society.

The parents of these children have been through the same mill, and they are severely damaged themselves and ill-equipped to guide, teach, interest, or socialize their children."[5]

Conceptualizing clients as inadequate, in need of the most minute and extensive guidance, not only justifies the exercise of power; it also justifies surveillance of the client's home: "The shifting of treatment from the clinic to the home was based on the assumption that clinic appointments are alien to the experience and culture of this 'nonmotivated' social class. They are alien to them because psychopathology is part and parcel of other social-economic-cultural problems and of their way of life."[6] Treatment in the home was also justified on the basis of the unique way poor people conceptualize personal boundaries: "Their sense of privacy begins at a different point from that of middle-class families, which begins at the portals of the home."[7]

The poor were seen as severely limited in their capacity to keep appointments, develop contracts, and use language in "talk therapy": "Just as children act out their problems in play therapy, so would their parents, who are immature, inadequate, confused, insecure, and in rivalry with each other and with their children. They function on the same emotional level as their children, have the same emotional needs, and respond to recognition of achievement in the same ways as their children."[8] So while social work might ordinarily help a client to articulate alternative solutions, to assess short-term gains against long-term losses, "this level of casework is usually too abstract and complex for the client who suffers from the basic cognitive deficits common among the poor." The poor need to be helped at the most concrete level, at the level appropriate to them.

In particular, the poor need demonstrations on how to live. This does not mean simply that they need to be shown how to do x or y, but rather that everything they do needs remodeling, reorientation, correction, and not as a matter to be discussed at a later time in an office, but wherever the action originates, at the moment of its occurrence. This approach requires a local or neighborhood base, "in which client and worker meet each other in a variety of ways. The agency would be there for reasons beyond (but including) help for family problems, and the worker would become a perceptible part of the daily lives of the local people."[9] This approach blurs the distinction between social workers and clients, with social workers finding themselves sometimes playing the part of friend, sometimes parent figure,[10] yet always acting as "a model with whom adults can identify, acting as flexibly as necessary in allowing for parental dependence while teaching and reinforcing change and self-mastery."[11]

The Language of Helping

The central method of justifying the new level of penetration was to portray the target population as more cognitively and socially impoverished than ever before. At the same time, the language was not so extreme as to warrant persecution or prosecution. The goal was not to repress the poor. It was to save them. They were lowered only to be uplifted, protected, nourished. So while the imagery was often extraordinarily negative, it was also veiled, sugarcoated. The central camouflage was the notion of rehabilitation itself. For every degrading comment made, there was a linkage to a modality of help that somehow stripped that comment of its hostile edge. Reciprocally, any suggestion that the remedies themselves might be too radical, too intrusive, or too controlling were nullified by linking them to what was already said of the client's moral and social failure. Any suspicion about the remedies, in other words, was resolved by linking them to the client's degraded status.

Notice, in the following four sentences, how subtly and effortlessly the statements of need (the negatives) and the remedies (the methods of control) commingle and mutually define one another: "The caseworkers made an effort to work with all the families . . . by talking frankly with them, particularly with the men, about how a mature person lives, what responsibilities he assumes, what he expects of him, and how by doing these things he may thereby become a more efficient and happier person. These men had poor relationships with their parents. They had never had an opportunity to learn appropriate behavior with a mature father figure or by osmosis in daily living in a well-patterned home. They had to be taught the simple, elementary rules of normal adult behavior." [12]

The first and last sentences, taken by themselves, may sound extraordinarily presumptuous; after all, they declare that social workers should impose their values on clients. Instead of asking the client what he believes and how he wishes to live, social workers are to inform him "what society expects of him," so he can "become a more efficient and happier person." However, when these directives are read in conjunction with the middle sentences (the statements of need)—e.g., that these men "had never had an opportunity to learn appropriate behavior with a mature father figure"—they appear well intentioned, even compassionate. In other words, if the authors had simply strung the clients' deficiencies together, their motives could easily be called into question. But because the negatives are framed in relation to some mode of helping, they are seen as diagnostic, as explanation, not degradation.

Consider how this passage from a paper by David Hallowitz published in *Social Casework* frames "poor black children" and their families in an extremely negative way, yet because the central motivation appears to be to help, we are more likely to see the author as caring than bigoted:

> Many poor black children suffer extensive emotional deprivation, and
> they often do not have the limits, controls, and supervision by loving par-
> ents that they need for normal psychosocial development. Children and
> parents may have developed severe personality and characterological im-
> pairments. The child's poor ego and superego development, inadequate
> capacity for reality-testing, and impulsive acting-out behavior may have
> reached such proportions that it is impossible to treat him effectively on
> an outpatient basis, even with the variety of counseling and treatment
> modalities that have been developed.[13]

The most interesting thing about this language is not the uncomplimen-
tary description of "poor black children" and their families. Nor is it the explicit recommendation to provide them with the most extreme method of
control—inpatient treatment. What is interesting is that we gloss the repres-
sive consequences of such statements because they appear to arise from
benevolent motivation. The underlying message should be unambiguous.
After all, one class of people is described as more disturbed and deviant than
another; one class of people requires more control and surveillance. To say
that many poor black children "suffer extensive emotional deprivation" and
"do not have the limits, controls, and supervision by loving parents that they
need" makes it clear that "normal" children—those who are not poor and
not black—are less likely to be emotionally deprived and are more likely to
have limits, controls, and supervision set by loving parents. Yet, the invoca-
tion of helping makes it almost impossible to identify this language as self-
serving power. Recognizing how people are blemished appears as the pre-
condition for cleansing them; recognizing that black children do not have
loving parents, that they have lower reality testing and higher impulsive acting out, appears as the first step in liberating them of these imperfections.

Here is a passage from a paper titled "Casework with Multiproblem Families," which shows another way social work managed to appear innocent. It
disguised its repressiveness by continually embedding negative statements
about clients in a positive context:

> The families, particularly the mothers, cannot be adequate models to
> their children nor meet their needs because in many ways they are like
> their children and give priority to their own imperative needs. There is
> marked disorganization, immaturity, and lacunae at various stages of de-
> velopment. They do have, however, islands of relatively intact functioning
> that represent fragments of greater maturity. They can function partly at
> different levels of development. Although they are so deprived that they
> are in constant rivalry with their children, they can give them limited care
> and do have hopes and aspirations for them. Their relationship to their
> children does have some warmth in spite of their inconstancy and incon-
> sistency. They can hold and feed and clothe them well at times, and do not

always treat them like dolls. They do appear to have some latent values, and do make some sporadic, unsystematized attempts to learn about their children, themselves, and their community via television, newspapers, advertisements, magazines, and some books. They have a genuine but latent yearning to trust and relate, to learn to be better mothers. It is this motivation that must be nourished initially.[14]

The author of this passage compliments the poor as she demolishes them. Poor families may be immature and dysfunctional, but they *do* have "islands of relatively intact functioning that represent fragments of greater maturity." The poor may act like siblings to their own children, but "they *can* give them limited care and *do* have hopes and aspirations for them." These parents do not *always* treat their children like dolls. These parents "appear to have *some* latent values, and do make *some* sporadic and unsystematized attempts to learn about their children" (italics added). Because the sentences are organized as if to affirm the positive traits of the poor—so that social workers might better perceive strengths that require "nourishing"—the author's bias and hostility are almost completely hidden.

Perhaps the most effective and widespread strategy for disguising degradation was the case description. The stories were often so detailed that it was impossible to imagine them as lies, as somehow made-up or biased. After all, they were simply stating the facts as received on an individual case. Yet the negatives were presented in such a way that the single instance was seen as somehow typical, as a stand-in for a whole class of people. Consider this "case illustration"—the *only* "case illustration"—from an article by Ben Orcutt titled "Casework Interventions and the Problems of the Poor." It concerns Mrs. R., an "obese" black woman with ten children, who was admitted to a state hospital:

> Mrs. R. was diagnosed as a chronic schizophrenic, undifferentiated type. She was hospitalized at the request of the family court when at a court hearing both she and her husband were charged with child neglect. Her bizarre delusional responses led to recommendation of hospitalization. Mrs. R. spoke of being unable to take care of her ten children, ranging from two-year-old twins to a fourteen-year-old daughter on whom she relied. Her child care was erratic, and at times she could not feed, change, or train the twins, nor could she touch or acknowledge any of the children. She refused to prepare her husband's meals and refused sexual relationships, fearing pregnancy. She used a contraceptive preparation which had been ineffective. Mr. R. had withdrawn from her verbally and emotionally, and generally was away from home. He had deserted her four years before, but returned when ordered by the court to face a jail sentence or return home.
>
> Mrs. R. is essentially nonverbal; her voice has a strained, unnatural sound. She distrusts people and is aloof and withdrawn. She complains of

the heavy strain of family responsibility. Mr. R. does not see himself as a helpmate and does nothing to maintain the family or marital relationship, nor does he give physical care to the children. Clinic appointments, household chores and management, and discipline are left to Mrs. R. She says she resents this and her husband's criticism of her being a poor housekeeper, but she does not speak out about it. She tends to withdraw and appears apathetic.

The six school-age children all have learning difficulties and are in special classes at public school. One child, age ten, is severely retarded and cannot dress herself. All the children in the family are functioning below normal expectations. Little is known of Mrs. R.'s early life beyond the fact that she was the youngest of nine children and was born on a farm. She moved to the city with her mother during her teens after her father died. She worked in factories, was self-supporting, and lived with her mother until age twenty-six, when she married her present husband. Her mother has subsequently died, and there is no extended family in the city. In the hospital, in addition to appearing isolated, she evidences some delusional ideas.[15]

It may not be possible to describe "the poor" in general as "obese," "schizophrenic," "bizarre," "nonverbal," "withdrawn," "aloof," "delusional," "apathetic." It may not be possible to say that poor women in general neglect their children, speak in voices that have "a strained, unnatural sound," refuse to prepare meals for, or have sex with, their husbands. Yet these terms can be applied to one poor woman, and she can then be called typical. As the author put it, "This case illustration is similar to a magnitude of cases known to hospitals and to voluntary and public agencies that serve people from low-income groups in areas of a central city."[16]

We can see how well psychiatric and psychoanalytic terminology fits this rhetoric. It gives social work the capacity to affix the most negative images and meanings onto the poor without appearing oppressive or even uncharitable. To illustrate, the authors of an article on how to perform social work on the parents of juvenile delinquents[17] divide these clients into a series of categories (e.g., "oral erotic personality," "oral sadistic personality," "anal character structure," "anal erotic personality," "anal sadistic personality") that have the look and feel of medical diagnoses, of scientifically derived truths. Yet, when one pauses to think about them, such language is as polar and degrading as anything appearing in the most oppressive political propaganda. The difference is that when despots refer to their political enemies as "vermin," "dogs," "mechanized robots," or "international maggots and bedbugs,"[18] there is no ambiguity regarding the malevolent intent. However, when a social worker refers to a client as an "anal personality," as one who "sets up a situation with the child in a typically anal way by giving and withholding," in which "the child is offered as an extension of the parent, like a good bowel movement," the hostile relationship is completely masked by the rehabilitative one.

A Manichean Universe

Among the benefits of the language of helping, it extends and enlarges authority at the same time it disguises authority.[19] Consider social work's almost ubiquitous reliance on jargonized counterterms. These expressions describe a lack or failure in the client, and usually begin with a prefix such as *in- non- dis-*, or *dys-*. Some examples include *inadequate, inappropriate, nonverbal, disorganized, disadvantaged, dysfunctional, multideficit, multiproblem, lack of self-awareness, emotionally deprived, maladaptive*. This language legitimizes social workers' political and social biases by showing that they are not against clients but are against their inappropriate behavior; not against the poor but against their lack of self-awareness; not against mothers on ADC but against their overdependency; not against the hard-to-reach but against their multideficits. Social workers are not in favor of maligning, defaming, coercing, or controlling but, rather, of making the inadequate adequate, the disorganized organized, the abnormal normal.

Social work jargon defines and supports belief in a Manichean universe, a system comprised of two distinctive, homogeneous camps, in which the "maladapted" exist in opposition to the "adapted," the nonverbal against the verbal, the abnormal against the normal. And just as the language of deficits, of *in-* and *non-* and *mal-*, defines clients, it also defines the social workers who assign these labels. For if clients are the negative pole of this duality, who else can be the positive pole if not the social workers who control the language? What silently downgrades the objects also upgrades the subjects. By continually describing clients as "maladapted" and "abnormal," social workers make it apparent that there is such a thing as normal adaptation and that they embody this ideal.

Through the description of the poor's vices and deficiencies, a moral drama is staged in which one group is portrayed as inferior so that another can be portrayed as superior. To the degree the poor are portrayed as "inconsistent" and "harsh," the middle class are displayed as "consistent" and "mild." The more "authoritarian" and "rigid" the poor appear, the more "democratic" and "equalitarian" appear the contrast group.

Consider the dichotomization produced by a paper titled "Social Work Practice with Very Poor Families."[20] According to the text, the poor use child-rearing techniques that are characterized by "inconsistent, harsh, physical punishment." The middle class, on the other hand, use "mild, firm, consistent discipline." The poor base their family patterns on "fatalistic, subjective attitudes, magical thinking"; the middle class on "rational, evidence-oriented, objective attitudes." The poor rely on "authoritarian, rigid family structure—strict definitions"; the middle class rely on "democratic, equalitarian, flexible family behavior patterns." The poor use "limited verbal communication, relative absence of subtlety and abstract concepts, a physical action style"; the middle class use "extensive verbal communication, values placed on complexity, abstractions." As for sex, the poor have "ignorance of physiology of reproductive system" and "distrust of sex," while the middle class is characterized by "acceptance of sex, positive sex expression within marriage by both husband and wife valued as part of total marriage relationship," and "understanding of physiology of reproductive system."

The language of aggressive social work, while overtly a language of helping, was thus responsible for defining the polar extremes of a moral order in which Normality confronted Abnormality. The more effective social workers were in getting images of moral culpability, weakness, and brutality associated with the poor, the more effective they were in getting images of moral superiority, strength, and sensitivity associated with themselves. Judging the poor, therefore, went hand in hand with creating and authorizing a class of judges.

Whether the negative characteristics of one client were being described, or whether it was the poor as a class of people, these descriptions always appeared to mask an alternative interpretation of what was happening in clients' lives. By focusing on the characteristics of clients, on *their* pathology, *their* delinquency, *their* failures, attention was diverted from the conditions external to them that constrained and limited their choices. The point is that aggressive social work's discourse on the negative traits of the poor legitimized the existing social order by deflecting attention from the unequal distribution of social resources and opportunities responsible for turning some people into clients and others into their judges.

CHAPTER 7

Lobotomy

Lobotomy many times offers sudden, amazing, almost magical relief to hopelessly anguished, distraught, symptom-driven patients. However, the social worker must keep in mind that the prognosis for this change and the maintenance of improvement will be largely determined by his preliminary investigation and the thoroughness and promptness of post-operative social service.

Herbert A. Cahoon, *Journal of Psychiatric Social Work* (1952)

The right to break reality into polar segments—normal/abnormal, functional/dysfunctional, sane/insane—existed long before the era of aggressive social work. But how confidently that right was claimed in the 1950s! There was the belief that normality was immediately recognizable, seeable, and seizeable, that it was a thing to be prepared and administered, that it could be imposed on anyone.

As for examples, there is probably none better than lobotomy. On the one hand, it shows that other professions were finding new ways to penetrate, that it was not just social work. On the other, it shows how social work worked with teams; how it augmented psychiatry, psychology, and nursing; how it shared, cooperated, collaborated. Although the lobotomist (a physician) occupied center stage, a large supporting cast (consisting of psychologists, nurses, occupational therapists, and social workers) was needed to secure and facilitate his performance. They arranged scenes, prepared props, made sure everyone knew where to stand and what to say, so that when the physician entered, his performance could appear effortless.

True, lobotomy is an extreme instance of the fraudulence of scientific claims, but it also reveals the unseen consequences of professional teamwork. That so many social workers collaborated to diagnose, persuade, treat, and rehabilitate so many people, in the name of a medical procedure those same professionals now consider physical mutilation, provides the most compelling exposure of social work's proclivity to adapt itself to the value systems of which it is a part. What I wish to illustrate through the medium of lobotomy is how social work, by blinding itself to alternative interpretations of what was taking place, contributed to a program that oppressed the poor in the name of helping them. (Most lobotomies were conducted on state hospital patients; the procedure was considered especially effective on females, Jews, and "Negroes.")[1]

Myth and Spectacle

I begin by considering the sources of lobotomy's appeal. Why was it so popular at midcentury? Why were more than seventeen thousand lobotomies performed between 1949 and 1951?[2]

First, consider that in October 1949, Egas Moniz, the Portuguese neurologist, won the Nobel Prize in medicine for inventing the lobotomy, resulting in enormous prestige and public acceptance of this operation as a treatment of severe mental disease.

Second, mental patients appeared much more disturbed then than now. Padded rooms and tube feeding were in frequent use, incontinence of urine and feces was common, many patients wore thick leather handcuffs as restraints, great canvas camisoles, locks, straps, "muffs," "mitts," and other devices.[3] "They were drilled, counted, searched and herded and many of those best able to work spent their lives scrubbing floors. . . . Depressives on suicide caution cards were stripped of their possessions, spoon fed and marched from one room to another." Not only were patients credited with the most exotic-sounding symptoms—echolalia, flexibilitas cerea, catatonic stupor—there was always the threat of disorder and violence: "It was rare for members of staff to walk around disturbed wards unaccompanied."[4]

Third, people thought lobotomy worked. Consider these newspaper headlines[5]:

> Surgeons's Knife Restores Sanity to Nerve Victims
> Wizardry of Surgery Restores Sanity to Fifty Raving Maniacs
> Brain Surgery Is Credited with Cure of 50 Hopelessly Insane
> Forgetting Operation Bleaches Brain
> No Worse Than Removing Tooth

Fourth, the benefits of lobotomy could be recognized from afar. After surgery "the corners of the mouth are no longer turned down, the brow is not furrowed, nor do the lower eyelids droop so as to reveal schlera beneath the cornea."[6] There were all these photos within psychiatric texts and journals of frowning, frightened-looking men and women, dressed in hospital smock or pajamas, underlined by captions reading "patient . . . before lobotomy" or "patient . . . with catatonic schizophrenia."[7] To their right were the "after" photos, revealing those same people "one year [or sixteen months] after operation," dressed in civilian attire, hair neatly coiffed, their faces beaming with joy and confidence. The message: those who undergo lobotomy may be so unlike what they once were that they seem to belong to different lives, even different species.

In a word, lobotomy seemed incredibly efficient. By all appearances, no social or psychological therapy had ever been administered so cheaply yet so profoundly, so quickly yet so permanently. For example, in the summer of 1952, a single physician lobotomized 228 patients in West Virginia—in effect "cleaning out" some of the worst back wards of that state hospital system—during a single twelve-day period. Each lobotomy took only ten minutes to perform and cost no more than $10 per patient.[8]

In the context of the "war against mental illness," lobotomy appeared as the most decisive of initiatives, a summa of effectiveness. Like ballet, it provided the illusion of a world controlled by movement, not words. When the lobotomist spoke, it was in images: First, the patient was placed on the operating table and given two to four electroconvulsive shocks within a period of four minutes. Electroconvulsive shock was the preferred mode of anaesthesia "because of the ease with which it can be administered to unruly patients, because of a quicker clotting of blood, and because of the temporarily beneficent effects of shock therapy in reducing overactivity in the patient."[9] As the convulsions subsided, a towel was placed over the patient's nose and mouth. Then, standing behind the patient, the physician elevated the right eyelid and introduced the point of the leukotome (ice pick) into the conjunctival sac; it was almost always sterile due to the free flow of tears in response to the electro shock, tears being bacteriostatic. A few taps of the carpenter's mallet drove the leukotome through the orbital plate. The second leukotome was introduced in the same way on the left side. The leukotomes were inserted into each opening to a depth of 2.5 inches, swung through the brain at a 20-degree arc medially and a 30-degree arc laterally, undercutting almost the whole orbital complex of the brain without severing any sizable arteries.[10]

In this spectacle, the physician conveyed potency, courage, decisiveness. He was the hero-leader, and social work (along with nursing), the ideal aide-de-camp: preparing things, bringing them out, laying them out, so when the leader's work was done, all that was left was to admire his beautiful performance without wondering where it came from. The most remarkable (and reassuring) feature of the operation is that patients are unable to formulate any ideas about the changes that have occurred in them; they also "forget incidents in their psychotic period that stand out in sharp detail in the memories of their relatives."[11] All memory of imperfection is vanished. Even their wrinkles disappear. After the operation the patient's face and head are completely smooth. There are no stitches or scars.[12] Like Christ's seamless robe, there is no sign of the human operation of assembling. In all the "after" photos the characters wear smiles, their cheeks swollen with the fullness of flesh and happiness. Their hair has been cleaned, combed, curled, arranged so as to impose the traditional signs of order and symmetry. What do these changes signify? Quite simply, the label of normality. They show that the insane person has become sane.

The Social Work Connection

From the beginning, both social work and lobotomy were aimed at decreasing the size, scope, and intensity of the asylum network in the United States. Both existed to shorten the period of hospitalization, to facilitate discharge. All the visions concerned emptying wards, returning patients to family life, making people manageable in private homes. Consider that without the increased likelihood of returning the patient to the community, there is scarcely any reason to perform this operation in the first place. For example, how do we measure the success of the West Virginia Lobotomy Project, if not by noting that 85 of the 224 survivors were out of the hospital by 1953, and more than 50 others had been out of the hospital for short periods? (I use the word *survivors* because 4 of the original 228 patients died—2 from internal hemorrhage immediately following the operation, and 2 from dehydration.) Such an outcome was defended not only in terms of patient benefits but in taxpayer dollars: "The cost of the 1952 project was $2,300. Based on a per diem cost of $2.04 in the state hospitals of West Virginia, the savings to the state in the year following the 1952 project were $48,000." [13]

Here is how the social workers from one hospital speeded discharge following lobotomy:

> Rehabilitation plans began immediately after the patient's admission to the Boston Psychopathic Hospital, at the first interview between the social worker and the patient and his relatives. The home situation, work experience, and financial problems were discussed. An attempt was made at this time to ascertain what skills the patient possessed, and the occupational and nursing services were at once informed of the patient's work potentialities and experiences. . . . An attempt was made at this time to arrange for special training for those patients who, after operation, had to be self-supporting if they were to live outside the hospital.[14]

But social work not only mobilized and coordinated team communication while patients were hospitalized; it also mobilized and coordinated services after their discharge. That was how Miss S., who was originally diagnosed as having dementia praecox, hebephrenic type, managed to reenter the labor force. She was tried as a typist in the hospital's clinical laboratory, where her difficulties were discussed

> with the social worker in weekly conferences. Although Miss S. was slow in learning and less able to take responsibility than the "average person,"

in this tolerant atmosphere she accepted criticism and suggestions; as time went on she gained speed and began to remember techniques used before her illness. She gradually improved and became friendly with her co-workers, who showed interest in her long accounts of prewar Europe.

After three months of work in the laboratory, Miss S. appeared ready to look for a job. Finally, by her own efforts, she obtained a secretarial position which she filled satisfactorily.[15]

Lobotomy is connected to social work because it made use of all the values and techniques described in the earlier chapters—sharing information, home visiting, normalization. Because it transferred interest from the body to the mind, from the public institution to the private dwelling, from segregation to inclusion. Because there is no line drawn with the social worker on the one side and the client on the other: "We try to avoid all barriers, make contacts pleasant and minimize an atmosphere of authority. We do not wear uniforms. We insist upon this minimum of rules: (1) courtesy, (2) truth, and (3) respect for the rights of others." [16]

True to social work's tradition of charity visiting, the purpose of lobotomy is not to inflict pain or punishment. It is always kind: to replace a brooding disposition for an ingenuous one, to trade a bit of cognitive capacity for an agreeable mood, to transform "a state of perpetual anxiety and distress to one of calm acceptance of the inevitability of all things." [17]

True to that same tradition, lobotomy is consistent with what in earlier chapters was called "disindividualized power." This means that although lobotomized clients appear as individuals to the social worker, she does not appear as an individual to them. Instead, she is a stand-in for the needs of the physician and hospital, or better still, the community and society: "As social workers, we have accepted as one of our basic principles the tenet that people are individuals. We must go still further and accept the principle that some individuals are unable to express their need for help or of using the help that is available to them. The needs of society demand help for such individuals." [18]

In keeping with these principles, social work practice in cases of lobotomy is not characterized by critical inquiry and dissent but rather by teamwork and cooperation. For example, when the doctor tells the patient and family that lobotomy is needed, this is handled "with the psychiatric social worker present at the conference so that she can reinforce in later interviews what the doctor has said. The psychiatric social worker must be so competent in representing the hospital and what is happening in respect to the patient, his progress, and treatment that it is possible to reduce the need of the relative always to have access to the doctor; for the relative seeks the doctor not only in relation to the patient but, more often, for help in his own emotional reaction to this traumatic situation." [19]

We need to understand why the psychiatrist makes the social worker his representative and stand-in: Because "whatever she does, she follows the physician's lead in his therapeutic plan. If he asks the worker to give merely supportive therapy to a relative or to assist in manipulating the home situation, she, of course, does so in such a way that there is an integration of constructive movement between the work with the family and the patient's progress. At the same time she keeps the physician informed of important changes and utilizes the knowledge she gains in her conferences with the physician in ensuing her casework with the relatives or with the dynamics of the situation."[20]

And if at times the social worker does not agree with or understand the physician's order, that does not pose an obstacle in itself: "There are two reasons for this, the first being well-known—namely, that the psychiatric social worker may not be entirely familiar with the psychodynamics of the situation. The second reason is that the psychiatric social worker, as such is the case, may interfere in the rapport established between the patient and physician and must, therefore, be cautious in lending her efforts to the interpretive situations. It may be added that in many cases she can be of vital assistance and value to the psychiatrist through her close personal relationships with members of the family and others of importance in the case."[21]

First of all, social work smoothes the way by reducing anxiety and opposition from the patient: "She knows that this is a difficult period for the patient and so helps him in expressing his feelings and fears. Illness itself, especially mental illness, places one in a position where a great deal of support is needed in carrying out plans."[22] Here is how such support was indicated to one patient: "I pointed out to Mrs. H. that she told me she was afraid of many things and that it must be hard for her to do the things she liked because of these fears. She agreed with this. I told her that the hospital had doctors who would be able to help her with these fears, who were interested in seeing that she got well again and was no longer afraid."[23]

That social work attempts to calm patients' fears prior to lobotomy should not be taken to mean that their consent is a prerequisite for surgery. Consent is always desirable, of course. But in working with this type of client, there are other considerations, such as the obligation to live in harmony with others. "In reality, none of us is free to do as he chooses," wrote Rudolf Boquet in the *Journal of Psychiatric Social Work*.

> We are all bound by the restrictions, mores, and folkways that influence our decisions in the society in which we live. In our society an individual is hospitalized for a mental illness when he has ceased to function socially and economically in a manner which is generally considered acceptable to his immediate environment. The hospitalized patient is therefore bound more rigidly by the restrictions of society. He has lost to some

extent his right to self-determination because of circumstances beyond his control. By virtue of his admission to a mental hospital, it is acknowledged that he is temporarily or permanently incapable of coping successfully with the varied problems in his life.[24]

If anyone's consent is required for lobotomy to proceed, it is not the patient's but the relative's or guardian's. This, of course, is social work's specific area of expertise: "Although some relatives readily agree to give permission for the operation, some may request that it be given, others find it difficult to make a decision. In all cases, there is probably some guilt and tremendous concern about taking this step. A caseworker may find that relatives require help which at this point can relieve anxiety and indeed set the stage for a more accepting and satisfactory environment for the [patient's] eventual return."[25] Sometimes workers overcome resistances by accepting relatives' fears, by recognizing how difficult this decision is. At other times, it may be "necessary to arouse guilt in order to forestall further resistance. . . . I indicated that a person with this sort of illness is likely to get worse later on and that I hoped Mrs. G. would not do anything now that she would later regret."[26]

Once the operation is completed, contacts with family members focus on reorienting their attitudes toward the patient. The purpose is not simply to keep them in touch with the patient's progress but to help them anticipate the homecoming, to inform them that very specific forms of support and patience are required. For example, family members must learn to expect a certain amount of inertia from the convalescent:

> Whoever has charge of the patient will have to pull him out of bed, otherwise he may stay there all day, although there is no reason for him to do so. It is especially necessary for somebody to pull him out of bed since he won't get up voluntarily even to go to the toilet, and only alertness on the part of those who care for him will prevent a lot of linen going unnecessarily to the laundry. Once the patient has been guided safely to the toilet he may take an hour to complete his business. Often he has to be pulled up off the seat. "I'm doing it; I'm doing it" he says. "Just a little while; I'm nearly finished." Usually he finishes in just a little while, but the passage of time means nothing to him, and he stays on, not thinking, merely inert. If other members of the family are waiting for use of the bathroom, this type of behavior can be exasperating.[27]

One helpful hint is for family members to remove the keys from the bathroom door so patients do not lock themselves in:

> The husband of one of our patients had to climb through the transom to get his wife out of the tub eleven hours after she had locked herself in the bathroom. This was exceptional, the longest period for bathing usually

being about three hours. Even after such ablutions it is not unusual to find "vast patches of unirrigated soil." The patient has stayed in the bathtub playing with the soap or rag, or merely absorbed in watching the water dripping from the hands and has not made a thorough job of bathing. The playfulness of some of the patients while they are in the water is still further trying to members of the family who are insufficiently foresighted as regards the wearing of old clothes. Patients are as little children and they enjoy squirting water around.[28]

The goal of social work visitation is to help relatives accept and welcome their lobotomized son or daughter, husband or wife. As the following vignette from Sonya Friedman's "Casework Treatment of Relatives of Lobotomized Patients" illustrates, this often involves helping family members reinterpret or reframe behavior that might otherwise appear peculiar or objectionable:

At the time that Mr. C. left the hospital in November, 1949, he was delusional and in poor contact. However, he was not violent. His sister, who was unmarried, gave up her job and remained at home to care for him. Although she was controlling and allowed him very little freedom, Mr. C. responded well to her. However, he was extremely resentful of his father who was also in the home and frequently threatened him with violence. *The social worker's role at that point was to help the father accept his son's expressions of hostility.* Mr. C. gained a great deal of satisfaction out of teasing his father and blaming him for preventing him from going to school. As his father's attitude changed the patient gained less satisfaction from teasing him and this became a minor problem.

Mr. C. regressed immediately after returning home and required fundamental retraining in his bathroom and eating habits. *The worker helped the family through this period by interpreting the meaning of his behavior and the methods as prescribed by the doctor for handling this.* The next problem with which the worker helped the patient was to establish a routine in the home in order to best keep the patient occupied. (Italics added)[29]

The point is that social workers did not simply increase the likelihood of returning lobotomized patients to the community; they increased the likelihood of relatives and other community members accepting these convalescents. Note, for example, that even though many of the patients who were "successfully" discharged from the West Virginia Lobotomy Project did not adjust very well, their relatives raised few objections: "It was remarkable in some cases that the families had been able to put up with the lazy, slovenly person that had been released from the hospital; nevertheless, in most instances there was a remarkable lack of complaint heard, either from the patient or from the relatives. A general air of relaxation seemed notable."[30]

Why did relatives not complain about the "lazy, slovenly person" returned to them? Presumably because social work prepared the way:

> A program of group education of relatives was conducted weekly by a social worker. At this meeting, the common postoperative characteristics of lobotomy patients, such as slowness, lack of initiative, outspokenness, wetting, and seizures, were pointed out. The relatives were told that wetting is usually temporary, that lethargy often improves greatly, and that convulsive seizures may be readily controlled by medication. Emphasis was placed on the fact that although the patient may have personality deficits, he is usually much happier as a result of the operation.
> These group education sessions gave the family members an opportunity to air their anxieties and to take comfort from other families whose problems resembled their own. Not only did family members become educated in the care of the patient, but they were led to feel that the hospital's interest in the patient extended far beyond the point of discharge.[31]

By talking about lobotomy in this way, it becomes depoliticized: Social work empties it of history and fills it with nature. Social work gives lobotomy a natural justification; it gives it a meaning that is not one of explanation but one of a statement of fact. If I hear *the fact* of lobotomized patients' "slowness, lack of initiative, outspokenness, wetting, and seizures," I am very near to finding that it goes without saying: I am reassured. If I make lobotomy natural, I abolish complexity, strip it of contradiction and depth, see it as wide open and wallowing in clarity. That patients often die as a result of lobotomy,[32] that lobotomy is mostly practiced on the poor,[33] on minority groups and women,[34] is forgotten. That lobotomy is not simply directed against "illness" but against dissent, against originality and difference,[35] is similarly evaded. Instead, lobotomy is laid out as self-evident, like the weather or the seasons, something whose existence is inevitable, requiring acceptance, tolerance.

What does it mean that psychiatrists themselves debated the ethics of lobotomy but that social work did not?[36] It means simply that social work represents the principal of consensus, self-negation, cooperation: "Workers are early taught not to superimpose their own opinions, wishes, or decisions upon their clients, and to see themselves as offering help and support rather than intervention."[37] Social work represents the democratic process, which means that "all must be bound by the validity of group decision."[38] It stands for the search for a common denominator, the belief that people are products of a biological, psychological, and social continuum, that they are knowable and malleable.[39] In short, social work cancels difference.

Part 3
Empowering Social Work

CHAPTER 8

The Rhetoric of Empowerment

The empowerment tradition has inspired its social workers to listen to clients and neighborhood members at great length before shaping programs and services. Empowerment work has long been premised on the study of clients' or constituents' articulated concerns and demonstrated needs, study involving attentive, systematic, and skilled inquiry into the meanings, consequences, causes, correlates, forms, and scope of problems. Empowerment-based social work depends upon the best concepts and methodological skills of the assessment tradition in social work.

Barbara Levy Simon, *The Empowerment Tradition in American Social Work* (1994)

From the mid-1970s, social work has been in a discursive ferment over the concept of "empowerment." Social workers had to use the word *empowerment* as often as possible; they had to speak of empowerment not simply as an ethic but as a thing administered, inserted, regulated for the greater good of all. It was both an end and a means-to-an-end; it was applied to all situations and justified every intervention.

This compulsion can be traced in part to social work's need to atone for past excesses. First, in the early 1970s, critics such as William Ryan and Murray Edelman showed that social workers had reason to be embarrassed. Their efforts to help people "caught in the cycle of poverty" were called a brilliant strategy for perpetuating the very inequalities they so ostentatiously sought to erase:

> They indignantly condemn any notions of innate wickedness or genetic defect. "The Negro is *not born* inferior," they shout apoplectically. "Force of circumstance," they explain in reasonable tones, "has made him inferior." And they dismiss with self-righteous contempt any claims that the poor man in America is plainly unworthy or shiftless or enamored of idleness. No, they say, he is "caught in the cycle of poverty." He is trained to be poor by his culture and his family life. . . . With such an elegant formulation, the humanitarian can have it both ways. He can, all at the same time, concentrate his charitable interest on the defects of the victim, condemn the vague social and environmental stresses that produced the

defect (some time ago), and ignore the continuing effect of victimizing social forces (right now).[1]

A second source of embarrassment was the black Civil Rights movement. The rise of the concept of black power made it unacceptable to speak of minority populations as "maladjusted" or pathological. According to the new way of speaking, minority groups needed equal rights, dignity, power. What they did *not* need—at least from social workers and other government agents—was nurturance, parenting, sound advice, role models, therapy, all the things that social workers have always offered in prodigious quantity. Now it was society that needed rehabilitation, not individuals. As Bill J. Tidwell expressed in the *Journal of Education for Social Work*, "The basic challenge that the new thrust by black people presents to social work, then, is to reconstitute its assumptions and modify its technology so as to be more realistic about the dynamics of power and their relationship to the problems and needs of the black community."[2] He concluded, "We must emphasize that the problems of some client groups do not stem from social maladjustment and are not amenable to rehabilitative or cooperative solutions." Instead, social workers must learn to accept "that a vital part of the societal function of social work must be to remove the structural and attitudinal constraints that make our democratic system into an abusive and oppressive one to large segments of the population."

Now, to adapt Tidwell's analysis to the perspective of this book: the basic challenge to social work is not to "reconstitute its assumptions and modify its technology" in order to focus on the "structural and attitudinal constraints that make our democratic system an abusive and oppressive one," but rather to find ways to appear that it is doing just this, so that it can continue to do what it has always done, namely, to meet with individuals of oppressed classes, to hear their secrets, observe their family interactions, support their conformity, and challenge their resistance.

Social work's solution—the tactic of deception (and self-deception)—is to continuously speak of the institutional causes of racism and poverty (here is where the term *empowerment* has to be inserted), all the while keeping the discourse focused on individual-level interventions.[3] So the discourse on racial oppression—on the external causes of inequality—is matched to a counterdiscourse on how to successfully influence the lives of people of color, not as a part of a mass, but on a person-by-person, family-by-family basis. Any suspicion that the diagnosis (institutional racism) is not in tune with the cure (individual rehabilitation) is partly dispelled by the nonoppressive, empowerment vocabulary added to the individual-level interventions.[4] According to that rhetoric, empowering individuals means always attempting to interpret clients' actions in a positive way, to affirm, to be empathic and supportive, to deflect blame and guilt, to "keep hope alive by acknowledging and discussing external causes of oppressive conditions . . . , en-

couraging the client's own words . . . , accepting the client's problem definition . . . , having the client name and own her strengths."[5] However, nothing
could completely obscure what was indeed taking place: social workers in-
serting themselves into clients' lives, initiating actions, judging outcomes,
controlling terminologies and meanings.

Winning Confidence

As in earlier times, care must be taken to address the disempowered respectfully: "Because the white worker may be initially regarded with suspicion,
as a potential enemy until proven otherwise, it is necessary to observe with
singular care all the formalities which are the overt indications of respect."[6]
In the words of Doman Lum: "When the social worker engages the minority client, he or she must observe certain relationship protocols, such as addressing the client with his or her surname, making formal introductions,
acknowledging the elderly or head of household as the authority, and conveying respect through other means. Rather than focusing initially on the problem, the social worker should practice professional self-disclosure, whereby
a point of interest common to the client and the worker becomes a means of
forming a relationship."[7]

White social workers must avoid any appearance of a patronizing or superior attitude. Above all, they must not pretend to have a knowledge of the
client's culture that they do not have, nor attempt to use clients' street argot
or dialect in an effort to convey their cultural sophistication or familiarity:
"Assuming the language of the client in contrast to one's own is to risk 'coming on too strong.' Not only the phrasing used but also the style of delivery
has to be natural to be accepted without ridicule by the interviewee. The
'tone' is very difficult for an outsider to come by."[8]

Social workers Enola Proctor and Larry Davis used hypothetical dialogue
to illustrate how a white social worker's failure to acknowledge ignorance of
a black client's vernacular creates the impression of arrogance and incompe-
tence, and how openness about cultural differences, and a genuine desire to
understand, create trust:

> *Client.* Like I was saying, Fred, I miss my main squeeze very much even
> though I've got so many hammers after me.
>
> *Worker* [*incorrect follow-up*]. Well, Joe, it sounds like you're in good spir-
> its. I am surprised in light of the fact that last week you were unhappy over
> your wife leaving you. Are you feeling better because of the woodworking
> you're doing?
>
> *Worker* [*correct follow-up*]. Just a minute, Joe. I think that I might have
> missed something here. Perhaps you'll be good enough to explain to me

one more time what you meant. In particular, what did you say about hammers—are you making something?[9]

The central message is that only by openly acknowledging their misunderstandings or failure to comprehend can white workers have any chance of creating the level of rapport needed to win the black client's trust: "Rather than concealing oneself behind professional policies and practices, the worker meets the client as a human being and initiates the relationship. Rather than focusing on the client's problem, the goal is to humanize the relationship by disclosing a topic common to both of their backgrounds. Professional self-disclosure lays the groundwork for the reciprocal response of self-disclosure by the client."[10] Of course, "suspicion and mistrust . . . anxiety about the unknown, and shame about admitting the need for assistance are natural feelings of clients generally." But "for people of color, those feelings are exacerbated by racism and discrimination."[11]

Because blacks' expectations of prejudicial attitudes from professionals have been repeatedly confirmed, they are much more likely to respond to social workers by "playing it cool," by maintaining a cover, a distance, a reserve.[12] Thus, the social worker's only hope of penetrating the black client's veneer is to act conspicuously different—to be authentic, vulnerable, completely open. In the opinion of David Burgest, writing in *Social Work Practice with Minorities*, "clients of color can accept genuine and authentic feelings, actions, and behaviors of social caseworkers."[13] The social worker's honesty is the single most effective tool for overcoming the effects of institutional racism: "Empathy, the key ingredient of the helping relationship, neutralizes the client's powerlessness. . . . Essential in building trust and developing a relationship that will foster growth and change, empathy becomes an anesthetic for the pain of the client's loneliness and his feelings of abandonment and powerlessness."[14]

The only problem with this formulation—at least from the perspective of people of color—is that it makes resistance to "genuinely" empathic social workers appear spurious, self-defeating, pathological. When there is any conflict between dark-skinned clients and their empathic social workers, the social workers' position appears as the only legitimate one. According to these rules, empathic white social workers can "confront the client when *true* feelings of warmth, genuine concern, and empathy have been expressed but have been misinterpreted or distorted by the client"[15] (italics added).

The strategy is brilliant. To ensure the appearance of equality, we say that social workers can practice with dark-skinned people if their interventions are based on genuine warmth and empathy. However, to guarantee that the appearance does not become reality, there is a second, unstated rule: that only social workers have the authority to determine whether their own or anyone else's feelings are genuine. Here is an illustration from Ruth Middleman and Gail Goldberg Wood's *Skills for Direct Practice in Social Work*:

Jackie, a young black woman, told me that she is very angry at the office manager where she works as a secretary because the woman treats her as if she is dumb. She said the woman lectures to her, explains things three and four times, and sometimes even asks her to repeat back the instructions. Then she sat back and glared at me. *I said, "What you just told me about the white woman who treats you like you are dumb is something like what you feel is going on between us, but you're reluctant to say so."* "What makes you think that? she asked. "Because you were glaring at ME the whole time you talked about it," I replied. She laughed. "I do get pissed off at you for stuff like that sometimes," she said, still grinning. *"Well, next time I piss you off like that, would you tell me if you can?"* I asked. She nodded, then added, "If I can." [16]

This interchange appears innocent enough, at least regarding what takes place between the social worker and client. But consider how social work readers might respond to these images. The mandate is unambiguous: they can and should use their true feelings as a resource for exposing clients' false assertions. "Clients may need help to articulate their problem situations, and 'caring confrontation' by the worker may facilitate that process." [17] The fact that the client herself, in the vignette, acknowledges the accuracy of the social worker's confrontation makes this vision of social work authority especially convincing. That the client is black and the social worker white not only shows that white social workers can understand what black clients say; it also shows that they understand what black clients do not say and, further, that they may confront them on their deceptions.

Semanticide

Curiously, then, the stated goal is to empower clients, but there is at the same time all this talk of confronting, penetrating resistances, gaining client cooperation. Empowerment social work mandates the maximization of client self-determination, but "the social worker always holds in reserve the right to reject a client-identified problem when the client's formulation conflicts with the social worker's ethics." [18] It is also permissible to reject client formulations "when, deep down inside we believe a client is not acting in his or her own best interests," [19] or when clients appear to undermine the helping process—when they attempt to dictate who will be involved in treatment, when they attempt to dictate the mode and frequency of sessions, and when they avoid focusing on topics of critical importance: "Irrespective of practice setting social workers encounter clients who, for various purposes, attempt to manipulate them. Failure to discern manipulative ploys enables clients to gain varying degrees of control in helping relationships and constrains the maneuverability of the social worker, thereby undermining the helping process." [20]

In other words, the ethic of client empowerment in no way prevents social workers from leading and directing clients. First, "because clients seldom present a single or a clear problem, workers have considerable freedom to select and focus on a specific problem or set of problems."[21] Second, social workers have an explicit obligation to oppose or interrupt client initiatives when it is believed that

> Clients lack information that, if available, would lead them to consent to interference.
>
> Clients are incapable of comprehending relevant information, either temporarily or permanently.
>
> Clients consent to paternalistic intervention prior to the interference.
>
> The harmful consequences that are likely without interference are irreversible.
>
> A wider range of freedom for the client can be preserved only by restricting it temporarily.
>
> The immediate need to rescue overrides prohibitions against interference.[22]

Apparently, social workers have it both ways. They claim the moral imprimatur of client self-determination, continuously describing their interventions as "empowering," but retain their prerogative to plan and strategize, direct and control. According to the new vocabulary, clients who follow suggestions and plans formulated by social work are not "yielding" or "submitting" to social work but are "empowered" by it. Here is an example from a paper by Donna Weaver titled "Empowering Treatment Skills for Helping Black Families":

> Mr. and Mrs. P. are a common-law couple with four children. Mrs. P. brought her teenage son to the agency because she could not handle his violent temper and constant acting-out behavior. The social worker believed that it was extremely important for Mr. P. to be involved in the family session. After numerous telephone calls and several letters, the social worker was unable to persuade Mr. P. to attend the family sessions. However, she persisted in trying to engage him in counseling despite his extreme resistance. Mrs. P. told the social worker that her husband was very suspicious and distrustful of social service agencies. He was a very proud man and did not like outsiders prying into his affairs. He felt that as the man of the family he should be able to handle his family's problems without the help of a social worker. This kind of survival technique is used by many black fathers and husbands who have been made to feel powerless in an oppressive society.
>
> The social worker recognized this attitude as typical feelings of many black males. However, she believed that she could help him recognize that he would not lose control of his family by joining them in treatment. By empowering him to feel that she could not fully understand or help

resolve the family's problems without his influence and full participation she was finally able to convince him that he was a viable and significant component of the treatment process. Once involved, Mr. P. was very co-operative and actively participated in all of the counseling sessions.[23]

The penultimate sentence in the vignette deserves special attention because of the way the term *empowering* is used: "By empowering him to feel that she could not fully understand or help resolve the family's problems without his influence and full participation she was finally able to convince him that he was a viable and significant component of the treatment process." In other words, the social worker convinced the resistant client that she (not he) could be fully effective in "resolving" his family's problems only if he cooperated with her. She asked him to abandon his position and go over to hers so she could do what she believed she must. Whether her goals and methods were better than his—*truly* better than his—is unanswerable and irrelevant. What matters is that the social worker's desire to include the father in family sessions was never held up to doubt. On the other hand, the father's contention that "he should be able to handle the family's problems without the help of a social worker" was blithely dismissed as a "survival technique . . . used by many black fathers and husbands who have been made to feel powerless in an oppressive society." The point is that what the language of social work calls "client empowerment" can easily be described in a different language as making the client "give in" or "give up."

One of the characteristics of power generally is to hold the weak accountable for transgressing rules established by the powerful for their own advantage. Social work's unique contribution is to get others, the weak and powerful alike, to agree that it is the weak who are acting inappropriately in situations in which they are dominated. Here is how a social worker managed just this as she tells her client, Steve, why his lateness for their appointments is unacceptable:

When I confronted him on his constant lateness he apologized, saying that the only available parking spaces at this time of night were several blocks away. Steve, a cerebral palsy victim, wears a leg brace and walks slowly. I said that he did not have to park so far away; that there are handicapped parking spaces right by the front door. He looked at me like I was crazy. "Steve," I said, "You are entitled to use the handicapped parking spaces right next door." He said that they are not for him, that he's just like everyone else, that his parents and his teachers always told him and that's what he believes. *I said he may be like everyone else in most ways, but that he is handicapped when it comes to walking at an average speed for an adult.* I also said that it was not fair for him to pretend that he wasn't handicapped at my expense, that I have had to wait fifteen minutes for him all three times we had appointments. I said that he could be here on time if he used the handicapped parking spots to which he is entitled.[24]

Social workers who hold clients responsible for rules of their devising and under their control are engaged in power. In this instance, the client had to account for being late, for refusing to use the designated parking space, and for refusing to label himself handicapped. The social worker had good reasons: "I also said that it was not fair for him to pretend that he was not handicapped at my expense, that I have had to wait fifteen minutes for him all three times we had appointments." What the social worker gains here is fairly easy to understand. She got her client to agree to behave according to her rules. But there is something else much more significant going on. She transformed what could easily be seen as an exercise in power, her power, into an exercise in empowerment. "The social worker does not patronize her able client," wrote Middleman and Wood, the authors who used this story, "and as seen below, the client examines for the first time in his life the way in which this taboo regarding the word 'handicapped' has kept him frightened. Ultimately, through several further sessions with the social worker, the client recognized that via the taboo, he had been depriving himself of rights to which he is entitled. He now exercises his rights." [25]

The social worker showed her client how to overcome his fears. He resisted at first but eventually realized that before one can be free, one must obey; before one is empowered, one is humble. That is the central paradox of empowerment theory: to become who one truly is, and do what one truly wants, one has to absorb another's definitions, interpretations, and prescriptions. The proof comes from the client's own grateful testimony—from the tears in his eyes:

> "I never thought of myself as handicapped before," he said. "Then it can hurt to hear me say it now," I replied. "It scares me," he said. "If I can think of myself that way I might use it as an excuse to not do well in school or at work. I only do well because I believe there's nothing I cannot do." "You make it sound like magic, Steve," I said. "Actually, you do well in school and at work because you are intelligent and work hard." "Yes," he acknowledged, "but maybe I would not work as hard if I let myself believe I'm handicapped." "Is that what's so scary about the word handicapped?" I asked. He nodded and there were tears in his eyes. [26]

The rhetoric of empowerment is, of course, quite different from earlier social work language, which simply described impoverished and minority people as inferior. The current language shifts its emphasis to the social worker's own "cultural sensitivity." Instead of discussing client defects, the new discourse focuses on social work virtues—on its empathy, sensitivity, courage. When defects are discussed today, they are located within society. The problem is defined in terms such as "institutional racism," the "white middle-class power structure," "the failure of social systems to create opportunities for competence to be displayed or learned." [27]

What stays the same are the methods of intervention. We have the same division between subject and object. As before, one group acts, the other is acted upon. One party heals, the other suffers. The focus of change is not the institutional structure but the client's way of dealing with it: "The person who is the help-seeker (learner, client, etc.) must attribute behavior change at least in part to his or her own actions if one is to acquire a sense of control necessary to manage family affairs. This is what we mean when we say a person is *empowered*." [28] So the defect, the problem to which social work activity is directed, is *still* located within the client. Only now when the defect is changed or removed, we do not say that the client has been healed or rehabilitated; we say that the client has been "empowered." Again, social workers have it both ways.

The technique is not new. John Wesley Young, in his book *Totalitarian Language: Its Nazi and Communist Antecedents*, called it "semanticide"— the practice of redefining terms to make politically questionable activities appear wholesome and acceptable. By referring to some official practice in language that makes it appear to be the opposite of what it really is—for example, signs at Auschwitz and Dachau proclaiming "Work makes you free"—people are encouraged to ignore or forget the evidence of their own senses.[29] But while the best-known examples of semanticide represent the willful and malevolent perversion of language, social work's is almost always innocent and well meaning.

Consider this vignette from Barbara Bryant Solomon's *Black Empowerment: Social Work in Oppressed Communities*. It shows how a hospital social worker came to the aid of a black client, Mrs. Smith, who was being steamrolled by the "white power structure." According to the social worker's account, the doctors wanted to send Mrs. Smith's husband to a nursing home before he or his wife were ready. Here the social worker pleads their cause in a staff meeting:

> I stated that the staff seemed to be acting hastily in view of a six-month hospitalization. I asked for more time to work for the family, particularly with Mrs. Smith, to help her prepare for the transition. Furthermore, both she and Mr. Smith had wanted to try having him stay at home. The staff stated that he was in no condition to do so. I suggested that Mrs. Smith should at least be given a choice in the matter.
>
> When Mrs. Smith was ushered into the meeting, the matter of choice never came up! She was peremptorily told what the plan for her husband was as made by the staff—to a nursing home and that was that! At that moment I shared with Mrs. Smith the terrible powerlessness inherent in our positions. Mrs. Smith is black, poor, and relatively uneducated. I was a social work student—perhaps the least influential of all the persons in the room, not only by student status but by virtue of the secondary role of social work in a medical setting. Some of the staff had expressed their hostil-

ity toward me openly before the Smiths were brought in. The head nurse
questioned whose needs were being met by my suggestion that Mr. Smith
have the choice of returning home if he wished. I decided to explore some
issues with the Smiths later. The odds against us were too great in that
staff meeting.

Mrs. Smith left the room crying and I followed. Spontaneously, I began
to cry with her. We went to my office where we talked and drank coffee
and cried some more. She indicated that she wanted to get back to her
husband who had been returned to the ward because she knew he would
be upset and would not want to talk to anybody but her. I agreed that she
should go but also indicated that I was willing to help them do whatever
they wanted to do.

We can see that this white social worker has been warm, empathetic, and
genuinely vulnerable with a client of a different ethnic background. We have
the evidence of tears, the invitation to drink coffee and cry together, the confession of powerlessness: "I shared with Mrs. Smith the terrible powerlessness inherent in our positions. Mrs. Smith is black, poor, and relatively uneducated. I was a social work student—perhaps the least influential of all
persons in the room." Only to the most jaded of critics could there be any
suggestion of manipulation or deception. The social worker's expressions of
sincerity could not have been a cover for some underlying disrespect, some
subtle intrusion or familiarity. Indeed, the only conceivable way that the social worker's displays of feeling could be criticized is that they may have been
too conspicuous—placing the social worker at the center of the story instead
of the client, legitimizing and empowering her status instead of Mrs. Smith's.
Let us read on:

The Smiths still indicated that they wanted to have Mr. Smith home
on a trial basis. After fighting administrative red tape and continuing staff
hostility, plans were made for Mr. Smith to be discharged to his home. He
was able to spend one night at home with his wife, having dinner with her,
touching the things he remembered and loved. In the middle of the night,
he had a respiratory attack and had to be rushed to an emergency hospital.
He was transferred to a nursing home several days later and one week
later, he died. Sometime later, Mrs. Smith called me to let me know how
much she appreciated the fact that her husband had been able to have that
one night at home and how devastated she would have been if he had died
in a nursing home never having been home again at all. It was as if the
fight against the institutional power block (which became less powerful
as she began to realize her strength, i.e., her "rights" and her ability to
obtain support from me and my supervisor in the struggle) had given her
new confidence in her ability to survive without her husband. Her last
comment to me was: "I'll miss him, but I'm not as depressed as I was.
I'm taking care of myself, and things are going to be alright."

The most curious element of the narrative is the social worker's claim to be empowering her clients. Forget that Mr. Smith had a "respiratory attack" his very first night at home and died a week later. Forget also that he might not have deteriorated so rapidly had the social worker not been successful in getting him discharged against medical opposition. For the sake of argument, let us emphasize the positive: through the social worker's intervention Mr. Smith *did* get to spend one night at home with his wife ("having dinner with her, touching the things he remembered and loved"). What I want to know is how such an outcome *empowered* the clients?

First of all, was not the social worker the one who fought administrative red tape and staff hostility? And was not Mrs. Smith's role restricted to that of the silently suffering (and grateful) witness to this drama? Yet the social worker makes it appear as if this battle was a transformative, empowering experience for Mrs. Smith: "It was as if the fight against the institutional power block (which became less powerful as she began to realize her strength, i.e., her 'rights' and her ability to obtain support from me and my supervisor in the struggle) had given her new confidence in her ability to survive without her husband."

And where was Mr. Smith in this process? The social worker implies that she knew what he wanted—indeed, she knew it so well that she was ready to battle for it—yet we are not told how she arrived at such certainty. Why was he so casually glossed? True, he is black, uneducated, poor, severely ill—identities that are traditionally simplified, patronized. But there is another reason for this omission. The social worker is "empowering" him. We therefore see here the mainspring of her authority—the *license*—operating in the open. Thus she battles, cajoles, confronts, in the name of a person she does not appear to know, without losing any of her plausibility. So he died after one night home. No matter, we have here the image of a social worker who made every possible sacrifice, who fought to the last breath, thanks to the most potent of signs: empowerment.

What this story indicates is how the language of empowerment legitimizes social work. Indeed, if some transformation occurred in the black client as a result of her association with this empowering process, it is that white social workers can be trusted. As the social worker put it, Mrs. Smith became aware of her "ability to obtain support from me and my supervisor in the struggle" against "the institutional power block." Furthermore, it demonstrates how the process of storytelling can be used as a method of legitimizing social work's practice with people of color by (1) reducing social work's self-blame, by (2) creating images of shared fate and shared consciousness between blacks and their white social workers, and by (3) demonstrating that white social workers can effectively assume personal responsibility for improving black clients' lives. Such stories show that social workers know what people of color want and are the ones who can give it to them.

The Fiction of Freedom

But the authority to influence minority-group clients—to tell them what is true or false—does not merely come from social workers' belief in themselves and their mission. It also comes from their position in society and the social agencies that employ them. They are permitted to say "this *is* that, and that" and may "seal every object and every event with a sound,"[31] not because of their personal characteristics, their charisma or logic, but because clients often have no choice but to be docile and compliant. We know, for example, that a large number of social work clients are assigned by courts, that welfare recipients have to see social workers in order to maintain eligibility, that persons are often assigned to social work rehabilitation as an alternative to jail, that patients treated in hospitals often *must* see a social worker, that parents who wish to retain custody of their children *must* prove to the worker that they are wholesome and responsible.

What sets social work apart, however, is the fiction of voluntariness. In fact, the term *involuntary client* is rarely used by social workers, who prefer to label troubling clients *hostile, resistant, reluctant, unmotivated, hard-to-reach.*[32] As Charles Garvin and Brett Seabury phrase it in *Interpersonal Practice in Social Work*, "There is no such thing as an involuntary client as we defined a client as a person or persons who accept a contract for social services." By definition, clients are "persons who come for help to a social agency and who expect to benefit directly from it; who determine, usually after some exploration and negotiation, that this was an appropriate move; and who enter into an agreement—referred to as a contract—with the social worker with regard to the terms of such service."[33]

There is the belief that clients can say anything, when they like or where they like, that they can be completely open or closed, motivated or unmotivated, at will. This stance comes from social work's tradition of individualism—from locating defects and virtues in people rather than the systems that created them. The immediate benefit to social workers is that when clients do not respond to their interventions in the expected way, the fault does not lie with them, their interventions, or the institutions they represent, but with clients for failing to take advantage of the opportunity offered.

Now for the downside. Denial of clients' involuntary status, denial not only of clients' disempowerment but of social work's contribution to their disempowerment, makes social workers oblivious to clients' need to lie and manipulate: "Dealing with clients who use self-serving manipulation poses a problem for many social workers, whose training has equipped them to relate with empathy and warmth and to demonstrate care and emotional support."[34] Like prison guards who need to believe that their convicts truly like them, social workers are easily controlled by those over whom they exercise power. The whole point is that even when social workers appear to have unquestionable capacity to sanction and punish, their need to deny it, to see

themselves as "empowering" rather than "empowered," results in a ritual—
a power game—in which both client and social worker appear oddly controlled by one another.

In the following dialogue, a black client attempts to learn from the white
social worker what she must say in order to have her son returned to her. On
the surface, the social worker appears to have complete control because she
is the one who decides what recommendation to make to the court. On another, more subtle level, the client appears to be in charge because the social
worker is hopelessly unaware of the power relationship, that this involuntary
client will say anything to get her son back—things that are untrue, things
that only sound sincere, spontaneous, friendly.[35]

It begins with the client asking the social worker if she is the one who will
decide to give her son back. The social worker replies that the court will ask
her opinion as to how the mother and her son get along:

> *Worker.* I can tell the court that I think you know how you got into a situa-
> tion where the court thought it necessary to remove your child from your
> home and I can also tell the court that I am convinced that because of that
> knowledge, it won't happen again. But I can only say that if I really am
> convinced and that can only come from what you tell me.
>
> *Client.* You want me to say that I lose my temper sometime with Jim and
> I have learned how to control it?
>
> *Worker.* I do not want you to say anything that is not true. I am only say-
> ing that it has to be true that you know how you got into this situation and
> that you have figured out how to prevent it from happening again.
>
> *Client.* (*suspiciously*) Suppose I say that I got into it because that no-good,
> used-to-be friend of mine called the protective service people and lied on
> me because I would not loan her money. And suppose I say it won't hap-
> pen again because I'm goin to beat her ass for her if I ever catch her!
>
> *Worker.* Then I would want to talk to her about that plan of yours to see
> how workable it is. For example, how do you know some other "no-good
> friend" won't call the protective service people on you the next time you
> accidentally hurt Jimmy? Can you be sure that you won't accidentally hurt
> him again? How can you deal with his behavior so that you won't need to
> punish him or maybe not so often? . . .
>
> *Client.* I sure hope you got the answer to that cause I sure don't.
>
> *Worker.* I think that you do! And maybe if I can help you get at your an-
> swers, maybe you'll find out that you can prevent what has happened from
> happening again.
>
> *Client.* That's a pretty big order. (*Silence*) But I think that I would like to
> try. I want my kid back and I do not want to lose him again.
>
> *Worker.* Can you tell me what it is that you're saying you want to try?

> *Client.* Well, I guess I'm saying that I'm going to try to talk about all those problems I'm having and maybe if I can understand what's happening, I'll know how to handle Jimmy better . . . because, if it seems that I can, then you'll let the court know it so I can get him back.

> *Worker.* That sounds like a good place to start . . . maybe we can start with whatever problem of the many you mentioned, *you* think is the most important in terms of what happened between you and Jimmy.

What relation could be more imbalanced? One party has the other's child and will give him back (that is, recommend to the court that he be given back) only if the latter does something for her—in this case, says the right thing. Yet the power here does not appear negative, as an effort to exact obedience, to repress, to dominate. Rather, this power is positive: the social worker appears to truly want the mother to get her son back, and truly wants the client to say the right thing, not as something extracted by force, like a witch's confession, but freely, because she really means it. Moreover, the social worker appears ready and willing to help the mother find the very words that the social worker needs to hear. So if there is a test of some sort going on here, it is one in which considerable coaching is allowed. Thus the social worker tells the client that she must use her own words ("if I really am [to be] convinced and that can only come from what you tell me"), and the client asks what words she must claim as her own ("You want me to say that I lose my temper sometime with Jim and I have learned to control it?"). The social worker offers more guidance ("I don't want you to say anything that is not true"), and the client, catching onto the game, tells the social worker the kind of preparation she needs ("I sure hope that you got the answer to that cause I sure don't").

Doublethink

The client faces a formidable challenge. If she is to get her child back, she must not only say what the social worker wants to hear but convince the social worker that her performance is natural and sincere—that the words she speaks are *her* words.[36] The client must appear as if her compliance comes about independently of the social worker's power to deny her her child.

The social worker's challenge is equally formidable. Though she has obvious power over the client, she must find a way to preserve belief in the client's voluntariness—that the words that the client is required to say are freely chosen. Her challenge is to convince herself that it is possible to bring the client over to her side, not as a matter of obedience or appearance, but genuinely, heart and soul.[37]

Here's where doublethink comes in: to preserve belief in the client's capacity to speak freely and sincerely, both the social worker and client continually struggle to erase and deny the role of power in the interview. It is not simply the client attempting to fool the social worker; it is also the social worker needing to be fooled. The client only needs to create the appearance of sincerity; the social worker needs to believe in it. Thus the social worker coaches the client on how to display the required sincerity and naturalness ("And maybe if I can help you get at your answers, maybe you'll find out that you *can* prevent what has happened from happening again"). In turn, the client's role is to feed the required lines back in the required way—not as a parrot but as one who has been "empowered" by the social worker and is grateful for this gift ("Well, I guess I'm saying that I'm going to try to talk about all those problems I'm having and maybe if I can understand what's happening, I'll know how to handle Jimmy better").

Both the mother and the social worker use doublethink in this situation but in different ways. The mother has to internalize the social worker's meanings and logics, suppressing her own language of resistance; the social worker, because she assiduously masks her own exercise of power, has to suppress the possibility that the mother indeed has a language of her own. While it is difficult to imagine someone in a worse bargaining position than a parent whose child is being held hostage, at least the mother in this vignette knows that power is being withheld from her and can thus develop a strategy of some sort. But the social worker, who needs to deny that power is operating, has no such opportunity. She needs to believe that the client can choose her words freely and, further, that she can help the client (empower her) to say what she really means.

The point is that social workers, in exercising power, are caught in its machinery just as much as clients. The rhetoric of client empowerment makes social workers vulnerable—manipulable—by masking from them their own exercise of power. As evidence of this vulnerability, consider the volumes of literature on social workers' burnout, all those pages devoted to accounting for social workers' own mental and physical exhaustion. It may very well be true that social work is too emotionally demanding;[38] that there are too much red tape and paperwork,[39] too little appreciation from clients,[40] too few criteria for measuring accomplishment.[41] But the psychological cost of doublethink, requiring the continual suppression of experience and thoughts, must also take its toll.

We have already discussed how social workers have it both ways: appearing empowering while practicing power. What needs to be recognized now is that any gain from this juxtaposition of opposites does not belong to social workers. Although the language of empowerment masks what might otherwise appear as coercive, the masking is actually directed at social workers more than anyone else. To do social work, social workers have to learn to ignore their exercise of power, to hide their memories in complex amnesias, to alter their sense of time, place, and person.

Consider that client "self-determination" serves as social workers' "professional password,"[42] as the object of their "every effort" (1993 *NASW Code of Ethics*). At the same time, social workers are trained to recognize in themselves an explicitly formulated body of knowledge on what clients need and do not need, what clients should and should not do. So social workers who are pledged to help clients define themselves, according to their values, on their terms, are simultaneously obligated to recognize in themselves the right to encourage and discourage, to support and oppose, whatever clients may formulate as their needs and choices. They are trained to exercise power—"inferences, evaluation, and problem definition must lead to action. . . . Something must be done with what is known."[43] And they are trained to deny their exercise of power—"The client has a right to be free in making his [or her] own decisions and choices. . . . The social worker has a corresponding duty to respect this right, in theory and practice, by refraining from any direct interference with it, and by positively helping the client to exercise that right."[44] This is why social workers are so often obscure with clients about what they can and cannot do—why they are accused of beating around the bush, why they so often appear hypocritical:

> *Client.* Are you going to be the one to decide whether I get my child back or not?
>
> *Worker.* The Court will ask my opinion about how you and your child will get along if he is returned.
>
> *Client.* How will you know about that?
>
> *Worker.* I hope *you* will let me know about that.
>
> *Client.* O.K. I'll tell you. It's going to be great. . . .
>
> *Worker.* But I do not know it will be great.
>
> *Client.* I just told you, didn't I? You said that if I let you know . . . didn't you?[45]

Because they are vested with knowledge on how to judge and manage clients' lives yet are obligated to always support clients' self-determination, social workers are forced to live by two mutually exclusive mandates: to use and not to use knowledge; to practice and not to practice power; "to be conscious of complete truthfulness while telling carefully constructed lies."[46]

An article by Ann Weick and Loren Pope in *Social Casework* illustrates this point. The story concerns V, a forty-year-old woman who sought help from a social worker after her husband left her:

> After approximately two months of treatment in which she was encouraged to trust her own "internal wisdom," her own perceptions of interpersonal events in her life, as well as to respect the various feelings she

experienced, she wrote a letter to her current therapist between sessions. The following excerpt captures the gist of her experience with a therapist who respected the client's experiences and right to determine for herself what she should do to resolve her problems.

> This is the first thing (in my gut) that makes sense at all—for it supplies the missing link to how come I cannot live and I cannot die, how come I have to but am afraid. I'm very afraid—mostly of myself. You provide enormous affirmation of my substance in addition to allowing me to hurt, cry, be helpless, and talk about the bad stuff without labeling me as manipulative. I've never so much as said I'm a rotten person (in a therapy context) and not had my words challenged (making me have to defend and thus strengthen my own bad feelings). . . . Mostly I was given a choice to "let go cooperatively" and thus replace such an encompassing bad feeling with instant counter-feelings. I pulled this off from time to time. [Even though] Mary Martin never actually thought she could fly—she did give a good performance. So did I. My other option was to own and carefully guard my feelings (although they were horrible, they were mine). However, if that was my position, I was labeled (accused of being) "gamey," childish, manipulative, bad, dependent . . . and the bottom line was if I did not give up my bad stuff, my whole integrity regarding therapy was highly in question. It clearly was not OK to stay in therapy and resist giving up rotten feelings. . . . I had to hide hurt, pretend it was gone, and that only reinforced its power over me.
>
> "Thank you my good friend. You're courageous to be driving me through such a minefield. . . . I sure as hell hope you know that map. I do not ordinarily go on odd journeys unless I trust my guide with my very fiber. I trust you." [47]

The social worker appears wonderfully empowering to his client, allowing her "to hurt, cry, be helpless, and talk about the bad stuff without labeling [her] as manipulative." Yet he also appears to have perfect knowledge and complete control—"Thank you my good friend," his client writes, "You're courageous to be driving me through such a minefield. . . . I trust my guide with my very fiber." The contradiction, of course, appears in the client's descriptions of her social worker. But where did she learn that social workers need to be praised simultaneously for their permissiveness and their directiveness, their wisdom and their openness, if not from exposure to social work's own doublethink standard? Accordingly, after the social worker has read the client's letter, he appears to tell her she has given him too much power, and herself not enough. Yet even as he makes these statements, he appears to also be saying the very opposite:

> In the following session, her therapist expressed his appreciation for her trust in him and also expressed his concern that she had apparently put him in the position of "driving me through such a minefield," when in

fact he had been *following* her. "You know your own minefield," he said, "much better than I could ever know it. I've been following your lead. You have pointed out where the mines are buried. Further, I do not need courage for that, just an abiding respect for your sense of what you feel and what you want for yourself now. I suppose," he continued, "you might need my trust of your internal wisdom as we travel through the minefield together, and I'm certainly willing to lend it to you until you are convinced that you can trust that wise place in yourself."[48]

When taken at face value, the social worker appears predictably warm, straightforward, clear. But consider that the sentences that are used to gently correct the client's language, to tell her what she *really* did and what he *really* did and what it all *really* means, are the same sentences by which he insists that he has all along been following her lead, that she knows her own minefield, and that she should trust her own internal wisdom. What we have here is a contradiction captured in flight. He is empowering her as he corrects her. He repudiates her self-determination at the very moment that he insists she has always had it.

My point is not that the social worker is imposing his interpretations on the client (that he is dominating her). What I wish to convey is that the social worker's very own statements are imposed on him. Whatever system of rules and obligations is operating here originates neither in the social worker nor in the client but in the discourse itself—in the procedures that demand that certain things be said and repeated, and other things be unsaid and left forgotten. Both parties appear dominated but not by each other. Neither is to blame, yet each is a victim.

CHAPTER 9

The New Excuse

What happens when a complaint comes to the child welfare agency and a social worker is handed the job of doing something about it? What do you say when you knock on a door and a strange woman opens it and stares suspiciously at you? . . .

The wise caseworker begins with . . . the firm conviction that it is his job to find out what is happening to the children. . . .

This is not a simple task—few abusive parents will admit under these circumstances that they have done anything other than discipline their children in normal fashion. Two things help the caseworker: one, observation of the family and household and, two, the defective reality judgment of the parents. No amount of protestation by the parents can disguise the fear in these families, the frozen stillness of the children, the anxious corroboration of the passive parent to every belligerent statement of the aggressive partner. The children watch and listen with the wary tension of frightened animals. When a parent asserts "My children love me. They're always wanting to be with me. Isn't that true?" the children hastily proclaim their devotion, their words at variance with their anxious faces.

Leontine Young, *Wednesday's Children: A Study of Child Neglect and Abuse* (1964)

Aggressive social work did not die or wither away. It was improved. Through the admixture of the most vivid and detailed images of child abuse, social workers found an entirely new, much more compelling series of excuses and justifications for visiting and inspecting the unwilling poor in their homes. Instead of "multiproblem" families "at risk" to do something vaguely dangerous and depraved, there were now the most meticulous descriptions of injuries, wounds, blood and gore.

By the mid-1980s as many as two million investigations per year were being explained through this new language.[1] But what mattered most was not the sheer volume of child abuse investigations. What mattered was that not all classes of people were equally vulnerable. Although the new child abuse rhetoric continually proclaimed that this "disease" was classless, that it "afflicted" families of every race, creed, color, and economic status,[2] the truth is that the vast majority of child abuse investigations were (and are) performed on families in the lowest economic brackets. For example, in 1970, David Gil found that 37.2 percent of families in which child abuse was substantiated had been on public assistance at the time of the investigation, and that nearly 60 percent were on welfare either during the investigation or as recently as one year prior.[3] Eight years later, the American Humane Association showed that 45 percent of the homes in which investigators located child abuse were on public assistance.[4] Most of the investigated families lived at the poverty level, and only 9 percent had household income levels that approximated the national median.[5]

It is true, of course, that child abuse imagery has always been used by social workers as a "very good reason" to make a home visit. But the early images were sharply circumscribed, almost invariably portraying child abuse as a direct consequence of poverty, drunkenness, industrial exploitation, step-parenting or foster parenting.[6] While early formulations recognized the harmfulness of child abuse, it was a harmfulness that was seen as situational, as easily identified, contained, and managed. A parent could commit the most gruesome offense—for example, chaining a six-year-old child to the bed ("the child screamed all day, had tried to get out of her chains, had been cut, and Mrs. Anderson [the mother] refused to take her to the doctor")[7]— yet there was not the slightest hesitation or ambiguity regarding why the deed occurred: "The [mother's] worry of lack of food, her own ill health, and the dread of eviction, had been more than she could stand."[8] While early analyses often traced child maltreatment to the abuser's character defects, the attributions were almost always simplistic, one dimensional, and glossed by such terms as "low-intelligence," "slackness," "ignorance" ("whatever is wrong with the mother's care of the children is not due to marital difficulties but rather to slackness and ignorance").[9]

By the 1960s, however, the psychodynamics of child abuse were entirely redefined. What had once been regarded as immediately seeable and knowable had quite suddenly become complex, ephemeral. There were endless musings on unconscious motivations, forces and counterforces, reversals and paradoxes: "Probably the crux of the problem of distinguishing the non-abusing from the abusing parent lies in the fact that in the latter when there is significant environmental and intrapsychic stress, with a contest between ego ideal and superego, the punitive superego wins out."[10] Instead of child abuse being seen as principally situational, the result of poverty, unemployment, stress, or the like, "it was perceived that there are certain personality deficits that distinguish most abusing and neglecting parents from all other people and that explain the phenomena. In the context of this approach, the parent-client is regarded as a patient, whose 'illness' involves his or her entire personality and who is the object of treatment."[11]

What changed everything was the publication of "The Battered-Child Syndrome" in 1962 in the *Journal of the American Medical Association.*[12] This article by C. Henry Kempe and associates succeeded in reframing child abuse not only as a killer disease but also as one that is contagious, of epidemic proportions, and wildly unpredictable: "It is likely that [the battered-child syndrome] will be found to be a more frequent cause of death than such well recognized and thoroughly studied diseases as leukemia, cystic fibrosis and muscular dystrophy and may well rank with automobile accidents." That prediction, from a *JAMA* editorial published in the same issue as the Kempe et al. paper, marked the beginning of an avalanche of scholarship and journalism devoted to exploring and documenting the magnitude of this threat. For example, *Index Medicus* lists only one child abuse article prior to 1962. Between 1962 and 1980, 1,234 articles are listed on that topic.[13]

Even more significant than all the talk of the "alarming numbers" of bruised and battered children was the continual incantation of hiddenness. The major difference between the old and the new rhetoric was that in the past child abuse was portrayed as easily recognized and explained. Now the emphasis was on how difficult it was to spot; how people were reluctant to report abuse; how perpetrators, victims, and professionals denied, concealed, rationalized. As Kempe and his associates phrased it in the opening paragraph of their paper, "It is a significant cause of childhood disability and death. Unfortunately, it is frequently not recognized or, if diagnosed, is inadequately handled by the physician because of hesitation to bring the case to the attention of the proper authorities."[14] That this paper was based on analyses of x-rays of broken bones is entirely consistent with the message that child abuse cannot be identified through superficial examination—"the bones tell a story the child is too young or too frightened to tell."[15]

Why is child abuse hidden? Because parents are resistive: "*No amount of questioning will bring an admission.* There is seldom a witness to child abuse, so that questioning of relatives, neighbors, and others is equally fruitless. In fact, as time goes on the parent becomes more secure in telling his story. It becomes more believable to him and others"[16] (italics added). Child abusers go on at length about how a child fell down the stairs or out of a bed; they show how Johnny hit his head in a certain way; they show the bed he fell out of and the object he collided with on the way down. But, most disconcerting of all, physicians all too often believe such stories:

> A young child had been brought to the hospital with multiple burns and scars. One of the scars appeared to be someone's initials. The parents were most concerned about the child, and gave a history of skin problems. The physicians searched for some kind of skin disease that would produce lesions similar to those seen on the child. They found none, and now discharged the child when the lesions healed. A few days later she was back at the hospital, DOA (dead on arrival) from head trauma. The pediatrician related that they really knew that the lesions were from burns, but *they*

wanted to believe the parents' story and so searched for medical evidence that would support their story.[17] (italics added)

The lesson here is not only that child abuse must be investigated but that it must be investigated by experts. Moreover, it requires professionals who not only know how to gain people's confidence and learn their secrets but are unafraid to report what they learn—even if these reports are based on conjecture and suspicion. According to the new rhetoric, even the smallest hesitation can cost lives, no child is safe, and no parent or caregiver can be presumed innocent before the investigation is complete. "The social worker may feel that he is expected to enter a family with the notion that the parents are 'guilty' until proven innocent. If one wishes to use these terms, the statement is correct. Medical evidence of a serious traumatic injury which goes unexplained must lead to a strong suspicion of abuse, and a definite need to protect the child. *The social worker must feel comfortable approaching the family with the assumption that abuse has occurred"* [18] (italics added). The bias should not be in favor of the suspect's innocence; "the bias should be in favor of the child's safety; everything should be done to prevent repeated trauma, and the physician should not be satisfied to return the child to an environment where even a moderate risk of repetition exists." [19]

What we now explore is how social workers put the new credo "guilty until proven innocent" into action. This chapter's central question is how social workers manage to convert suspicion of child abuse into the certainty of child abuse. Conceptualizing the "child abuser" label as a mosaic constructed out of bits and pieces of imputations, bound together by a logic specifically selected for getting the job done, we explore how the child abuser's point of view is documented and displayed, and how evidence is organized on paper to create the conviction that specific behaviors with specific meanings have occurred. These dynamics are addressed through the examination of sixty case records documenting physical abuse and sixty documenting sexual abuse. They come from a state-run social service agency and represent investigations conducted during a two-year period in the 1980s. They were randomly selected from all case records of child abuse by a "babysitter" (someone who took care of a child in a private home but who was not a member of the child's family, was not a boyfriend or girlfriend of the child's parent, and was not employed in a registered or licensed group care facility).

Documenting Child Abuse

At the beginning of each record, the social worker described the physical injuries believed to have been inflicted on the child by the suspect. To illustrate this reporting style, one three-year-old boy who was spanked by a babysitter was described by the physician as having "a contusion to the buttocks and small superficial lacerations." However, the social worker who used these injuries as evidence of child abuse described them as follows:

> The injuries gave the appearance of an ink blot, in that they were almost mirror images of each other, positioned in the center of each buttock. The bruising was approximately four inches long by about two and a half inches wide, and was dark red on the perimeter and had a white cast to the inside of the bruise. There was a long linear line running across the bottom of both buttocks extending almost the entire width of the child's buttock. There was lighter reddish bruising surrounding the two largest bruises on each buttock and faint bluish-red bruising extending up to the lower back. The bruising would be characterized as being red turning to a deeper reddish-purple than true bright red.

This unusually graphic style of presentation gave the bruises a special status. They were no longer simply bruises but now appeared grotesque, thus placing the person who did this into the special social category reserved for the strange and malevolent. A parallel line of reportage is apparent in the sexual abuse cases. To the degree that the available information permitted, reports contained no obscurity in the descriptions of sexual interactions. No detail of what happened appeared too small to be pursued, named, and included in the records as evidence. As this excerpt from a social worker's recorded interview with an eight-year-old girl illustrates, even such features of the event as the size, hardness, and overall appearance of the suspect's penis assumed critical importance within interviewers' frames of reference:

S.W. How did the bad touch happen? Can you think?

Child. I cannot remember.

S.W. Did you ever have a kiss?

Child. No.

S.W. Anybody?

Child. Uh uh.

S.W. Did you have to touch anybody?

Child. Yeah.

S.W. Ah, you had to touch 'em. Where did you have to touch 'em?

Child. Down below.

S.W. Oh, down below. Do you have a word for that body part?

Child. A thing-a-ma-jig.

S.W. A thing-a-ma-jig. OK, let's look. . . . Is P. [the suspect] a man?

Child. Yeah.

S.W. OK, let's take a look at that man doll. Can you show me on the man doll what part you're talking about?

Child. This part.

S.W. Oh, the part that sticks out in front. We have another word for that. Do you know the other word for that part?

Child. Dick.

S.W. Yeah. Dick is another word for it. Another word is penis.

Child. Penis?

S.W. Yeah.

Child. Oh.

S.W. Can you tell me what—Did you see his body? Did you see his penis with your eyes?

Child. No.

S.W. OK. Did he have his pants on or off?

Child Unzipped.

S.W. Unzipped. I see. How did his penis happen to come out of his pants?

Child. By the zipper.

S.W. I see. Who took his penis out of his pants?

Child. He did.

S.W. What did you have to touch his penis with?

Child. My fingers.

S.W. I see. How did you know you had to do that?

Child. He told me to.

S.W. What did he say?

Child. Itch it.

S.W. Itch it. I see. Did he show you how to itch it? How did he have to itch it? One question at a time. Did he show you how to itch it?

Child He said just go back.

S.W. So you showed me that you're kind of scratching on it.

Child. Um hum.

S. W. Did anything happen to his penis or his thing-a-ma-jig when you did that?

Child. No.

S. W. OK. When he took his penis out of his pants, how did it look?

Child. Yucky.

S. W. Yeah, I know you think it's yucky, but um, what does yucky mean? Can you tell me with some other words besides yucky?

Child. Slimy.

S. W. Looked slimy. OK. Was it big?

Child. Yeah.

S. W. Was it hard or soft?

Child. Soft and hard.

S. W. Explain how you mean that. . . .

How did social workers establish that child abuse occurred when the victim, the child, was too young to explain what happened, the suspect denied committing child abuse, and there were no witnesses? In these instances, social workers argued that injuries occurred during the time the suspects were taking care of the children. The parents of the injured children testified that the children were sent to the babysitters in good health, without any marks, but returned with a noticeable injury. This allowed the social worker to determine responsibility through the following formula: if a babysitter cannot produce any plausible alternative explanation of the child's injuries, the babysitter must be responsible for the injuries.

But in most cases the children who had allegedly been sexually abused did not have conspicuous or easily described injuries. This would appear to limit severely social workers' capacity to document that a suspect committed sexual abuse when the suspect denied the charges, when the child was too young to provide coherent testimony, and when there were no other witnesses. However, this was not always the case. Like the investigators described by Harold Garfinkel, who were able to determine the cause of death among possible suicides with only "*this* much; *this* sight; *this* note; *this* collection of whatever is at hand,"[20] social workers showed the capacity to "make do" with whatever information was available. In one case of sexual abuse, for example, there were no witnesses, no admission from the suspect, no physical evidence, and no charge from the alleged victim; still, "evidence" was summoned to establish the babysitter's guilt. Here, the social worker cited a four-year-old's fears, nightmares, and other "behavior consistent with that of a child who was sexually traumatized by a close family friend." Additionally, the babysitter in question was portrayed as a "type" capable of doing such things: "Having no physical evidence, and no consistent statement from the alleged victim, I am forced to make a conclusion based on the credibility of the child as opposed to that of the perpetrator. This conclusion is supported by similar allegations against him from an independent source. It is also supported by behavioral indications and what we know of his history."

In a second case, a social worker showed that information pointing to the suspect's homosexuality and history of sexual victimization could be used to support charges of sexual abuse when other kinds of evidence were lacking: "Although the babysitter denied having sexual contact with this child when interviewed, he did leave a note to the effect that he was attracted to males and thought that he was homosexual, and records indicate that he, himself, was sexually abused at the age of eight. Based on the interview done, the past history, and his own previous victimization, this worker feels that he did, in fact, penetrate and perpetrate himself upon the victim."

In most cases, however, portraying the suspect as a "type" was not critical to the finding of child abuse. The rationale for labeling was primarily constructed out of witnesses' testimony showing "who did what to whom."

The Accused Is Guilty

Since the children and alleged child abusers often had different versions of what happened, social workers needed a decision rule to settle the question of who had the correct story. The rule used for resolving disagreements was fairly simple: the child's version was considered the true one. The children were called "credible" witnesses when describing assaults done to them because it was assumed they had nothing to gain by falsely accusing the babysitter. The babysitters, on the other hand, were seen as "noncredible" (when they attempted to establish their innocence) because they had everything to gain by lying. Even children as young as two and three years old were believed in preference to their adult babysitters. In fact, the main reason given for interpreting children as superior witnesses was precisely their youth, ignorance, and lack of sophistication. As one social worker observed, "It's my experience that a four-year-old would not be able to maintain such a consistent account of an incident if she was not telling the truth." Particularly in cases of sexual abuse, it was believed that the younger the witness, the more credible his or her testimony was. Social workers made the point that children who were providing details of sexual behavior would not know of such things unless they had been abused.[21]

The children's accounts were rejected in only three instances. In one case, two teenage boys claimed they witnessed a babysitter abuse a child as they peered through a window. Both the babysitter and the child said this was not true. The social worker did not feel it was necessary to explain why the babysitter would deny the allegations, but the child's denial was seen as problematic. Therefore, the social worker offered the following rationale for rejecting the child's account: "The child's refusal to say anything is not unusual because her mother was so verbally upset when she was informed of the allegations." A child's version of what happened (his denial of abuse) was rejected in a second case on the grounds that he was protecting a babysitter described as his "best friend." Finally, a twelve-year-old female who repeatedly denied that anyone had touched her sexually was seen as noncredible because of her "modesty." As the social worker put it, "She did seem to have a very difficult time talking about it, and I feel she greatly minimized the incident due to her embarrassment about it."

In general, however, testimony from children was treated as the most credible source of evidence of what happened, since most social workers believe that children do not lie about the abuse done to them. By contrast, babysitters were presented as credible witnesses only when they agreed with the allegations made against them. When they testified to the contrary, they were portrayed as biased. What does not happen, therefore, is the child implicating someone, the accused saying nothing happened, and the investigator siding with the accused. This suggests an underlying idealization that precedes and supports the ones operating on the surface of most cases: *the accused is guilty.*

Here, it might be useful to draw an analogy between the child protection workers' "investigative stance" and that of welfare investigators responsible for determining applicants' eligibility.[22] In both cases, investigators adopt a thoroughgoing skepticism designed "to locate and display the potential discrepancy between the applicant's [or suspect's] subjective and 'interested' claims and the factual and objective (i.e., rational) account that close observation of agency procedure is deemed to produce."[23] However, an important difference should be noted: during the conduct of welfare investigations, the investigated party is referred to as the "applicant," indicating that the investigation could end in a determination of either eligibility or ineligibility; by contrast, during the conduct of child abuse investigations, the investigated party is routinely identified as the "perpetrator," suggesting a previously concluded status. To illustrate, these notations documented one worker's activities during the first two days of a child abuse investigation:

> 3/24: Home visit with police, interviewed parents, child not at home—perpetrator not in home.
> 3/26: Interview with detective J. at police station with CPI and child. Perpetrator arrested.

While in theory individuals accused of child abuse may be only "suspects," at the level of practice they are "perpetrators." This discrepancy between theory and practice is more than an example of how the formal structures of organizations are accompanied by unintended and unprogrammed structures.[24] In this instance, social workers are formally enjoined to gather evidence about "perpetrators," not "suspects." Consider these lines from the agency's official handbook: "Information collected from the person [witness] should include precise description of size, shape, color, type, and location of injury. It may be possible to establish the credibility of the child, the responsible caretaker or the *perpetrator* as a source of this information. . . . The *perpetrator* and victim may be credible persons and need to be judged on the basis of the same factors as any other persons" (italics added).

The implicit message is that the goal of the child abuse investigation is not to determine an individual's guilt or innocence but to find evidence to be used in recording or "documenting" what is already taken for granted: that parties initially identified as the "perpetrator" and "victim" are in fact the "perpetrator" and "victim." Strictly speaking, then, the goal is not to determine "who did what to whom," since that information is assumed at the outset, but, rather, to document that agency rules have been followed, and that the investigation was conducted in a rational, objective manner.

More Decision Rules

A decision rule was also needed to determine the babysitter's intentions. While babysitters were portrayed in the allegations as malicious and exploitive, many babysitters offered a different version of their motivations. Among the babysitters accused of physical abuse, twenty-five acknowledged hitting the children but also claimed they intended no harm. Three said they were having a bad day, were under unusual stress, and simply "lost it." They attributed their violence to a spontaneous, noninstrumental expression of frustration. For example, one male caregiver took a two-year-old to the potty several times but the child did not go. Later he noticed that the child's diaper was wet, so he hurried him to the potty. However, just before being placed on the potty, the child had a bowel movement. At that point the caregiver lost his temper and hit the child.

One woman who was labeled abusive claimed she was ill and never wanted to babysit in the first place. She only agreed to take care of a two-year-old girl because the girl's mother insisted. The mother had an unexpected schedule change at work and needed child care on an emergency basis. The abusive event occurred soon after the babysitter served lunch to the child. While the sitter rested on the couch in the living room, she observed the girl messing with her lunch. The sitter got up and tried to settle the child. When this did not work, she took away the girl's paper plate and threw it in the garbage. At that point the girl began to cry for her mother. The babysitter returned to the living room to lie down on the couch, but the girl followed her, wailing for her mother. When the girl reached the couch, the babysitter sat up and slapped her.

Other babysitters described their violence in instrumental terms: their goal was to discipline the children, not to hurt or injure them. They said that whatever injuries occurred were the accidental result of hitting (in one case, biting) the children harder than they meant to do. Some sitters indicated that the only reason children were injured during a disciplinary action was that the children moved just as they were being hit, exposing a sensitive part of the body to a blow. Others protested that the child's movements made it impossible to aim the blows accurately or to assess how hard they were hitting. In one case, the sitter said she was trying to hit the child across the buttocks with a stick, but the child put her hand across her buttocks to protect herself, receiving "nonintentional" bruising and swelling to the hand. A different sitter asked that the social worker consider that at the time of the violation he did not know it was against the law to beat a child with a belt. Another said he had been given permission to spank the child by the child's mother and was only following her orders. This was confirmed by the mother. After a two-and-a-half-year-old bit another child, his sitter bit him to show him "what it felt like." The sitter argued that she had done this in the past and had even told the child's mother. Thus, she believed that this was tacitly approved. Still another babysitter claimed that he struck in self-defense the eleven-year-old girl who was in his care. He said that when he told her it was time for bed she began to bite and kick him. He said her injuries resulted from his efforts to calm and restrain her.

To sift out the babysitters' "official" intentions from the versions offered by the sitters themselves, several social workers explicitly invoked the following reasoning: physical damage to the child would be considered "intentional" if the acts that produced them were intentional. Thus, a social worker wrote, "I am concluding that this injury to the child was non-accidental in that the babysitter did have a purpose in striking the child, that purpose being to discipline her in hopes of modifying her behavior." While close examination of this logic reveals an absurdity (the injury was seen as "intentional" despite the fact that it was produced by an act aimed at an entirely different outcome, "modifying her behavior"), the practical consequence of such a formula was a simple method for determining a suspect's intentions: if a babysitter was known to intentionally hit a child, causing an injury, the social worker could conclude the babysitter intended to cause the injury. Through such a formula, the most common excuse utilized by babysitters to account for their actions, that the injury was the accidental result of a disciplinary action, was interpreted as a confession of responsibility for physical abuse.

To give another example of how this formula provided a shortcut to determining intentionality, one social worker concluded her recording as follows: "Physical abuse is founded in that the caretaker did hit the child on the face because she was throwing a temper tantrum and left a bruise approximately one inch long under the right eye. This constitutes a non-accidental injury. The bruise is still visible after five days."

In cases involving allegations of physical abuse, the problem of figuring out what the babysitter was really contemplating at the time of the violation never came up as a separate issue because the alleged perpetrator's motivation to injure the child was seen as the operational equivalent of two prior questions, "Does the child have an injury resulting from a blow?" and "Did the babysitter intentionally strike the child?" When each of these questions was answered affirmatively, intent to harm the child was inferred. Thus, it was possible for a social worker to observe, "It was this writer's opinion that the babysitter was surprised at the injury she left on the child by spanking the child," and yet later conclude, "the injury occurred as a result of a non-accidental incident."

One record included comments from witnesses stating that a babysitter pushed a five-year-old boy after the child socked a cat. All agreed that the injury was not a direct consequence of the push but resulted when the child lost balance and fell over. Despite the social worker's explicit recognition that the injury was neither planned nor anticipated (she wrote that "the injury will probably not be repeated due to the sitter's awareness of the seriousness of disciplining a child by reacting rather than thinking"), the report of physical abuse was, nonetheless, founded "due to the fact that the injury occurred in the course of a disciplinary action."

In another record, a male babysitter admitted to spanking a child, causing red marks on his buttocks. Although the child's father said he "did not believe the sitter meant to spank as hard as he did," and the police officer who was present concluded that "based on the information obtained in this investigation, I could find no intent on the sitter's part to assault this child," the social worker found the determination of physical abuse nonproblematic. Since the child received the injury in the course of a spanking, child abuse occurred.

There were only two cases of sexual abuse in which the alleged abuser acknowledged touching the child in a manner consistent with the allegations but at the same time denied sexual intent. In one of these cases, the alleged abuser said he only touched a ten-year-old boy's genitals in the process of giving him a bath. In the other case, the alleged abuser claimed he only touched the girl's body as part of an anatomy lesson, to show her where her rib and pelvic bones were located. Both of these accounts were dismissed as preposterous. The social workers expressed the opinion that sexual intent was the only possible reason anyone would enact the types of behavior attributed to the accused in the allegations. In short, an equation was drawn between specific behaviors attributed to the accused and their states of mind. If it was established that the babysitter behaved toward the child in ways commonly understood as sexual (e.g., fondling), establishing intent, as a separate dimension of the investigation, was seen as redundant. Thus, social workers were able to conclude their investigation of sexual abuse, as one investigator did, by utilizing the following formula: "The child, a credible witness, indicated that her babysitter did fondle her genitals. Therefore, this is a founded case of intent to commit sexual abuse."

To summarize, in cases of physical and sexual abuse, the intent to commit these acts was seen as a necessary component of the specific behaviors used to accomplish them. Hitting that resulted in an injury to a child was always treated as if it was a direct indicator of the motivation to injure. Similarly, behavior commonly known as "sexual" was always treated as if it were identical with the suspect's intent to sexually exploit. The fact that social workers sometimes described suspects' surprise and horror at the physical damage their violence caused the child did not make the attribution of "intent to harm" more problematic because suspects' accounts were not organizationally defined as indicators of intent. The fact that fifty of the babysitters labeled as abusive denied performing the actions imputed to them and another fourteen were not interviewed at all (because they either could not be located or refused to speak to the social worker) demonstrated that it was possible to determine babysitters' intentions "officially" without confirmatory statements from the babysitters themselves.

Violence of the Letter

Some sociologists believe that wrongdoers have considerable capacity to defend and mollify attributions of deviance by offering excuses, apologies, and expressions of sorrow. For example, formulations such as Mill's "vocabularies of motive," Scott and Lyman's "accounts," Sykes and Matza's "techniques of neutralization," and Hewitt and Stokes's "disclaimers" reflect a belief in the almost limitless reparative potential of talk.[25] In the parlance of these sociologists, "deviant identities are negotiable." They are negotiable because attributions of wrongdoing are seen to depend not only on an assessment of what the wrongdoer did but on an understanding of his or her mental state during and after the violation. As Jack Douglas observes, "an individual is considered responsible for his actions if and only if . . . he has intended to commit those actions and knows the rules relevant to them."[26]

Yet examination of child abuse documents completely contradicts these presumptions. Though accused persons argued that the violation in question was unanticipated, unplanned, and contrary to what they wished, they were still labeled. "The timbers of fractured sociations"[27] were not repaired through talk. The reason has to do with the linkage of investigation and writing. Oral and written communication have different potentialities for conveying information and structuring argument. Because investigative agencies require social workers to defend their judgments in writing, social workers limit their investigations to the "recordable" features of clients' situations. This means that the contingencies of a case that best lend themselves to being described in written language (such as the client's behavior) are given the most prominence, and those contingencies most difficult to capture on paper (those aspects of a case best understood through face-to-face interaction, such as the client's feelings and motivations) are minimized or neglected.[28]

We also need to recognize that recordkeepers are reluctant to designate deviance on something as indefinite as "feelings"—theirs or the client's. The primary risk of citing the client's mental state at the time of the violation as a criterion for labeling or not labeling is that it makes the social worker vulnerable to accusations of subjectivity and personal bias. Since records are permanently available to supervisory scrutiny, social workers feel pressure to make written assessments defendable displays of competence.[29] For this reason, social workers must use records not only to display "what happened" but also to indicate that they performed their jobs rationally and objectively.[30] These practical considerations oblige social workers to place singular emphasis on the tangible aspects of the case—what the client's behavior was and what harm resulted—at the same time giving relatively little weight to the client's excuses, apologies, and expressions of sorrow.

Because testimony from the person most likely to disagree with the child abuser label, the accused, does not have to be considered, the labeling process is simplified. This is not to say that testimony from the accused might overcome the processes of institutional sense making; it is to suggest, rather, that because this testimony is not factored in, the designation of child abuse becomes more "cut and dried," defendable, and recordable. As a result, abuse that might otherwise be denied, excused, or justified, either in whole or in part, can then be fully attributed to suspects.

While it can be argued that simplifying the means by which suspects are labeled is desirable for a society concerned about keeping dangerous people away from children,[31] the negative consequences should be acknowledged. First, individuals who perform investigations belong to one social class and those who are investigated typically belong to another. Second, the control of writing gives investigators power over clients, making it impossible for people at risk of being labeled as child abuser to "negotiate" on an equal footing with labelers. Indeed, any disjuncture between suspects' and social workers' versions of "what really happened" does not have to be resolved prior to the attribution of child abuse.[32] Since investigators have the capacity to impose their interpretation of events on suspects, the only "resolution" needed from the investigators' perspective entails finding ways to make their decisions defendable in writing.

In weighing the effects of these recording practices, we need to remind ourselves that the child abuse record is not filed away and forgotten but becomes part of a permanent, centralized registry broadly accessible to professionals, courts, and police. Although the states regulate who shall and who shall not have access to the registry, in most instances the guidelines are quite general and vague. This statute from Massachusetts is typical: "Data and information relating to individual cases in the central registry shall be confidential and shall be made available only with the approval of the commissioner or upon court order. The commissioner shall establish rules and regulations governing the availability of such data and information."[33]

This blanket provision for "confidentiality," even when coupled with the mandate for the commissioner to establish rules and regulations, provides little protection for the rights of labeled persons. In most states, people are not given the opportunity to challenge the listing of their names. In fact, people are usually not informed that their names have been listed in the first place, and there is no statutory provision for the length of time a name remains on the list.[34] Moreover, the list is not restricted to those whose child abuse is "founded" through investigation, but often includes the names of families in which the report is unsubstantiated because evidence is insufficient or unavailable, the perpetrator could not be identified, the child or family could not be located, "or the situation of poor child care does not meet the established criteria of abuse and neglect."[35] So despite the failure to "prove" that a specific party or parties are guilty of a specific crime, the names of suspects remain on the registry simply because there is insufficient evidence supporting their innocence—there is no proof that child abuse did not occur: "The fact that a report is unsubstantiated does not mean that a child was not abused or neglected."[36]

As might be expected, the personal, social, and legal stigma resulting from being placed on a child abuse registry is enormous. Once the impression has been formed that a person is a child abuser, the expectation exists that he or she will continue to be abusive. Moreover, there is little a person can do to remove this identifier. It exists as part of a permanent record that can be recalled whenever a person's child care capacities or moral standing are questioned.[37] If, as Dorothy Smith argues, the creation of written records "mediates relations among persons in ways analogous to how Marx conceived commodities mediating relations among individuals,"[38] then for the relations (and identities) constituted by records, there is no intersubjective world in which members share the passage of time, and, in the words of Alfred Schutz, "grow old together." There is no interpersonal negotiation, only "fact" as sedimented in the records themselves.

To illustrate, an article appeared in the *Des Moines Register* on 29 November 1993 that told that story of a hairdresser's campaign to get herself off the Iowa Child Abuse Registry. Shirley Toomey's name was listed on the registry in 1988, some two years after investigators determined that she backhanded her twelve-year-old daughter, cutting her lip with her ring. First she attempted to convince social service officials that her daughter's injury was accidental and that she had never hurt her daughter before. Even her daughter testified in her behalf, stating that, while her mother was not perfect, she was no child abuser. Failing to sway the investigators, Toomey took her case to court. However, the judge who heard her case sided with the social service officials. Undeterred, Toomey next went to the Iowa Court of Appeals. This time, the court supported her: "Our courts recognize parents have the right, if they are so inclined, to inflict reasonable corporal punishment in connection with the rearing of their children." The appeals court judge not only concluded that keeping her name on file as a child abuser based on only one isolated incident was inappropriate but also admonished the social service department "to use more care, deliberation and sensitivity prior to labeling a parent's behavior as child abuse." However, the state asked the Iowa Supreme Court to overrule the Court of Appeals, resulting in a second reversal. "We believe the evidence is sufficient," declared the high court, "when the record is viewed as a whole to support the finding of the department that the incident involved was child abuse within the meaning of the law." Toomey next went to the U.S. Supreme Court, unsuccessfully contending that the state had illegally intruded on family life. As things stand now, Toomey can anticipate being on the registry at least another ten years. What concerns her most is not the loss of work or any financial costs resulting from the labeling. Rather, it is that her name has been forever associated with child abuse: "It makes me feel less than a person," she said. "It makes me feel like a loser, and I'm not, and I won't be a loser." She added, "I took a lot of pride in being a mother. What they've done is hurt me. I think they can pull those records out until the day I die, maybe after I die."[39]

Shirley Toomey's story may be taken as a personal tragedy, but the point is not that social work abused this or that individual; it is how some classes of people organize and manage others by making their interventions appear personal. Social work appears simply as a humanitarian effort to help children, yet poor people suspected of child abuse are much more likely to be investigated. Clients from low socioeconomic groups are much more likely to be routed to the court system; the children are much more likely to be placed in out-of-home facilities; and the parents are much more likely to be prosecuted.[40]

Through the urgency of child abuse rhetoric, one class of people is captured in writing by members of another social class. We can see how our reliance on writing to retain an accurate knowledge of the past makes this seizure severely consequential.[41] In a culture where biography is recorded, when there is disagreement about the recollection of events, the issue is not settled by appealing to some actor's memory. In such a culture, documents show what really happened.[42] Thus, when one people or social class takes charge of another's biography, they appropriate that people's history.[43] It is the technique whereby the true memory of an event is dissociated from those who lived it.[44] Ironically, then, although the stated intent of the child abuse investigation is to "strengthen family life," the most common result is the permanent registration of people's deficits. The most important consequence is that one population becomes vulnerable to a form of judgment to which the other is almost entirely immune.

CHAPTER 10

The New Record

> Keep in mind the purpose of all recorded entries. Consider: "Why am I writing this?" Keep entries focused and to the point. Answer the presenting problem or record the key elements of a situation by including significant, relevant information. Exclude inappropriate, irrelevant, or excessive details. . . .
>
> Details that might be misinterpreted or misused by others in the agency having formal or informal access to the case record should not be recorded. . . .
>
> Material that might be incriminating to the agency, should the client bring a suit for any reason, should not be recorded.
>
> **Susanna J. Wilson,** *Recording: Guidelines for Social Workers* **(1980)**

The Federal Privacy Act of 1974 gave clients the right to read their records—to make corrections, challenge interpretations, and question the methods of fact gathering and fact dissemination used on them.[1] Yet social agencies were not suddenly inundated with requests from individuals seeking access to their files.[2] Few clients took advantage of their newfound freedom because they did not know they had it.[3] Although most social agencies were allowing clients to see their files, they did not inform clients of the policy. To use Sheldon Gelman's terminology, record access policies in the United States were "full/passive."[4]

There is a second reason why the Federal Privacy Act caused little stir. If the social worker was still not permitted to have a relationship with the client other than that sanctioned by the agency, then, for all intents and purposes, the help seeker is the agency's client. The social worker is the agent of the agency. This means that anything the social worker is privy to, the agency is privy to as well. So what the social worker writes in the record must be understood by the client as being available to the social worker's supervisor, to other administrative personnel in the agency, and eventually to any agency personnel who might at some future time read the record. Moreover, if the social worker should be called to testify in court, nothing that has been written in the record is considered by the court to be privileged.[5]

All of this is openly acknowledged by social workers. What is not acknowledged, but is widely known, is that clients' records still could be distributed, studied, and discussed without clients' consent far beyond the confines of the court system and the agencies where records are officially housed. This book is proof of that. The previous chapter was based on the examination of over a hundred social work records from the 1980s. Yet no client was asked permission. I went through all the officially designated channels of permission seeking, from the director of the social work agency on down, but at no point was there any mention of clients' veto power.

A third reason why the Federal Privacy Act did little to empower clients has to do with the ways records were shared with them. It was not done to give dissidents a voice or to give clients an opportunity to take exception to social work readings of history. Rather, sharing records became another device to socialize clients—to make clients see themselves from the perspective of their recordkeepers; to gain clients' cooperation by making them feel that what their social workers say about them is true and well intended, scientific and nonbiased.

It should not be surprising then that the published accounts of what happened when records were shared with clients consistently point to the positive (cooperation-inducing) effects of this activity. Far from using their new rights to challenge records and social work practice, "clients who were actively involved in sharing records identified strongly with the project and became advocates for the project and for the organization. These same clients were less likely to challenge decisions and therefore posed less of a risk than did clients who were alienated from the agency."[6]

Sharing records is a way for persons who are being helped to learn either to trust their helpers or to recognize the impossibility of resistance. Even when clients were not positively inspired by their files, they are still less likely to respond with anger than with boredom or indifference.[7] In any case, once clients saw a part of their files, they rarely followed with a request to see the whole thing.[8] For those who did examine the whole file, they rarely asked to see it again.[9]

How does sharing records teach clients to be quiet and obey? How does it teach them to be "good"—to learn that the best antidotes for uncertainty and confusion are cooperation and belief?[10] The answer is that at the same moment that social agencies became legally obligated to share records with clients on demand, records were being rewritten in a solemn new language stripped of hearsay, speculation, and unverified historical information—all that in the past had made social service records so voluminous and interesting. As noted in the previous chapter, musings about intentions and motivations, feelings and interior experience, excuses and justifications, are now avoided. Now, "if a person tells you that he is an alcoholic, you must determine the behavioral referents to this term, that is, what specific behaviors-in-situations (or their absence) are referred to." [11] Now, if a client tells you he drinks, it is necessary to report how much, how often, how long, when this problem began, how it progressed, its patterns and interruptions, what is being done and how effective the intervention is. Anything short of calculated, quantified description risks making social work appear inefficient and ineffective:

> The first task for social workers, as individuals and in groups, is to prove that social work practice is capable of proceeding in a deliberate manner to achieve planned results. The specter that casework (or any other social work method) might be "a set of undefined techniques, applied to unspecified problems, with unpredictable outcome" must be laid to rest. Armed with the self-confidence that accompanies documentation, the profession faces the task of interpreting its activities to a myriad of others—paraprofessionals, team members of other disciplines, consumers of services, legislators, and funding sources. [12]

Because social workers in the 1970s and 1980s had become "accountable" to numerous untold inspectors and judges, including the clients about whom they wrote, they had to choose their words carefully. Social workers were now "restrained not only by their responsibility to protect their clients' right to confidentiality but also by a desire to protect the client and themselves if the client or family should read the document." [13] The solution was to efface the evidence that human beings were responsible for the assertions in the records. The new social worker says, it is not I the social worker who makes these assertions but reality itself. But where suppression of the authorial "I" and use of the passive voice had long been identified as features of social work style, now social workers attempted to lift the "I" from clients. "The era when social work agencies could keep detailed narrative records on each client has passed," wrote Jill Kagle in 1984. [14] Gone were records appearing as novels, oriented to describing and assessing the client's character. Gone too were such general goals as "enhancing self-esteem" or "increasing ego strength." In their place came an entirely new language of measures and specificity.

The Calculated Person

Let us begin by looking at the record of Jean, a mother of two small children. During her intake interview, she told the social worker that she has a problem with her children. She tunes them out and worries that she does not take very good care of them. Second, she said she does not make enough money from her factory job to pay her rent increase. A third worry is her boyfriend, Mike. He loves her, she says, but she does not feel the same way. She continues to see him because she does not wish to hurt his feelings. Jean says this is all making her very confused and depressed. She cries a lot, has trouble sleeping, and says she barely has enough energy to get through the day. Lately she has been thinking about suicide.

Here's how the social worker (using the PIE notational system) enters her assessment in the record.

> Factor I:
> · Parent role problem, responsibility/performance expectation type, moderate severity, one to five years duration, somewhat inadequate coping skills (presenting problem) (Code 1130.213)
> · Lover role problem, ambivalence/conflict type, low severity, one to six months duration, somewhat inadequate coping skills (Code 2120.133)
>
> Factor II:
> · Economic/basic needs system, insufficient financial resources in community to provide sustenance for self and dependents, high severity, one to five years duration (Code 5401.31)
> · Economic/basic needs system, shelter, other shelter problem (unavailability of affordable housing), moderate severity, six months to one year duration (Code 5203.21)
>
> Factor III:
> · DSM-III-R Axis I, 296.22, major depression, single episode, moderate severity
> Axis II, V71.09, no diagnosis [15]

Just as poetry, in Eliot's famous phrase, "can communicate before it is understood," Jean's record communicates before it is even read. Its look communicates: so many adjectives and adjectival phrases strung together—"Parent role problem, responsibility/performance expectation type, moderate severity, one to five years duration, somewhat inadequate coping skills"—make the writing appear as if it went through a syntactic compressor. The words do not appear to be written so much as riveted onto the page. Then there are all these mystery terms—Factor I, Factor II, Factor III, Code 5401.31, Axis II, V71.09—which proclaim in the clearest possible way that this literature is not for the consumption of the uninitiated. So even if Jean, thanks to the Federal Privacy Act, were to get permission to read the document, she would not only fail to see herself but she would also fail to see her mother tongue: the grammar of firm subject, active verb, seeable object has been exchanged for a language without sentences, without images, without actions or actors.

What the new record supplies is not so much information as an attitude— partly comforting and partly forbidding. It is comforting because it affirms that clients can be known, enumerated, coded. Each has a specific slot that is always there. Yet this language is forbidding because it allows no space for argument or compromise. No one, least of all Jean, can dispute the appropriateness of her "Code 1130.213" because no one can say what it means. That is the whole point. This language is designed to bring discourse to a screeching halt. It intimidates so successfully, first, because it carries the aura of science and quantitative measurement. Second, it draws its sureness from the fact that it has no metaphors or verbs. It is a language without associations or referents, without past or future. Instead of the throb of motive and desire, frustration and triumph, we have disconnected phrases. Instead of the crises of human consciousness, we have an inventory of words.

In short, this language gets its persuasive power from what it omits. Because every word refers only to itself, anyone attempting to argue with their selection and placement—say, that a term here is awkward, a trifle exaggerated, or simply does not fit—is risking the same ridicule that Voltaire heaped on Dr. Pangloss: "Things cannot be other than they are. . . . Everything is made for the best purpose." [16] Because nothing claims to be other than what it is—to be like something else or to be doing or becoming anything else— there is no possibility of falsification. Everything is exactly as it should be, no more, no less.

As a consequence, social work interventions in records of this sort do not have to be explained or formulated: their necessity appears self-evident. What is done follows logically and inexorably from the observations: "After observing the interactions of an individual client, family, or small group, the social worker records his or her observations in the appropriate cell: What emerges will be a picture of what positive behaviors should be reinforced, what negative behaviors should be extinguished, and what new positive behaviors need to be learned by the client." [17]

The Record of Mrs. A.

Like Jean, Mrs. A. is a single mother who feels she is not doing a good job taking care of her three preschool-age children. She does not get up in the morning to feed them; there are no regular mealtimes; and she often loses her temper, at which times she slaps and screams at whoever is nearest.[18] What I want to show now is how the social work interventions—or at least the recorded descriptions of them—do not assess such general questions as adaptation or adjustment, virtue or character. Instead, we see only the specific behaviors that occur too often, too seldom, at the wrong time, or in the wrong place. The primary purpose no longer seems to be to judge the person's moral status. Now the purpose is to take hold of bodies and divide them into parts, to regulate appearances, rest and motion.

Instead of telling the story of how Mrs. A. failed or succeeded, resisted or cooperated—images that had for so long dominated social work textbooks and journals—her record tells the story of the tendency, the interval, the behavior and its duration. There are scales, grids, and lists of tasks and task ratings that are organized into logical groups or combinations so interrelations and overlap can be identified. (Table 2 describes four tasks that the social worker indentified for Mrs. A. and rates her performance at these tasks.) The contemporary era did not invent these practices; categorization and quantification had long been of central importance in social work discourse. Rather, it accelerated the use, changed the scale, provided precise instruments.[19]

As the record for Mrs. A. shows, behavioral baselines are obtained at the beginning of service, and behavioral changes are measured during, at the close of, and possibly even after the period of service. That a client feels better, or that a new service program is working, is specified in concrete behavioral terms.[20] Records of changes in the target problems make it possible to determine nonprogress or retrogression, to determine whether the program moves too quickly or too slowly, the extent to which progress is stabilized, when the terminal goal is reached, whether the client has the requisite skills for behavior change, whether it might be necessary to move back to an earlier stage of intervention, and so forth.[21]

The new imperative is to "delineate which specific behavior will accomplish the desired ends, how the client will be behaving (i.e., what he or she will actually be doing) when the aims are achieved, and the conditions under which the behavior can be expected to occur."[22] An effort is made to determine how long the targeted behaviors last, when they originate and stop, their frequency and intensity. Thus, we have problem checklists, flow charts, inventories, matrices, scaling procedures, and rapid assessment instruments: the BPC (Behavior Problem Checklist), RBI (Rational Behavior Inventory), FSS (Fear Summary Schedule), AASF (Assessment of Adult Social Functioning), GCS (Generalized Contentment Scale), IAI (Index of Alcoholism Involvement), GSI (Global Screening Inventory), PASPH (Partner Abuse Scale: Physical), PASNP (Partner Abuse Scale: Non-physical), CAM (Child's Attitude Toward Mother), CAF (Child's Attitude Toward Father), IBR (Index of Brother Relations), ISR (Index of Sister Relations).

Through such devices, observation is automatically combined with classification, and classification automatically implies prediction and prescription. Social work interventions are now punctuated and sustained by knowledge that rests on brevity and clarity. Interventions are perfectly attuned to knowledge: "Correct action is reinforced and incorrect action is identified, so that it can be discontinued, modified, or replaced by other interventions. Blocked passages can be unplugged; an impasse between social worker and client assessed and negotiated; unworkable objectives revised; detours circumvented through exploration of alternatives; strategies and tactics reformulated in response to client resistances and situational limitations; and the lines of action thus adjusted and kept on their proper course."[23]

Table 2. Sample List of Tasks for Client

Task #1

Mrs. A. is to make up schedule for herself and children, setting down times for getting up, meals, housework, naps, etc.

Problem to which related __1__　Session formulated __2__

Origin of Task: Client _____　Practitioner __X__　Other (specify) _____

Client's Initial Commitment __4__ [a]

Task Reviewed: Session #__3__ _____ _____ _____ _____ _____ _____

Task Achievement Rating: __2__ [b]

Comments

She has done some work on schedule, but it was not complete. We finish it in a session.

Task #2

Mrs. A. is to get up at 9 A.M. to prepare her own and children's breakfast. If she does not, she is to get up when at first awakened by children.

Problem to which related __1__　Session formulated __3__

Origin of Task: Client __X__　Practitioner _____　Other (specify) _____

Client's Initial Commitment __4__

Task Reviewed:　Session #__4__　__5__ _____ _____ _____ _____ _____

Task Achievement Rating: __2__　__2__ _____ _____ _____ _____ _____

Comments

Session 4. She got up before nine on her own initiative and once when awakened by the twins (out of five days). She has been trying to get up but "cannot seem to quite make it." She began to do much better after Debbie began nursery school. This task, then, became incorporated as a part of task 4 (below).

Task #3

Practitioner will attempt to locate nursery schools and day care centers that might take Debbie.

Problem to which related __1__　Session formulated __2__

Origin of Task: _____　Practitioner __X__　Other (specify) _____

Task Reviewed:　Session #__3__ _____ _____ _____ _____ _____ _____

Task Achievement Rating: __4__ _____ _____ _____ _____ _____ _____

Comments

Mrs. A. had mixed feelings about this plan because of her problems in "getting going" in the morning, having to dress and take twins along to drop and pick up Debbie; worried about cost. . . .

Task #4

Mrs. A. will get up and get Debbie ready for nursery school pick-up by 9 A.M.

Problem to which related __1__　Session formulated __3__

Origin of Task: Client __X__　Practitioner _____　Other (specify) _____

Client's Initial Commitment __5__

Task Reviewed:　Session #__5__　__6__　__7__　__8__　__9__　__10__

Task Achievement Rating: __4__　__4__　__2__　__3__　__3__　__4__

Comments
Task Review, Session 7. Mrs. A. "overslept" two mornings the preceding week.
Volunteer driver rang bell and awakened her; waited until she got Debbie ready.
Brief telephone conference with driver after first morning on how to handle this
problem.

---

[a] Number refers to score on Commitment Scale.

[b] The Task Achievement Scale measures the client's success in carrying out the task:
    4 = completely achieved
    3 = substantially achieved
    2 = partially achieved
    1 = not achieved or minimally achieved

Source: William J. Reid, *The Task-Centered System.*

The record's structure is a symbol of social work certainty and efficiency,
as well as a sort of archetype of the structure and organization expected of
clients. If clients' behaviors have to fit various timetables and sequences, the
words on the page are also structured into tables and sequences. The new
record appears as an endless tableaux of cells, rankings, headings, and subheadings, each sentence housed in the appropriate district, no semanteme
superfluous or wanting, doing to words what must be done to clients: mark-
ing off spaces and priorities, organizing the petty and useless, breaking the
whole into its constituent parts.

The Dual Purpose

The purpose is both rhetorical and real: rhetorical because its effect is to silence and terrify critics, convincing them that social work possesses all manner of specificity and deliberation, and real because it addresses social work's
principle mission, that of keeping track of an individual's most personal details, of normalizing, supervising, and regularizing his or her smallest movements. So while the earlier social work could be literally oriented to describing and assessing the client's character—to assessing the client's worth as a
whole person—the new social work focuses on parts of the whole; it poses
the question of how the whole can be broken down and how each part can
be divided into new subdivisions.

In the new story line, each behavior or element of sociability has its own
measure, and each measure its own purpose. The social worker "begins with
a survey of both functional and dysfunctional behaviors in [the client's] environmental context. Gradually the worker begins to classify the various complaints and problems in terms of excesses and deficits, that is, those behaviors that are problematic because they occur too often, do not occur often

enough, or occur at the wrong times or place. These are crucial distinctions because entirely different intervention strategies may be selected when the goal is to increase as opposed to decrease behavior."[24]

The interventions do not have to be explained; they simply proceed from the classification scheme. It is no longer a question of understanding interventions but of perceiving their necessity and doing them according to the prearranged scheme: "For too long, social work has hidden behind the guise that 'treatment is an art' and 'recording is poetry.' What is needed now is a tool or an approach that will enable professionals to answer the questions: What is the problem? What are the client's goals in seeking treatment? Was treatment implemented? How long did it take? Was it effective?"[25] Because clients are portrayed as belonging to a little world of measures and typologies, against each of which normality or abnormality are immediately seeable and knowable, it is now possible to make judgments without the appearance of judgmentalism. Everything that is done now sounds as if it has to be done.

This does not mean that social workers ceased to make errors or ceased being portrayed as capable of making errors. The very opposite is true: "Error can occur at any stage . . . because of such factors as inaccurate information, biased observations, faulty hypotheses, improper testing, and unwarranted conclusions."[26] The difference is that now error is seen as identifiable and thus avoidable—that there are clear-cut methods for ascertaining and preventing the smallest missteps relating to statements, actions, and interventions. The following illustration from an article by Allison Murdach published in *Social Work* titled "Avoiding Errors in Clinical Prediction," relates the story of a social worker who assists a psychiatric patient arrange air travel and who is asked by the airline to sign a statement testifying that her client will not pose a risk to airline personnel or the passengers on the flight.

> To honor this request, the social worker met with the patient to evaluate her condition, discussed her progress with staff, and quickly reviewed her hospital records. While interacting with the patient and staff, the worker searched for patterns or cues that would indicate the presence of problems that would preclude air travel by the patient. Because none were found, the social worker felt that she could confidently predict that the patient was fully capable of making the flight. The worker then completed and signed the statement required by the airline company.
>
> While driving the patient to the airport, however, the worker suddenly felt she had made an error. She observed that, evidently as a result of anxiety, the patient was nervously gesturing and softly talking to herself while chain-smoking cigarettes. Because the worker realized that this behavior might alarm airline personnel and other passengers, she counseled the patient about the potential negative effect of such mannerisms. After counseling the patient voluntarily took a prescribed tranquilizer on arrival at the airport and agreed to control her behavior more carefully. Because the

patient now appeared calmer and in better control, the worker felt that the patient posed no risk and could proceed with her flight.

The story raises several interesting questions: Why does the social worker have to "honor" the airline's request that she guarantee the patient's benignancy? If cardiac, diabetic, and ear, nose, and throat patients are entitled to use public transportation just like anyone else, is it "honorable" to treat psychiatric patients differently? If not, perhaps the social worker's time would be better used to combat such discrimination. One cannot help but wonder, of course, how the airline was originally tipped off to the fact that this customer is a psychiatric patient—whether the social worker, with the best of intentions, alerted everyone that a *special* person was planning to come on board.

My point, in raising these questions, is not simply that social work still acknowledges it can make errors—it does—but to draw readers' attention to the type of error it worries about, and the way it is formulated. As before, the error is on the side of manipulating the individual, not on the side of manipulating the institution. What is new, however, is the immediacy with which "error" is apprehended and corrected. In this instance, the perception of error did not come from the discovery of some violent plan or motive. Nor did it hinge on the social worker's understanding of the client's personality or history. Rather, it hinged on the identification of behavior—on external signs. The social worker noticed "the patient was nervously gesturing and softly talking to herself while chain-smoking cigarettes." The critical signal, in other words, was these small divergences from the norm, these inappropriate gestures and mannerisms. Note also how clear-cut and immediate the solution was. The social worker told her client to behave herself, slipped her a pill, and that was that—"the patient voluntarily took the prescribed tranquilizer on arrival at the airport and agreed to control her behavior more carefully."

As we can see, the contemporary social work narrative is not characterized by some new, highly specialized jargon. In fact, there is a general movement against technical terms—what might be called "socspeak" or "psychspeak." What changed is the focus on measurable behavior, the shift from the client's interior to the exterior, from content to form. What changed also, especially as evidenced by the records of Jean and Mrs. A, is the orderliness of the language; its specificity and minuteness. Each area of human relations now appears descriptively separate from every other; each personal trait and way of relating is broken up and rearranged, with the person appearing as a sort of machine with many parts and overlapping identities, with each part and identity defined by the place it occupies in a series, and each place in the series by the gap that separates it from the others.

If we ask why the new social work narrative has no dominant theory or ideology, why contemporary social work is completely eclectic, the answer must be that its goal is not a certain way of defining poverty and poor people. The type of definition is almost irrelevant. What matters is that clients are subject to a constant, uninterrupted analysis. In other words, it is the process rather than the result that counts. Social work survives as simultaneously task centered and feminist, Marxist and gestalt, behaviorist and Freudian, because the critical consideration is not *how* divisions and subdivisions are formulated and discussed but simply that they *are* formulated and discussed, and done so continuously. What matters is the sheer quantity and variety of theoretical perspectives making possible an endlessly minute and complex discourse of causes, relationships, contingencies, and symptoms: "So many principles and procedures may influence the modification of behavior—e.g., positive reinforcement, insight, extinction, 'faith,' reciprocal-inhibition, social modeling, counter-conditioning, cognitive dissonance, situational manipulation, 'that it seems the best strategy at this point would be to consider that different kinds of responses may be governed by different principles and may require different procedures for their modification.'"[28]

It Applies to Social Workers, Too

The statement above shows what social workers do to clients. Yet are not social workers, by their own definitions, just as much the objects of analysis as the clients they assist? In other words, perhaps all this codifying and partitioning, this replacement of the interior with the exterior, applies to social workers as much as to anyone else—from their slightest movements and gestures to their most urgent purposes and needs. This is not to say social workers are no longer allowed to use their personal feelings and intuitions to influence clients. Rather, the problem is the vagueness, imprecision, and a lack of empirical evidence about their effects. Thus, to save—and to have a sound rationale for saving—the social workers' hearts and souls, bodies and gestures, for practicing social work, more rigor and certainly more precision about the meaning and applicability of their personal feelings had to be developed. This is why social work textbooks now offer the minutest directions concerning utterances, mannerisms, tones, postures.

Now, for example, social workers are provided lists of desirable facial expressions: direct eye contact is recommended (except when culturally proscribed); so are "warmth and concern reflected in facial expression," "eyes at same level as client's," "appropriately varied and animated facial expressions," "mouth relaxed; occasional smiles." By contrast, these facial expressions should be suppressed: "yawning," "frozen or rigid facial expressions,"

"inappropriate slight smile," "pursing or biting lips," "lifting eyebrow critically," "nodding head excessively," "staring or fixating on person or object,"
"eye level higher or lower than client's."

As for posture, the social worker's body should be "leaning slightly forward; attentive but relaxed," "arms and hands moderately expressive," using
"appropriate gestures." However, some types of posture are counterproduc-
tive: "rigid body position; arms tightly folded," "body turned at an angle to
client," "fidgeting with hands (including clipping nails or cleaning pipe),"
"squirming or rocking in chair," "slouching or placing feet on desk," "hand
or fingers over mouth," "pointing finger for emphasis."

The social worker's voice must also conform to specifications. On the positive side, it should be "clearly audible but not loud," "modulated to reflect
nuances of feeling and emotional tone of client messages." On the negative
side, "monotonic voice" is to be avoided, as are mumbling, inaudible and
halting speech, grammatical errors, prolonged silences, excessively animated
speech, speaking too loudly, clearing the throat too often, laughing nervously, and either slow, rapid, or staccato speech.[29]

It is certainly not the first time that social workers had become the objects
of detailed prescriptions and proscriptions. Nor is it the first time we see social work focusing on the processes of the activity rather the result, or the di-
viding up of behavior into the appropriate and inappropriate, the obligatory
and forbidden. What changed is the level of calculation involved; also, behavior is all written up, explicit, codified.

Now there are texts that tell the precise position in which a social worker
should sit in order to maximize congenial connection or rapport: "It involves
placing one's self physically at a right angle to the client, approximately 29 to
36 inches away. It also involves avoiding the desk, a potentially separating
middle-class and businesslike accoutrement that can be both a physical and
cultural barrier to communication."[30]

Now, we do not simply tell social workers that the disclosure of personal
information tends to increase clients' confidence in them; we specify that
confidence increases when social workers "display emotions congruent with
the content of the disclosure," when they "do not use self-disclosure as a response to client self-disclosure," and when they "do not disclose material
representing unexamined countertransference or reflecting instability or in-
competence." It is also important that "female therapists should use caution
in disclosing to clients who ascribe to traditional sex role stereotypes."[31]

Now, it is not enough for social workers to be empathic with clients. They
must attain stage five on the Empathy Scale: "Reflecting each emotional nu-
ance, and using voice and intensity of expressions finely attuned to the
client's moment-by-moment experiencing."[32] They must say specific words
and phrases: "Could it be that you're feeling . . . ," "I'm not sure if I'm with

you but . . . ," "Correct me if I'm wrong, but I'm sensing . . . ," "I'm not sure that I'm with you; do you mean . . . ," "What I think I'm hearing is . . . ," "To me it's almost like you're saying . . . ," "As I think about what you say, it occurs to me you're feeling. . . . "[33] They must subscribe to criteria, conditions, and specifications: "(1) unconditional acceptance, (2) openness in receiving, (3) recognizing the double layers of messages (their content and their feeling components), (4) accurate processing of information, and (5) clear and concrete feedback to the other."[34]

Even genuineness is organized, graded, dissected. According to the five-point Genuineness Scale, at level five the social worker is "freely and deeply himself in the relationship. He is open to experiences and feelings of all types—both pleasant and hurtful—without traces of defensiveness or retreat into professionalism. Although there may be contradictory feelings, these are accepted or recognized."[35]

You ask whether social workers have actually succeeded in controlling their responses in this way—say, attaining stage five on the Empathy and Genuineness Scales. Some have, of course. Still, all we can definitely affirm is how rapidly social work grew and multiplied over this century. If that is not evidence of social work's success, what is? Also, we cannot say their techniques were not tested when there is continual corroboration in texts, stories, and records—a steady stream of discourse reflecting social workers' certainty about what needs to be done, what they need to do, to whom they must do it, how often, at what levels and intervals. Surely no other profession has ever accumulated—and in such a relatively short span of time—a similar quantity of discourse on the administration of empathy, warmth, genuineness.

What social workers gained from this discourse is clear enough. On the one hand, the endless partitioning and coding, enumeration and serialization, accented their certainty. On the other, the placement of qualities such as genuineness and empathy in specific cells, which belong to rows and columns, which have their order and stages, their boldfaced headings and subheadings, freed them from seeing themselves as manipulative and controlling. How could this minute management of genuineness and empathy come from a profession that is not indeed genuine and empathic? How could there be any suspicion of hierarchical domination from someone struggling to move from stage four to stage five on the Empathy Scale?

The only penalty, for social workers at least, is that the focus on measurement and certainty makes them acutely vulnerable to judgment—their own judgment mostly. That the new discourse affirms the existence of stage five on the Genuineness Scale proves that this way of relating is both attainable and often attained. The social worker who does not meet these standards, who is not "freely and deeply himself in the relationship" or "open to experiences and feelings of all types—both pleasant and hurtful—without traces of defensiveness or retreat into professionalism," can only blame himself. Social workers' responsibility for controlling their genuineness, then, is the price they pay for the possibility of its perfect control. In other words, the more minute the specifications, the greater the chances that the social worker will not measure up, the greater the chances that failure—regardless of how small—will be noted. The individual social worker exists in a state of continual self-reproach.

CHAPTER 11

Self-Inoculations

> To assume a social worker can empower someone else is naive and con-
> descending and has little basis in reality. Power is not something that so-
> cial workers possess for distribution at will. Clients, not social workers,
> own the power that brings significant change in clinical practice. A clinical
> social worker is merely a resource person with professional training on the
> use of resources who is committed to people empowerment and willing
> to share his or her knowledge in a manner that helps people realize their
> own power, take control of their own lives, and solve their own problems.
>
> **Charles D. Cowger, "Assessing Client Strengths: Clinical Assessment for Client Empowerment"**
> **(1994)**

Social workers are reflective. They criticize their techniques, show concern about paternalism, worry over "social control" and "victim blaming." They are not stupid. Yet, the more social workers reflect on their
discipline's drawbacks, the more confident they appear in its essential perfectibility. It is like homeopathy: Social work cures doubts about its practice
by acknowledging the legitimacy of those very doubts. Social workers inocu-
late themselves with the contingent malady so they can survive the essential one.[1]

According to the formula, they take the established value or technique
that needs restoration and support, lavishly display its inadequacies, the in-
justices it produces, the dangers to which it gives rise. Next they confront
it with its most obvious excesses and contradictions; then, at the last moment, they save it in spite of, or rather by means of, these very contradictions
and blemishes. Here is an illustration from a chapter by Barbara Joseph in
Women's Issues and Social Work Practice:

> Mrs. J. refused to pay her rent until heat and repairs were forthcoming.
> The welfare worker, in the face of the situation, focused on the where-
> abouts of the children's father and searched for evidence of his living in
> the house, questioning children about his possible presence there, though
> the social worker's objective was, he said, to help, in keeping, of course,

165

with the system's mandate to enable families to live in health and decency. Mrs. J. ordered the worker to leave. He retaliated by withholding her check.

Her children, undernourished, underclothed, did poorly in school and often could not attend. The school's response was to 'blame the victim,' referring the mother to the social worker, who, in moral indignation, started neglect proceedings. The truant officer helped out by referring the mother to court for contributing to the truancy of her children. Mrs. J. went berserk in pain and fear for her life and the lives of her children.[2]

In this vignette, none of social work's meanness and tyranny is hidden. It is fully acknowledged that Mrs. J. "needed to liberate herself from the stereotypical categorization of professionals whose racist, moralist attitudes and behaviors functioned to prevent her from receiving the services she needed and was entitled to."[3] So what does the author suggest for Mrs. J.? That she stay as far away from social workers as she possibly can? Quite the contrary. The story that begins with a cry of indignation against social work comes full circle by bidding social work to rise to the challenge of saving its victim. Thus, the order of treatment for Mrs. J. "ought to include referrals to the neighborhood tenants' organization, the local welfare rights and legal aid offices, among others, and the requisite child care and escort and advocate services, so that the critical societal attitudes and institutional policies and practices could be dealt with concretely, politically, and legislatively, in common cause with other oppressed people."[4]

The moral of the story is clear: What is this trifling dross of social work, compared to its advantages? What does it matter, *after all*, if some social workers are a little brutal and a little blind, when there are so many good ones ready and willing to address client needs "concretely, politically, and legislatively, in common cause with other oppressed people." We see how Mrs. J. needed to rid herself of a prejudice that cost her dearly: "Then and only then could Mrs. J. be helped to assess the functional or dysfunctional consequences of her behavior in a way which enabled her to make rational choices for herself and her children in any situation, based on a real sense of herself, her strengths, her needs, and the real options and choices she had."[5]

Consider this defense of social work knowledge from a paper by Ellie Pozatek titled "The Problem of Certainty: Clinical Social Work in the Postmodern Era." The author begins by establishing as a basic principle the self-righteousness and narrow-mindedness of some practitioners because they "often assume a stance of certainty, that is, a belief that they actually know what a client is experiencing in the particular context of his or her life."[6] Then, she brings out the flag, showing that social work knowledge, however unattractive, is a way to rescue those very clients most harmed by it. She illustrates:

> A Hispanic family was referred by the Department of Social Services to a family therapy team for consultation. This family was facing a serious crisis around the question of being able to stay together, and the mother, Ana, was having a very difficult time because the father was incapacitated. When Ana's therapist, a social worker, was asked what it was like for him to work with her, he responded that it was difficult for him because she did not seem to understand him very well. He believed she "had a certain level of cognitive impairment." When asked about the language difference, he stated that Ana seemed to speak English fairly well. He did not think that language was the problem.
>
> A Hispanic clinician on the family therapy team discovered that although Ana did have fairly strong English skills, to express herself about difficult emotional issues she needed to speak in Spanish. Neither the social worker nor apparently his agency saw her inability to speak English as a problem; they viewed her cognitive impairment as a problem. Ana did not tell the social worker that her ability to engage in the therapy process was limited by her ability to fully express herself.[7]

This vignette shows without apology or disguise the image of a social worker as narrow-minded and arrogant. He says that the therapy is not going well because his Spanish-speaking client, Ana, cannot understand him. He says it is her fault: she must have "a certain level of cognitive impairment." But then, at the last moment, the magical hat is turned over, and out pops the image of a Hispanic clinician who discovers that "although Ana did have fairly strong English skills, to express herself about difficult emotional issues she needed to speak in Spanish."

The explicit message is that social workers should not proceed as if their knowledge is infallible (because, after all, their assessments are often inaccurate and harmful), but the implicit message is that correct answers do exist, and that social workers can possess them. By projecting social work error onto a certain type of social worker, the discipline as a whole escapes without notice. By positing the error as a trivial and awkward pustule, the evil is not located within social work but exorcised from it. Thus, social work's self-criticism outwardly appears to undermine social work's belief in itself, but upon closer scrutiny it preserves that belief by isolating sources of trouble and labeling them exceptional. Stories of social worker failure do not challenge social work's foundations but are elaborated in such a way as to reflexively affirm them. In other words, failures are used as resources for organizing, identifying, and explaining the "core meaning" of social work.

Critics conclude their attacks on social work, not by contemplating its essential harmfulness or absurdity, but by referring to its improvement and fullest realization. The silent understanding is that social workers need only see what their errors are, and resolve to eliminate them, for such errors to be eliminated. In keeping with this formula, the paper on "The Problem of Certainty" in social work does not end with an apology but with a series of injunctions and exhortations presuming the complete accessibility and perfectibility of social work knowledge:

> Respect the complexity and ambiguity of a client's life.
> Take into account the context of the therapeutic relationship.
> Bring an awareness of subjective cultural experience to work.
> Understand the client's experience as well as behavior.
> Develop a collaborative method for interpreting meaning.
> Recognize the power of prevailing discourse.
> Recognize that clients often make choices that contribute to the process by which they are marginalized.
> Adopt a therapeutic position of uncertainty.[8]

Once again, social work has it both ways, doublethink *in extremis*: "a therapeutic position of uncertainty" is recommended as if it were itself a certainty; a proclamation of ignorance is treated as a proclamation of knowledge. It claims "to know and not to know," simultaneously; it denies its knowledge base at the very moment it affirms it. In this way, social work has none of the costs associated with arrogance and paternalism. After all, it claims to know nothing. However, it comes away with all the benefits: unquestioned belief in its capacity to "understand a client's experience as well as behavior," to "respect the complexity and ambiguity of a client's life," to "bring an awareness of subjective experience to work," and so forth.

Nowhere is legitimation through self-effacement plainer than in social work's feminist critique. Here, social workers appear to deny the authority of knowledge and training ("We do not know anybody who learned feminist practice in a school of social work"), emphasizing instead that their relationship to clients is rooted in consciousness of "common ground" and "cocreative process."[9] Just as was done at the turn of the century, "common ground" and "cocreative process" are revealed by submerging differences between client and worker, by appearing more as friends than as professionals, by visiting clients at home, by covering and obscuring anything that might make the client feel that facts are being gathered and judgments made. As Jan Fook suggests in "Feminist Contributions to Casework Practice":

> The physical setting of the interview should be that which makes the least possible status distinction between client and worker, and encourages maximum sharing and co-operation. The office may be perceived by the client as a physical expression of the caseworker's higher status. However, in the client's home the worker enters as "visitor" rather than as "official" and may more easily relate as an equal person, rather than a professional. Similarly, interviews conducted while both doing the super-

market shopping (something many women do regularly), giving the other a lift somewhere, or over lunch in the park, could provide the setting to help equalize roles, and may breakdown the mystique of the "professional interview." [10]

How do social workers manage to convince themselves and their clients that this appearance of equality is not mere artifice but is genuine? By exchanging confidence for confidence, trust for trust. Social workers continuously draw attention to their feelings, testifying to their shared history of abuse and oppression, to their identification with clients' suffering, as well as to their own limitations and uncertainties:

> My social work practice begins with myself. In essence I have been a feminist, to some degree, all of my life. My foremothers and forefathers struggled in the wilderness to farm, minister, and teach. As the only descendant in two generations to wear the olive skin of my French-European ancestors, I was claimed by, or relegated to, various cultures throughout my life. I felt a kinship with the world and felt special to have been claimed by many others, yet I also experienced rejection by those who believed I was nonwhite. The name-calling inflicted upon me still resounds in my memory. Perhaps the pain was eased somewhat by the knowledge that secretly I possessed a certain status because I wasn't "one of them." I feel embarrassment that I too was influenced by those in power. I find common solidarity in my own experiences of oppression. I work from that place toward a greater humility, knowing that my existence is temporal and any status an illusion.[11]

One would be very wrong to treat such testimony as an attempt to demystify. Thanks to such confidences, the social worker appears more authoritative than ever. Far from the public disclosure of the details of the social worker's humanness and vulnerability making her appear as the equal of clients, as cut from the same cloth, it gives the social worker mythic status. To endow her with so much humility, to so fully expose the courage and self-torture that accompanies her professional status, makes the performance of social work appear miraculous.

This is not a contemporary invention. Social workers from the turn of the century were similarly inspired: "in view of all that bounty we received, in view of the beauty which has struck us dumb, in view of the flood of affection that we never have answered, we know what to do next." [12] True, the images and explanations are different today. But the effects are the same: enthusiasm, sincerity, intoxication. In both instances, then and now, social workers' intoxication obscures any recognition that power, not equality, is being performed.

Because the authority of the profession is never better displayed than when it is contradicted, social workers themselves raise many of the same questions I raise in this volume: How can anyone give power to another? Does not the very act of giving power to another add to the recipient's dependence on the giver? Don't the class-based institutional structures that give one people the capacity to empower another necessarily reinforce a system of class distinctions at the same time that they undermine the act of empowerment?[13] The difference is that for social workers the articulation of these questions is not a reason to halt the practice of social work. Rather, it is a license to continue. Just as the cuttlefish can safely resume its activities after it squirts its protective ink, social workers return to making their world after inoculating it with a few particles of uncertainty.

Do the contradictions of power and empowerment mean that social workers cannot help their clients? "Certainly not," answers Barbara Levy Simon in a paper titled "Rethinking Empowerment": "Social workers counsel, serve, assist, enable, catalyze, foster, nurture, mobilize, advocate, comfort, inspire, facilitate, broker, teach, train, lobby, and organize in myriad ways that help clients." Yet, she suggests, "the one function that social workers, or, for that matter, anyone else cannot perform for another person is that of empowerment. Empowerment is a reflexive activity, a process capable of being initiated and sustained only by the agent or subject who seeks power or self-determination. Others can only aid and abet in this empowerment process. They do so by providing a climate, a relationship, resources, and procedural means through which people can enhance their own lives."[14]

Reading these last lines, we cannot help but be struck by social work's bravery, by its willingness to be so open about its limitations. Social work is acknowledging that it cannot empower its clients. Clients have to do it for themselves. Still, we seek clarification. If social work can do everything it has always done ("counsel," "serve," "nurture," etc.) but cannot "empower," then these other things ("counseling," "serving," "nurturing") are obviously not "empowering." Now, if they are not empowering, does that mean they are "disempowering"? And if they are disempowering, does that mean they should be discontinued? Of course, these questions are never asked. Within the social work culture, the importance, or even the *possible* importance, of discontinuing social work is treated as irrelevant and fundamentally uninteresting.

To say that social workers are not "interested" in exploring the logical implications of their self-doubts is not to point to their error or to the opportunities they miss. What it means is that doubting always has a terminus point: when it reduces rather than increases social work's capacity to survive, when the self-inoculation creates a new disease more virulent than any present or future threat. In other words, self-criticism exists only to the degree it supports social work's legitimacy as a profession.

The stubborn belief in social work is essentially practical. Social work has no language with which to speak, think, or question, apart from itself. This does not mean, of course, that social work is different from any other domain of knowledge. When statisticians examine statistical issues, they do so through statistics. When experimental social psychologists examine the experimental method, they run new experiments.[15] And so it is with social work. Problems with the assumptions that organize social work are not examined outside or against those assumptions but through that self-same idiom. Social work's belief in its capacity to "do good" is a foundational assumption, much like the mathematician's belief in certain unquestioned and unquestionable axioms. Although at times the mathematician finds that 7 + 5 equals 11, this is not an occasion for revising the system. Rather, it is an occasion for restoring and preserving the system through explanation and excuse: perhaps there was a mistake in counting or someone was playing a practical joke. In any case, 7 + 5 must always equal 12.[16]

Social work transforms doubts about its practices by redefining them as "puzzle-solving" issues, as "insider" problems to be resolved by improving the procedures and methodologies already in place. In other words, any potential threat is nullified by assimilating it into the standard language by which social workers continually discuss new and better ways of conducting social work. Instead of ever considering ceasing its practice or ceasing to recognize the legitimacy of its practice, it attaches new formulas and motivations, new concepts and logics, to the existing practices. Thus, after acknowledging that social workers cannot empower others, the matter is not closed but leads to new questions on how social workers can "help" clients empower themselves, how social workers can share some part of empowerment, how empowerment can be replaced with "coempowerment," and so forth.[17]

What is the difference between empowerment and coempowerment or between social workers claiming to empower clients and social workers claiming to "help" clients empower themselves? It is the difference between attempting to live with an illness by means of denial, and attempting to live with it after an exorcism. It is the difference between avoiding confession entirely and recognizing that "a little confessed evil saves one from acknowledging a lot of hidden evil."[18] Thus, social workers always find themselves confronting a discipline that appears problematic in its particulars: How can we help clients without creating dependency? How can we articulate a common bond with people who speak a different language and belong to a different social class? How can we judge them without naming their weaknesses? How can we offer them guidance when they do not seek it? But, when it comes to examining its ultimate capacity for doing good, there are no such questions. Its right to observe, judge, and record is forever secure.

CHAPTER 12

Penetration

> Constructive interventions—and the earlier the better—reduce pregnancy, illiteracy, delinquency. Constructive interventions interrupt the fateful march from unmet needs to joblessness and crime. Constructive interventions offer a future to the futureless, a place in the sun for children of the shadows. And by making it better for them, we cut down the costs of their dependency—including the violence which all of us live with and fear—and therefore make it better for ourselves.
>
> **Judith Viorst, foreword to *Within Our Reach* (1988)**

Let us now forget homeopathy, exorcism, and cuttlefish. Forget also whether social workers are indeed happily inoculated, mystified, forever secure. There is still the overriding fact of penetration. No one can dispute that there are more reasons than ever before for going into people's homes, for interviewing family members, for uncovering secrets: child abuse, spouse abuse, elder abuse, sexual assault, delinquency, drug use, "risks" of every description. And no one can dispute that the poor are more comfortably and more frequently fitted to these vocabularies than any other group: "Poverty is the greatest risk factor of all. Family poverty is relentlessly correlated with high rates of school-age childbearing, school failure, and violent crime—and with all their antecedents. Low income is an important risk factor in itself, and so is relative poverty—having significantly less income than the norm, especially in a society that places such a high value on economic success. Virtually all the other risk factors that make rotten outcomes more likely are also found disproportionately among poor children: bad health in infancy and childhood, malnutrition, having an isolated or impaired mother, being abused or neglected, or having a decent place to live, and lacking access to the services that would protect against the effects of these conditions."[1]

I shall not attempt here to reconstitute the whole network of arguments and programs that make surveillance of the poor entirely different from, and much more intensive than, surveillance of the middle class. However, a few descriptions of recent initiatives and techniques should give some idea of the precocity of this phenomenon.

Let us begin by considering the current proliferation of programs described as "early identification" or "early intervention." The connotations are from the cold war: the preemptive strike, the early warning system. To identify inadequate parents before they harm their children, to identify children "at-risk" of being harmed before harm comes to them, to calculate the risks posed to and by the embryonic—these are the marks of a society that cares about children and families. But more significantly, the preemptive strike reassures us that we are efficient, thorough, on top of our game.

All of which is to explain why Congress passed PL 95-626 (the Adolescent Pregnancy Act) in 1978, creating the Office of Adolescent Pregnancy in Washington, authorizing all sorts of home visiting and counseling for pregnant and parenting teens. Then came PL 99-457 (the Education of the Handicapped Amendments of 1986), providing money for states to intervene in the lives of infants and children at increased *biological risk* (birth defects, low birth weight, Down's syndrome) and increased *environmental risk* (poverty, single parent, adolescent mother), suggesting a sort of equivalence between poverty and birth defects that no one had previously thought, but that seems to everyone to make perfect sense. The upshot of these laws is the increased likelihood of an impoverished single mother one day discovering a social worker at her door, inquiring about her child-care practices, the appropriateness of her living quarters, her boyfriend's drug use, the history of her compliance with welfare, and so forth.

Here is an illustration published in *Social Work in Health Care* in 1991.[2] According to the article, a pediatrician from a hospital pediatric clinic called the Little Sisters of the Assumption Family Health Service (LSA) to ask them to "assess the home situation" of a six-week-old baby, Jo-Anne, who appeared to be "failing to thrive":

> At the first home visit, the public health nurse and social worker/early child development specialist from LSA found Jo-Anne lying on her back in a dirty carriage in the corner of the room with a bottle propped along a side of a pillow. While the two other children were bickering over a cookie, the mother sat across the room by herself with her body turned away, avoiding eye contact most of the time. The baby was lethargic and wore a haunted expression, failing to either smile or make eye contact. When the social worker picked her up, she arched her back and began to scream in a high shrill voice. The mother paid no attention to the baby, saying in a monotone that she needed help finding a new apartment and dealing with her older child, Charles, whom she described as "bad" like his father, who was in jail for armed robbery and selling drugs. Charles had been abused by his father as a baby, suffered from severe eczema and was constantly provoking his mother with his poor motor coordination and impulse control. Although the two year old girl was able to express

herself quite well, she whined continuously, never seeking her mother for comfort but clinging to anyone entering the home.

Such accounts, as I have indicated earlier, play essentially on a notion of depth: people's problems are no longer stripped from the surface but from the darkest interior. All the images are based on an evocation of the intimate: first, there are the "unimportant irregularities and disturbances"[3]: the dirty carriage located in the corner, the baby's haunted expression, her bottle propped along the side of a pillow, children bickering over a cookie, the mother sitting by herself, her body turned away, avoiding eye contact. Then there are the shameful historical details: the baby's father, who is in jail for robbery and selling drugs, Charles's history of abuse, the mother's own history of deprivation. What we obtain through such description is confirmation that social work sees in depth, analyzes in depth, understands in depth. It confirms social work's hold over the world of the family: because all those things that make up a family's record of misery and misconduct are said,— better yet, they are documented in writing.

But social work does not stop with description and diagnosis. It offers remedies, cures, "intensified support services." Here is what was done with the mother of Jo-Anne:

> To reach the children, the LSA first had to win their mother's confidence through aggressive outreach. Initially, the LSA staff was very pessimistic about any changes the mother could make because of the depression and lethargy that seemed to blanket the household. However, using a variety of traditional and unorthodox behavioral, psychodynamic and supportive approaches, they soon noted positive signs indicating that the mother had the capacity to develop trust in another person. First, the mother agreed to their visits and let them in on a consistent basis. Second, she remembered when home visits were scheduled. Third, she called the workers by name and could differentiate between them. . . .
>
> The social worker worked . . . psychodynamically with the mother, encouraging her to speak about her past. She arranged with the local preschool center to re-enroll the four year old boy and intensified support services when the mother admitted that she had trouble getting up in the morning. For six weeks the social worker knocked on the family's door each morning and encouraged the mother to get up and prepare her son for school. From not having the child's clothing ready in the morning, the mother soon began to have him dressed and eating breakfast at the table when the knock on the door came.
>
> By the end of the first phase, the baby had reached the tenth percentile on the growth chart and the mother was using an alarm clock, purchased by the agency, to get up and get her son on the school bus. Having him out of the house gave her more time to attend to the baby and the middle

child. Frequent contact and the development of a structure had resolved the immediate crisis. The mother demonstrated that she was capable of accepting help.[4]

What does it mean that the social worker used "aggressive outreach" and "a variety of traditional and unorthodox behavioral, psychodynamic and supportive approaches"? An anthropologist, on hearing such terms, might suggest that their precise meaning is irrelevant. What matters instead is that this language is predictable and ritualistic, reaffirming that whatever the professional is doing, it is in the service of order, cooperation, normality. In other words, if there is any doubt that these methods do what they are supposed to do, it is dispelled in the banality of the prose, and in the signs of the mother's cooperation: first, that she "agreed to visits [by the nurse and social worker] and let them in on a consistent basis. Second, she remembered when home visits were scheduled. Third, she called the workers by name and could differentiate between them."

And what does it mean that the social worker visited the mother every morning for six weeks in order to make sure she was awake? Only that the home visit has magical powers. It is a totem remedy and so does not trouble about contradictions: to teach a client to wake up on her own by actually waking her up, to make sure she prepares breakfast by supervising her meal preparation, to guarantee minute to minute surveillance in all the ways she does not measure up—all this makes perfect sense. The proof is in the outcome: by the end of the vignette, the mother was waking up by means of an alarm clock (purchased for her by the Little Sisters of the Assumption), and her baby had reached the tenth percentile on the growth chart.

But beyond all the evidence of growth and success, one cannot help but wonder what an alternative interpretation of these interventions might look like—say, one less focused on the mother's poor discipline and parenting. Whatever else we may wish to say about this interpretation, we need to recognize that it validates a mythology of individual rather than collective failure. This language reinforces the belief that the client cannot manage her own affairs due to personal inadequacy: the exclusive target of intervention is the mother's aberrant behavior—her laziness, her detachment, her chaotic lifestyle—not the fact of her poverty. The political and social conditions of her life are not blamed—she is.

What is also left out is any consideration of the costs these interventions exact on clients. The language of the narrative makes it appear that this mother needs to be controlled for her own good—she needs someone in her house every morning to wake her up, to make sure she feeds and dresses her children: "Frequent contact and the development of a structure had resolved the immediate crisis. The mother demonstrated that she was capable of accepting help." While it is possible that the mother adopted social work's perspective and "accepted" its help, it is also possible that the mother had little choice, because social work's response to noncooperation—for not accepting its help—is isomorphic with surveillance itself. Noncooperation does not lead to social work withdrawal. It leads to the redoubled insistence on more visits.

Regardless of the conditions surrounding the mother's acquiescence in social work's intervention, its political utility is clear: people belonging to the dominant group are permitted into the homes of the subordinate; they observe intimate goings-on, record what they see, and share their observations with networks of other middle-class helpers. As before, the subject/object bifurcations are predictable and completely reassuring. Members of the dominant group are active, and members of the subordinate, passive: one party sees, the other is seen; one writes, the other is written about; one purveys knowledge and direction, the other gratefully absorbs and obeys. And while not all families involved in these programs are on the same economic plane, there is a continuing story of economic deprivation: living below the poverty level appears again and again as clients' distinguishing characteristic.[5]

Family Preservation

In 1980, Congress passed PL 96-272 (the Child Welfare Act) requiring all public child-welfare agencies to demonstrate, as a condition of receiving federal funds, that they are making "reasonable efforts" to prevent out-of-home placement of children. This means that before any child can be placed into a foster home, treatment center, or group residence, an attempt must be made to change the conditions of the home—to "preserve" the family. The Child Welfare Act also stipulates that public agencies must make "reasonable efforts" to return to the home those children who have been taken away from parents (for whatever reason) or risk loss of, or decrease in, federal funding. Accordingly, social work not only gets into people's homes to search for signs of child abuse and neglect; it also gets in during a rehabilitation stage, when an effort is made to show parents whose children were taken away how to care for them when they return.

The Child Welfare Act sparked a social movement. In 1982, there were 20 social programs specifically devoted to the ideals of family preservation; by 1988, that number increased to 333 programs nationwide.[6] Family preservation took off because it resonates so well with the political buzzwords *family values* and *pro-family*. Also, lobbyists claim it resonates well with the push for congressional budget cuts. According to media kits produced by the Edna McConnell Clark Foundation, family preservation costs less per family ($3,000 per family per year) than foster care, which it claims costs $10,000 per year, and residential treatment, which costs $40,000 per child per year.[7] Although home-based visiting is not specifically required by the Child Welfare Act, everyone understands that the office visit is somehow out of synch with the spirit of that law. "It seemed grotesque," one social worker wrote, "that disintegrating families, facing removal of children, should be subjected to further burdens, required to show up at inconvenient times in faraway places to meet with people, each of whom would deal, at best, with one small piece of their problem."[8]

Whether this reasoning is true or not is probably much less important than the fact that social workers, and the agencies that sponsor them, believe it is. Home-visiting the poor is kind. It is supportive. What is more, it increases the range of observations available to the courts, clinics, and hospitals, which depend on such data to decide on poor people's lives. Thus, social workers go into the foreign colony to see what they can see: "Examples of observations made during home-based assessment include safety; cleanliness; organization of the home; geographic proximity to public transportation, schools, stores, and place of employment; access to playmates for children living in the home; family interactions; and neighborhood safety. In families in which child sexual maltreatment is a concern, for example, child safety and privacy are more easily evaluated because living and sleeping areas and the availability of doors and locks can be observed and discussed with parents and children. Similarly, during an initial home visit, the practitioner might inquire about photographs or pictures in the family's home. Such inquiries provide opportunities to learn more about the family, friends, and possible social supports."[9]

What does it mean that people from one social class and culture peer into the neighborhoods and homes of people belonging to another? Surely, they do not do this because it is enjoyable. These travel instructions, written by social workers from *Homebuilders*, one of the nation's first and largest family preservation agencies, reveal how unwelcome home visitors feel. Like soldiers stationed in remote parts of a foreign colony, they experience continual threat, resistance, hostility. Anything is possible in this strange country:

Traveling by Subway
Traveling by subway can be a little more exciting than your average drive in the country. It's important to map out the journey carefully and know right where we're going. If the subway is empty or it's late at night or we're going through a particularly rough part of town, we sit by the doors between cars. If anyone scary comes in, we can go into the next car, or if we need to, pull the red emergency lever hanging down from the ceiling. We encourage workers to move if they feel the least bit uneasy. It's not important to worry about looking foolish. It's important to think about minimizing our risks, all the time.

Again, when we get off the subway, we need to know where we're going. We try to get detailed instructions. If we cannot, we see if someone can go with us the first time. It's a good idea to watch carefully for anyone suspicious. If someone may be following us, it is possible to use windows or mirrors to check. We tell our workers to cross the street if they feel nervous, and to stay away from bushes and dark corners. Cars can be good blockades. If someone does come after us, a parked car can keep them at a distance until we can attract attention or run away.

Entering the Home
When we enter apartment buildings, we look for curved mirrors near the ceiling to look in areas we cannot see directly, and listen for sounds of others nearby. If there's an elevator, we send it down to the basement and do not get in until it returns. Unfriendly people can program an elevator to take us to the basement no matter which button we push. When it arrives, they can take us out and mug us, or worse. Do not get in an elevator if someone suspicious is inside. Again, do not worry about looking foolish. Worry about being safe. Once you're in, stand as close as possible to the elevator panel so you can control the stops. If someone in the elevator starts acting strange, push the closest button and get off even if it is not the floor you want.

When we get to the door of a house or apartment, it's important to listen before we knock. It's good to stand to the side of the door so we won't be close, eye to eye with whoever opens it. When someone does open it, we need to wait to be invited in. We go slowly and let our eyes adjust to the light. Even if the door is ajar, it's not a good idea to just go in.

Meeting the Family
. . . Once we're in, we try to sit in a safe place, unless a family member indicates that he wants the worker in a certain seat. If so, we sit where they prefer. Otherwise, we're usually the most comfortable if we leave ourselves an exit and sit near a door. Most of us prefer to have our backs to a wall. Usually, living rooms are the safest places.

Guns are often in bedrooms. Kitchens are full of potential weapons.[10]

How can social workers help clients, if they feel so profoundly unwelcome and strange? The answer is that clients convince them that their interventions are effective, that their presence is supportive and preservative. This is the real, unsavory secret of home visiting. Not violations of the Fourth Amendment; not "illegal search and seizure"; not surprise house calls, three A.M. visits, forced entries and investigations. The secret is much less melodramatic. Families welcome social workers into their family, share with them the details of their home life, erase any sign of resistance, because they know that if they do not, their child may be taken away or not returned to them. In sum, the secret is coercion, the key elements of which include complete ambiguity regarding the goals of social work intervention ("a healthy family") with a completely unambiguous set of constraints for those who refuse to cooperate.

So however normal, banal, or friendly these interventions appear, they still depend on demonstrations of power. This fact is covered by ritual gestures that we have seen a thousand times. There is the forced politeness and graciousness: "We smile. We talk about positives like how nice their dog is, or how interesting we find their carving from Puerto Rico. We commiserate with them regarding the weather." [11] Then there are the exchanges of personal information: "We share neutral things about our lives: I have three sisters myself. I used to live in Brooklyn. I want to communicate that first we are going to relate to them person to person, before we phase into the helper-helpee relationship." [12] And, of course, there is writing, and the selective sharing of writing: "In keeping with the principle that family members are partners in service efforts, reports to the court and other agencies may be shared and discussed with the family, unless such reports include references to problems which the family is not aware of or which they cannot deal with. Workers are more careful to be accurate and to write with respect and concern for the family when they know they will be discussing their report with the family." [13]

Indeed, all the techniques detailed in the first half of this book—the ones associated with Mary Richmond, friendly visitors, and the "aggressive" social workers from the 1950s—were meticulously reinvented and adapted to suit these new projects. If we ask why this was done, the answer is simply that the techniques work; they encourage clients to talk and circulate freely, creating new opportunities for observation: "We need to be likable so that they will allow us into their homes and spend time with us and so that they will trust us with information that makes them vulnerable. We need to be likable so that they will support us as we support them." [14]

A Final Question

Are social workers responsible for manipulation and deception? Are they immoral? In my opinion, the answer is no. As noted in earlier chapters, social work does not depend on bravado or persuasive skills. It depends on evasion: principally, evasion of the fact of its power, and the fact of clients' powerlessness. Rather than being guilty of boldfaced lies, social workers are guilty of twisting the facts and misdescribing them. They systematically dismiss evidence, producing a gap between their self-conception and action: they describe themselves as empowering while their actions disempower. Their offense is not against morality because they do not consciously harm others or use them against their will. Their offense is against discourse, complexity, difference.

Irving Janis's word for this failure is "groupthink": social workers avoid making penetrating criticisms for fear of destroying an illusion of unanimity and the belief that they belong to a powerful, protective group. They believe that social work is fundamentally right and moral, so there is no need to explore alternative interpretations of their actions and intentions.[15] In short, they are reluctant to do anything that might threaten the sense of "we-feeling" and euphoria that comes with being a social worker and doing good.

Their offense is not willed but structural, being an inevitable by-product of their control of language—both written and spoken. Social work's capacity to endlessly spin favorable stories about itself, and to place them in records, books, and journals, condemns reformulation to silence and bad conscience.

The one incentive to change, I believe, is that social workers are victims, too. The deceptions, the manipulations, the need to live by two contradictory imperatives simultaneously, torture at the same moment they seduce. How much burnout results, how much pain, there is no guessing. Yet the message of burnout is clear: we cannot deny past and present complicity by telling flattering stories; nor can we resign ourselves to paralysis. The denial is too massive, the pain too great. Burnout—social workers' inability to successfully and permanently repress the contradictions they live by—creates the need to deal with questions that cannot, or will not, be asked. New, radically different understandings must be explored if they (and we) are to find a way out.

Introduction

1. Wall, "Mom Called an Abuser," 27 Nov. 1994, 1; "Joy Brown's Ordeal," 29 Nov. 1994, *Des Moines Register*, 6a.

2. Foucault, "Life of Infamous Men," 84.

3. According to Devine in *When Social Work Was Young* (1, 45), "The nineties of the nineteenth century and the next decade witnessed the transformation of organized charity into organized social work." This transformation occurred without much attention to theory or philosophy. Instead, the emphasis was on "the necessity for a complete and thorough original investigation from time to time, accurate clerical records of all visits, statements by applicants, relatives, and references of inquiries received, of all relief obtained or action taken."

4. Specht and Courtney, *Unfaithful Angels*, 160–61.

5. Ibid., 25.

6. Ibid., 170.

7. Ibid., 104, 6.

8. Ibid., 160.

9. Richmond, "Social Caseworker," 43.

10. Franklin, "Mary Richmond and Jane Addams," 518; Brieland, "Hull-House Tradition," 135; D. Levine, *Jane Addams*, 43.

11. Addams, *Democracy and Social Ethics*, 19–20.

12. There is, of course, the risk of overstating the difference between Addams and Richmond. Although Addams used the language of neighbor-to-neighbor helping, she was far from an egalitarian. As I note in chapter 1, she believed that well-to-do people have an obligation to help the poor. In her opinion, they have the required financial resources, as well as the appropriate sensibilities and education. Lasch argues very persuasively in *New Radicalism in America* (156–57) that Addams was at heart profoundly conservative and conventional. For example, if there was an

overabundance of juvenile delinquency in the Hull House neighborhood, Addams
felt that the problem could be diminished by providing young people "a more wholesome form of entertainment" such as the plays of Shakespeare and Moliere: "She
hoped incidentally that the artistic impulse thus developed might eventually be
brought to the service of industry so as to free it from 'its mechanism and material-
ism.' Better workers, better goods."

13. Pearrson, *Deviant Imagination*, 132–33.

14. Quoted in Franklin, "Mary Richmond and Jane Addams," 514.

15. Edelman, "Political Language."

16. Foucault, "Life of Infamous Men," 86.

17. The analysis of "forgetting" and "unconsciousness" derives mainly
from Pollner, Orwell, and Nietzsche. This passage from Nietzsche in "On Truth and
Lying" (250) sums it up: "Truths are illusions about which it has been forgotten that
they *are* illusions, worn-out metaphors without sensory impact, coins which have lost
their image and now can be used only as metal, and no longer as coins. . . . Now, of
course, man forgets that this is the situation; so he lies in the designated manner un-
consciously and according to centuries-old habits—and precisely *by this unconsciousness* by this forgetting, he arrives at this sense of truth."

18. Van Krieken, "Social Theory and Child Welfare," 407.

19. Foucault in *Power/Knowledge* (119) attempts to correct the belief that
power survives through threats and coercion: "If power were never anything but re-
pressive, if it never did anything but say no, do you really think one would be brought
to obey it? What makes power hold good, what makes it accepted, is simply the fact
that it does not weigh on us as a force that says no, but it traverses and produces
things, it induces pleasure, forms knowledge, produces discourse."

20. Foucault, "Nietzsche, Genealogy, History," 139–40.

21. Foucault, "Life of Infamous Men," 88.

22. Mills, "Situated Actions."

1. The Birth of the Investigation

1. Warner, *American Charities*, 372–73.

2. Lubove, *Progressives and the Slums*, 84.

3. Stewart, quoted in McMurry, "*I Am in a Consumption*," 177.

4. Abbott, *Tenements of Chicago*, 16.

5. Rosenwaike, *Population History of New York*, 63.

6. Campbell, *Darkness and Daylight in New York*, 44.

7. Simmel, "Sociology of the Senses," 360–61.

8. Quoted in Katz, *Shadow of the Poorhouse*, 158.

9. Spaulding, "New Immigration," 106–7.

10. Katz, *Shadow of the Poorhouse*, 158.

11. Gurteen, "Plan for Charity Organization," 38.

12. Sennett, "Middle-Class Families."

13. Ward, *Poverty, Ethnicity*, 43, 89.

14. Sennett, "Middle-Class Families," 388–89.

15. Riis, *How the Other Half Lives*, 207.

16. Ibid.

17. Cohen, *Visions of Social Control*, 13–39.

18. Foucault, *Discipline and Punish*, 252.

19. Brace, *Dangerous Classes of New York*, 88–89.

20. To illustrate how greatly settlement activity increased in the 1890s, we need only compare the number of new settlements organized in that decade with the number organized in the 1880s. According to Woods's *Handbook of Settlements*, twenty-four new settlements opened in New York State during the 1890s. This compares with only three settlement openings in New York during the 1880s.

21. Riis, *How the Other Half Lives*, 8, 41.

22. Addams, "Subjective Necessity," 17.

23. Ibid., 10–11.

24. Campbell, *Darkness and Daylight in New York*, 91–93.

25. One of the most vivid evocations of darkness in relation to the poor and their homes is found in Poole, *Plague and Its Stronghold* (13), where he emphasizes the connection between darkness, disease, danger: "But for the light trickling through grimy panels in doors, these halls are forever dark. It is in halls like these that the germs can live two years or longer. It is with halls like those that one clean room cannot bring safety."

26. Banks, *White Slavery*, 147–49.

27. Riis, *How the Other Half Lives*, 59, 61, 54, 5. My analysis is quite similar to that in Platt, *Child Savers* (41): "The 1880's and 1890's represented for many middle-class intellectuals and professionals a period of discovery of the 'dim attics and damp cellars in poverty-stricken sections of populous towns,' and of the 'innumerable haunts of misery throughout the land.' The city was suddenly found to be a place of scarcity, disease, neglect, ignorance, and 'dangerous influences.' Its slums were the 'last resorts of the penniless and the criminal'; here humanity reached the lowest level of degradation and misery."

28. Pfohl, " 'Discovery' of Child Abuse."

29. Campbell, *Darkness and Daylight in New York*, 175–77.

30. Riis, *Children of the Poor*, 152.

31. Ibid., 146.

32. Buzelle, "Charity Organization in Cities," 6–7.

33. This quotation is from Rauch, "Unfriendly Visitors," in which she shows that in the early days of charity visiting, most of the volunteers were from the upper classes. Most came from families in which the head of the house was engaged in some form of business. There were no weavers, spinners, drovers, teamsters, firemen or policemen. They lived in single-family homes in the best neighborhoods, and most had at least one servant. They came from old families and had almost no immigrants or minority group members among their ranks.

34. Elsing, "New York Tenement Houses," 42–43.

35. Addams, "Objective Necessity," 21.

36. Campbell, *Darkness and Daylight in New York*, 100.

37. Riis, *How the Other Half Lives*, 192–94.

38. Tucker, "Andover House in Boston," 179.

39. Gray, "Applications for Relief," 52.

40. Devine, "Value and Dangers of Investigation," 195.
41. Ibid., 198.
42. Ibid., 193.
43. Rauch, "Unfriendly Visitors," 249.
44. Ibid.
45. Ibid., 249–50.
46. Levi, "Religion and Social Service," 299.
47. Hamlin, "Friendly Visiting," 332.
48. Foucault, "Subject of Power," 214.
49. Foucault, "Life of Infamous Men," 83.
50. Norton, "Friendly Visiting," 30.
51. Foucault, "Life of Infamous Men," 84.

2. The Social Work Gaze

1. Pumphrey, "Mary E. Richmond," 382.
2. Gutridge, "Investigation," 361.
3. Woods, "University Settlements as Laboratories," 7–8.
4. The panopticon design calls for a prison building that encircles an open yard. The cells in the prison ring have two windows traversing the entire thickness of the building. One window faces outside, allowing light to illuminate the cell, and another window faces the interior yard. At the center of the interior yard stands a tower with windows occupied by a keeper who can see into the illuminated cells.
5. Richmond, *Social Diagnosis*, 153.
6. Norton, "Friendly Visiting," 28.
7. Robinson, *Changing Psychology*, 139.
8. Ibid., 107.
9. George, "Minutes and Discussions," 510.
10. Foucault, *Discipline and Punish*, 213.
11. Richmond, *Social Diagnosis*, 107.
12. Rannells, "Psychiatric Social Worker's Technique," 83.
13. De Schweinitz, *Art of Helping People*, 77–78.
14. Ibid., 78–81.
15. Z. D. Smith, "Education of the Friendly Visitor," 449.
16. Hutchins, "Best Mode of Investigation," 44.
17. R. E. Thompson, "General Suggestions," 177–78.
18. Rannells, "Psychiatric Social Worker's Technique," 83–84.
19. The central paradox of such injunctions is that they utilize the rhetorical style of religious/ethical imperatives—as if, for example, treating the poor person's house as sacred is an end in itself and must never be violated. The truth is that social workers were famous for visiting whenever it suited them—say, whenever they should happen to be in the neighborhood. We see this in the chapter 3, in which we examine actual patterns of visitation. In some odd way, social workers saw no contradiction between viewing the poor person's home as sacred (in order to gain entry and accomplish their tasks) and forcing their way in *when they had to*. This case entry

from 1923 describes one such visit: "Visited Mrs. Jenkins. It was next to impossible to get in. Mrs. Jenkins talked from behind the door and insisted repeatedly that Bobby was not going to work and that she did not want any help. After long conference at the door and much persistence, Mrs. Jenkins consented to visitor's coming in—the argument that won being that any conversation at the door might be heard by neighbors" (Breckenridge, *Family Welfare Work*, 203).

20. Hutchins, "Best Mode of Investigation," 44.

21. P. V. Young, *Interviewing in Social Work*, 67.

22. Birtwell, "Investigation," 131.

23. Ibid., 133.

24. Tenney, "Aids to Charity Visitors," 202.

25. Gray, "Applications for Relief," 55–56.

26. Hutchins, "Best Mode of Investigation," 44.

27. Strode and Strode, *Social Skills in Case Work*, 34.

28. Gray, "Applications for Relief," 55–56.

29. Ibid.

30. De Schweinitz, *Art of Helping People*, 65–67.

31. This metamorphosis is particularly notable when reminiscences are used as a means of learning about the elderly: "The past which they enjoy describing supplies the very background that is essential to him who is trying to understand their problems, and at the same time serves as an introduction to the other facts which it may be necessary to obtain" (De Schweinitz, *Art of Helping People*, 67).

32. Brisley, "Attempt to Articulate Processes," 158.

33. Deihl and Wilson, "Can Listening Become," 100.

34. Salsberry, "Techniques in Case Work," 155.

35. Ibid.

36. De Schweinitz, *Art of Helping People*, 68.

37. Ibid., 68–69.

38. Salsberry, "Techniques in Case Work," 155.

39. Ibid., 156.

40. Webb and Morgan, quoted in P. V. Young, *Interviewing in Social Work*, 59–60.

41. Rannells, "Psychiatric Social Worker's Technique," 119.

42. P. V. Young, *Interviewing in Social Work*, 83.

43. Richmond, *Social Diagnosis*, 130–31.

44. Rannells, "Psychiatric Social Worker's Technique," 97–98.

45. R. E. Thompson, "General Suggestions," 177. By the 1920s, approximately nine out of ten social workers were women. This unequal division was rationalized in this manner: "Women are undoubtedly better fitted to visit homes, to unravel tangled domestic situations, care for little children, counsel the growing girl, minister to many special types of need. And as regards the general problems of society, although from one point of view woman may be less disposed to disturb the settled order, especially as it relates to family, religion, and the mores and is, therefore, less likely to be a social reformer or revolutionist, nevertheless, since she regards many of our existing institutions, especially of government and industry, as not due to her devising, she often has less of that blind and almost worshipful reverence for

them which men as a rule seem to absorb from their environment and which renders most men rather blind and insensitive to many crude and barbarous features of government and industry as at present carried on" (Tufts, *Education and Training*, 70–73).

46. Richmond, *Social Diagnosis*, 464–65.

47. Ibid.

48. Birtwell, "Investigation," 132–33.

49. Ibid., 133.

50. Ibid.

51. Ibid.

52. Ibid., 132.

53. De Schweinitz, *Art of Helping People*, 65.

54. Z. D. Smith, "Education of the Friendly Visitor," 448.

55. Birtwell, "Investigation," 134.

56. Ibid., 137.

57. Orwell, *1984*, 32.

58. Sears, *Charity Visitor*, 37.

59. Orwell, *1984*, 176, 33.

60. Ibid., 33.

3. A Network of Writing

1. Gordon, *Heroes of Their Own Lives*, 295.

2. Katz in *Poverty and Policy* provides a detailed examination of the case record of a family that was seen in 1909 by the Society for Organizing Charity (SOC) in Philadelphia. The quoted excerpts and case data are taken from that study, especially 41–42, 52.

3. Foucault, *Discipline and Punish*, 189.

4. Richmond, *Social Diagnosis*, 110.

5. Sears, *Charity Visitor*, 43–44.

6. Ibid., 44.

7. Byington, *Confidential Exchange*, 4.

8. Watson, *Charity Organization Movement*, 125.

9. Byington, *Confidential Exchange*.

10. Fox, "Lines of Social Contact," 1036.

11. Byington, *Confidential Exchange*, 3.

12. Spencer, "Sociological and Practical Value," 227. By the close of the second decade of the twentieth century, the Social Service Exchange in Minneapolis had discovered a new way to exchange information: When newspaper articles appeared containing the names of an individual or family registered with them, these items were immediately clipped and mailed to the social service agencies responsible for originally registering that individual or family. "Vital statistics were handled in somewhat the same manner as the news items. After clearing and recording the additional information in the file, further information slips were sent to all the organizations having registered the cases, notifying them of births, deaths, and divorces." The most notable result of this new practice was that social workers had increased oppor-

tunity to prevent marriages involving inappropriate partners (usually underage girls). And when prevention was impossible, other forms of remedial action were taken. For example, "Nellie, a feeble-minded girl of sixteen, was placed in the State School shortly after the ceremony was performed, and her feeble-minded husband left for his former home in a neighboring state" (Harlin, "Social Service Exchange," 21).

13. Sears, *Charity Visitor*, 3.
14. P. V. Young, *Interviewing in Social Work*, 194.
15. Ibid.
16. Strode and Strode, *Social Skills in Case Work*, 165.
17. P. V. Young, *Interviewing in Social Work*, 193.
18. Hamilton, *Theory and Practice*, 65–66.
19. American Association of Social Workers, *Social Case Work*, 11.
20. Devine, *Principles of Relief*, 348.
21. Sheffield, *Social Case History*, 9–10.
22. Pumphrey, "Mary E. Richmond," 381.
23. Richmond, *Friendly Visiting*, 188.
24. Bruno, "Case Record," 452–53.
25. Sheffield, *Social Case History*, 29.
26. Ibid.
27. Ibid., 29–30.
28. Gordon, *Heroes of Their Own Lives*, 13.
29. Richmond, *Social Diagnosis*, 383.
30. Ibid., 399.
31. Ibid., 404.
32. Ibid., 416.
33. Ibid., 428.
34. Ibid., 431.
35. Ibid., 441.
36. Ibid., 444.
37. Mary Richmond believed that "as much information as possible be obtained from official records, neighbors, landlords, or employers without involving the client or his close relatives, since interrogation might be upsetting" (Pumphrey, "Mary E. Richmond," 383).
38. Warren, "Voyage of Discovery," 170–71.
39. Ibid., 171.
40. Quoted in "Public Records," *The Family*, 183.
41. Ibid.
42. Taft, "Social Worker's Opportunity," 152.
43. From the second through the fourth decades of this century, several books were published by social workers on how to write records in which the actual records of social agencies were reproduced as models. The following case record comes from Ralph, *Record Keeping*, 31–32.
44. Foucault, *Discipline and Punish*, 214.
45. Edelman, *Politics as Symbolic Action*, 72–74.
46. Merleau-Ponty, *Phenomenology of Perception*, 54.
47. Breckenridge, *Family Welfare Work*, 166–79.
48. Cohen, *Visions of Social Control*, 40.

49. Taft, "Social Worker's Opportunity," 151.

50. In support of this claim, malpractice suits are far less often directed against social workers than other professionals (see Jones and Alcabes, "Clients Don't Sue").

51. P. R. Lee, "Future of Professional Social Work," 2.

52. Cannon, *Social Work in Hospitals*, 3.

53. Hall, *Social Work Year Book, 1933*, 223.

54. Hall, *Social Work Year Book, 1929*, 148.

55. Hall, *Social Work Year Book, 1933*, 494.

56. Odencrantz, *Social Worker*, 41–45.

57. Rannells in "Psychiatric Social Worker's Technique" (112–16) provides an interesting vignette detailing social work's "resistance fighting" function. Readers interested in other examples of how social workers conceived themselves as "resistance fighters" should look at American Association of Social Workers, *Interviews*, and P. V. Young, *Interviewing in Social Work*.

58. Murray, "Case Work," 341.

59. Strode and Strode, *Social Skills in Case Work*, 85–86.

60. Cabot, *Social Work*, 7.

61. Walker, *Child Welfare Case Records*, 259–60.

62. Foucault, *Discipline and Punish*, 216–18.

4. Self-Mystification

1. Kempton, "Skill in Case Work," 261.

2. Pollner, *Mundane Reason*, 122–23.

3. Nietzsche, *Genealogy of Morals*, 253.

4. Cabot, *Social Work*, 183–88.

5. Devine, quoted in Watson, *Charity Organization Movement*, 153–54.

6. De Schweinitz, *Art of Helping People*, 62.

7. Strode and Strode, *Social Skills in Case Work*, 171.

8. Tufts, *Education and Training*, 98.

9. Keiser, "Analysis of an Interview," 17–18.

10. Goffman, *Presentation of Self*, 71.

11. Keiser, "Analysis of an Interview," 17.

12. Cabot, *Social Work*, 186.

13. Mills, "Situated Actions."

14. Kempton, "First Contact and Social History," 112.

15. Springer, "How We Behave," 219.

16. Smith, "Education of the Friendly Visitor," 449.

17. Barthes, *Mythologies*, 16.

18. J. Lee, "Why Have School Visitors?" 302.

19. Oppenheimer, *Visiting Teacher Movement*, 169.

20. Cannon, *Social Work in Hospitals*, 113.

21. Ellis, *Visiting Teacher in Rochester*, 108, 109, 125.

22. Pear, "Social Values," 219–22.

23. Froman, *Language and Power*, 82.

24. Johnson, *Visiting Teacher in New York City*, xi–xxii.

25. This mythology may increase social work's power and authority, but as Kenneth E. Reid argues in "Nonrational Dynamics" (601), there is a price paid at the level of the individual social worker. He explains: "Case examples in textbooks generally describe situations in which the helper successfully assists the client to resolve the issues with which he is struggling, because of the correct intervention at the proper time. Like the thirty-minute situation comedy on television, there may be seemingly overwhelming odds, but by the end, all is well.

"Unfortunately, for a vast majority of the individuals and families who seek help at voluntary and public agencies, the potential for success is often limited. By the time the worker comes into contact with them, they may have passed unsuccessfully through a whole series of helping systems. As the worker attempts to assist the client with a problem, he may find himself frustrated because the process is neither smooth nor fast. Differing from the case example in the textbook, the problem or issue seems to resist resolution.

"A mechanic or a carpenter may attribute his lack of success to inadequate tools; the helping person can only look to himself. It is his own personality that is the therapeutic tool, and for this reason the means of treatment are more difficult to separate from the self. The helping person is, therefore, prone to confuse the limitations of his professional capacity to heal, with his sense of personal worth."

26. Strode, "Client Co-operation," 24–25.

27. Ibid., 25.

28. De Schweinitz, *Art of Helping People*, 110.

29. Halbert, *What Is Professional Social Work?* 14.

30. Ibid.

31. Edelman, "Political Language."

32. G. H., "Bad Penny," 94–95.

33. Foucault, *Power/Knowledge*, 133.

34. Halbert, *What Is Professional Social Work?* 106–7.

35. Woodroofe, *From Charity to Social Work*, 92.

36. Katz, *Undeserving Poor*, 7.

37. Davis, "Mental Hygiene," 60.

38. Buzelle, "Individuality," 187.

39. Ibid., 187–88.

40. Gurteen, "Plan for Charity Organization"; Lowell, *Public Relief and Private Charity*.

41. Marcus, "Social Attitudes," 139.

42. Quoted in Castel, Castel, and Lovell, *Psychiatric Society*, 42.

43. Richmond, *Social Diagnosis*, 244.

44. Odencrantz, *Social Worker*, 26.

45. Cannon, *Social Work in Hospitals*, 35–36.

46. Myrick, "Psychological Processes in Interviewing," 26.

5. Reaching the Hard-to-Reach

1. Overton and Tinker, *Casework Notebook*, 32–33. Alice Overton originated "aggressive social work" in New York City in the early 1950s as the coordinator of an experimental project sponsored by the Youth Board and the Department of

Welfare. An annotated bibliography on this topic was published in 1970 (Schlesinger, *Multi-Problem Family*) and contained 322 reference items.

2. Overton and Tinker, *Casework Notebook*, 66.

3. Ibid., 13.

4. Lindenberg, "Hard to Reach," 29.

5. Stevenson, "Children without Fathers," 78.

6. Franks, "Shall We Sneak Up"; C. Thompson, "Indiana Stops Federal Welfare Abuses."

7. Axinn and Levin, *Social Welfare*, 235.

8. Buell, *Community Planning*, 48.

9. Axinn and Levin, *Social Welfare*, 236.

10. Stevenson, "Children without Fathers," 80.

11. Quoted in Bell, *Aid to Dependent Children*, 62–63.

12. Franks, "Shall We Sneak Up."

13. Reich, "Public Assistance Recipients," 332.

14. *Johnson* v. *United States* 333 U.S. 10 (1948), 14.

15. Overton, "Aggressive Casework," 54–56.

16. Hallinan, "Coordinating Agency Efforts," 12.

17. The social service exchange declined during the 1950s and 1960s, from 320 exchanges in 1946 to 220 in 1956 to 175 in 1959 (Litwak and Hylton, "Interorganizational Analysis"). One explanation for the decline is that the social service exchange failed the "hard-to-reach" or "multiproblem" family. Because most of the service to these families was highly fragmented, crisis oriented, episodic, and symptomatic, social workers felt that more ongoing planning was needed. Thus, instead of merely pooling information on these families in a central clearinghouse, interagency conferences were introduced to coordinate service delivery. These conferences included family agencies, recreation centers, schools, courts, corrections, day care and homemaker services, public welfare and health agencies, and the housing authority. According to Hallinan in "Coordinating Agency Efforts," in advance of each meeting, an up-to-date summary of the case situation to be discussed was mailed to each agency representative, and requests were also made for the agency representatives to discuss their specific experience with the family in question. Information was then shared at the meeting, and all the community agencies agreed to do their part to make the plan succeed.

18. Overton and Tinker, *Casework Notebook*, 24.

19. Ibid.

20. Sunley, "New Dimensions," 67.

21. Overton and Tinker, *Casework Notebook*, 64.

22. Regensburg, "Reaching Children," 108–9.

23. Glasser, "Prisoners of Benevolence," 118.

24. Overton and Tinker, *Casework Notebook*, 13.

25. Overton, "Families Who 'Don't Want Help,'" 307–8.

26. Tinker, "Casework with Hard-to-Reach Families," 167.

27. Ibid.

28. Bandler, "Casework with Multiproblem Families," 164–65.

29. Simmons, *Protective Services for Children*, 56.

30. Dick and Strnad, "Multi-Problem Family," 349.

31. Wilste, "'Hopeless' Family," 16.
32. Haas, "Reaching Out," 42.
33. Wilste, "'Hopeless' Family," 19.
34. Orwell, *1984*, 210–11.
35. Haas, "Reaching Out," 43.

6. Framing the Poor

1. Perman, "The Role of Transference," 48. This passage was also singled out in J. A. B. Lee, "Helping Professional's Use of Language."
2. Henry, "Motivation in Non-Voluntary Clients," 134.
3. King, "Family Therapy," 203.
4. Ibid., 204.
5. Ibid., 203–4.
6. R. A. Levine, "Treatment in the Home," 20.
7. Bandler, "Casework with Multiproblem Families," 163.
8. R. A. Levine, "Treatment in the Home," 22.
9. Sunley, "New Dimensions," 66.
10. Lance in "Intensive Work" provides a detailed example of the "parenting" approach to social work. Although the family was referred to social service for a very specific problem—the father sexually assaulted his adolescent daughter—the social worker's involvement was global, diffuse, oriented to providing them "the kind of basic parenting they have missed."
11. McKinney, "Adapting Family Therapy," 332.
12. Dick and Strnad, "Multi-Problem Family," 353.
13. Hallowitz, "Poor Black Family," 459.
14. Bandler, "Casework with Multiproblem Families," 161.
15. Orcutt, "Casework Interventions," 93–94.
16. Ibid., 94.
17. Simcox and Kaufman, "Treatment of Character Disorders," 393.
18. J. W. Young, *Totalitarian Language*, 87.
19. Edelman, "Political Language."
20. Chilman, "Social Work Practice," 14.

7. Lobotomy

1. Greenblatt, "Psychosurgery," 21.
2. Shutts, *Lobotomy*, 203.
3. Maisel, "Bedlam 1946," 102–3.
4. Dax, "History of Prefrontal Leucotomy," 20.
5. Valenstein, *Great and Desperate Cures*, 157.
6. Freeman et al., "West Virginia Lobotomy Project," 941.
7. Ibid., 941–43.
8. Ibid., 942; Shutts, *Lobotomy*, 214.
9. Freeman et al., "West Virginia Lobotomy Project," 940.

10. These specifications describe the technique of the "transorbital" lobotomy, the method used in West Virginia (see Shutts, *Lobotomy*, 180).

11. Freeman et al., "West Virginia Lobotomy Project," 941.

12. Although the transorbital lobotomy is indeed seamless, other forms of lobotomy, which involve entering the brain through the top of the skull, require sutures and bandages.

13. Freeman et al., "West Virginia Lobotomy Project," 942.

14. Hyde et al., "Problems in Rehabilitation," 233.

15. Ibid., 235–36.

16. Ibid., 238.

17. Freeman and Watts, "Prefrontal Lobotomy," 805.

18. Boquet, "Use of an 'Intrusive Technique,'" 31.

19. Bosserman, "Trends in Casework Treatment," 62.

20. Kirkham and Thompson, "Practicing Psychiatrist and Psychiatric Social Worker," 104–5.

21. Ibid., 105.

22. Kaplaw, "Role of the Social Worker," 33.

23. Ibid., 31.

24. Boquet, "Use of an 'Intrusive' Technique," 32.

25. Friedman, "Casework Treatment of Relatives," 65–66.

26. Kaplaw, "Role of the Social Worker," 24.

27. Freeman and Watts, "Prefrontal Lobotomy," 801.

28. Ibid., 802.

29. Friedman, "Casework Treatment of Relatives," 30.

30. Freeman et al., "West Virginia Lobotomy Project," 941–42.

31. Hyde et al., "Problems in Rehabilitation of Patients," 232–33.

32. Roughly 2 percent of lobotomized patients died soon after surgery (Freeman et al., "West Virginia Lobotomy Project").

33. Hollingshead and Redlich, *Social Class and Mental Illness*, 267.

34. Seventy percent of the West Virginia lobotomies were performed on women (Shutts, *Lobotomy*, 159).

35. The circumstances surrounding the lobotomy of Frances Farmer, a prominent movie actress from the 1940s, illustrate how this technique was used as a method of subduing those who resisted authority (see Shutts, *Lobotomy*, 182–83).

36. Almost from the moment of lobotomy's invention, a very vocal contingent of physicians registered their complete opposition to the procedure. For example, the *Medical Record* of May 1940 carried an editorial titled "The Lobotomy Delusion," in which lobotomy was called "radically wrong . . . meddlesome surgery . . . a violation of the Hippocratic Oath."

37. Slear, "Helping Psychotic Patients," 169.

38. Connery, "Climate of Teamwork," 60.

39. Ibid., 59.

8. The Rhetoric of Empowerment

1. Ryan, *Blaming the Victim*, 6–7.

2. Tidwell, "Black Community's Challenge," 65.

3. From their survey of contemporary social work journals, McMahon and Allen-Meares ("Is Social Work Racist?" 537) concluded that this literature "decontextualizes minority clients, intellectually removing them from the racist context in which they live." A second curiosity, according to McMahon and Allen-Meares, is how social work literature focuses "on mere change in the awareness of social workers" as if some transformation within the social worker psyche would result in broad-based social change. These observations led the authors to conclude that "taken as a whole, the literature portrays the social work profession as naive and superficial in its antiracist practice" (537).

Rosen and Livne ("Personal versus Environmental") conducted a related study on how social workers perceive client problems. Social workers from twelve agencies ($N = 176$) were given a standardized client intake summary and were asked to draw up a treatment plan for the client, addressing the client's problems, desired outcomes, and interventions. The main finding was that workers' assessments of problems and what needed to be done were markedly biased in favor of personal problems and interventions over environmental problems and interventions.

4. Stempler provides in "Effects of Aversive Racism" (466–67) an illustration of how social workers emphasize personal transformation and consciousness raising among themselves as a key to social work practice: "Only with such revisions in our knowledge and our thinking can we bring personal guilt as members of a racist culture into the open and destroy its insidious effect on us as workers. We reach this point so we can deal with our black clients as persons not objects.

"When we have accomplished this objective, we will stop quaking in fear when a black youth demands his rights. We will also stop trying to block out the guilt we feel when his father plays the game white society has invented for him, 'yes, sir'–ing us to death while hating us all the while. In short, we will begin to see our society as a multiracial one."

5. J. A. B. Lee, *Empowerment Approach*, 32.
6. Kadushin, *Social Work Interview*, 308.
7. Lum, *Social Work Practice*, 69.
8. Kadushin, *Social Work Interview*, 309–10.
9. Proctor and Davis, "Challenge of Racial Difference," 318–19.
10. Lum, *Social Work Practice*, 103–14.
11. Ibid., 69.
12. Kadushin, *Social Work Interview*, 306.
13. Burgest, *Social Work Practice with Minorities*, 119.
14. Pinderhughes, "Cross-Cultural Social Work," 312, 16.
15. Solomon, *Black Empowerment*, 311.
16. Middleman and Wood, *Skills for Direct Practice*, 158–59.
17. Cowger, "Assessing Client Strengths," 265.
18. Tolson, Reid, and Garvin, *Generalist Practice*, 57.
19. Reamer and Abramson, *Teaching of Social Work Ethics*, 15.
20. Hepworth, "Managing Manipulative Behavior," 682.
21. Rosen, Proctor, and Livne, "Planning and Direct Service," 166.
22. Reamer, "Concept of Paternalism," 261–67.
23. Weaver, "Empowering Treatment Skills," 103.
24. Middleman and Wood, *Skills for Direct Practice*, 161–62.

25. Ibid., 161.

26. Ibid., 162.

27. Dunst, Trivette, and Deal, "Enabling and Empowering Families," 3.

28. Ibid.

29. Arendt, *Origins of Totalitarianism*, 468–74.

30. Solomon, *Black Empowerment*, 309–11.

31. "The masters' right of giving names goes so far that it is permissible to look upon language itself as the expression of the power of the masters: they say 'this *is* that, and that,' they seal finally every object and every event with a sound, and thereby at the same time take possession of it" (Nietzsche, *Genealogy of Morals*, 20).

32. Rooney, *Work with Involuntary Clients*, 7.

33. Garvin and Seabury, *Interpersonal Practice*, 82.

34. Hepworth, "Managing Manipulative Behavior," 675.

35. Solomon, *Black Empowerment*, 335–37.

36. See Garfinkel, *Studies in Ethnomethodology*, 122; also, Goffman, *Presentation of Self*, 71.

37. "We are not content with negative obedience, nor even with the most abject submission. When finally you surrender to us, it must be of your own free will. We do not destroy the heretic because he resists us; so long as he resists us we never destroy him. We convert him; we bring him over to our side, not in appearance, but genuinely, heart and soul" (Orwell, *1984*, 210).

38. Ratliff, "Stress and Burnout."

39. Pines and Kafry, "Occupational Tedium."

40. Edelwich and Brodsky, *Burn-Out*.

41. Cherniss, *Staff Burnout*.

42. Trower, "Consumer-Centered," 191.

43. Meyer, *Assessment in Social Work*, 39.

44. Sheafor, Horejsi, and Horejsi, *Techniques and Guidelines*, 91–92.

45. Solomon, *Black Empowerment*, 335.

46. Orwell, *1984*, 32.

47. Weick and Pope, "Knowing What's Best," 15.

48. Ibid.

9. The New Excuse

1. American Humane Association, *National Analysis*, 1988.

2. Pelton, *For Reasons of Poverty*, xiv.

3. Gil, *Violence against Children*.

4. American Humane Association, *National Analysis*, 1978

5. Ibid.

6. Conrad and Schneider, *Deviance and Medicalization*.

7. Rue, "Case Work Approach," 278–79.

8. Ibid., 279.

9. Ibid., 282.

10. Steele and Pollack, "Parents Who Abuse," 123.

11. Pelton, *For Reasons of Poverty*, 27.

12. Kempe et al., "Battered-Child Syndrome," 962.

13. Nelson, *Issue of Child Abuse*, 63.

14. Kempe et al., "Battered-Child Syndrome," 17.

15. Ibid., 18.

16. Thomson et al., *Child Abuse*, 34.

17. Ibid.

18. Ibid., 32.

19. Kempe et al., "Battered-Child Syndrome," 24.

20. Garfinkel, *Studies in Ethnomethodology*, 18.

21. Eberle and Eberle, *Politics of Child Abuse*.

22. Zimmerman, "Fact as a Practical Accomplishment."

23. Ibid., 131.

24. Bittner, "Concept of Organization."

25. Mills, "Situated Actions"; Scott and Lyman, "Accounts"; Sykes and Matza, "Techniques of Neutralization"; Hewitt and Stokes, "Disclaimers."

26. Douglas, "Deviance and Respectability," 12.

27. Scott and Lyman, "Accounts," 46–47.

28. Kahn, *Court for Children*; Lemert, "Records in Juvenile Court."

29. A. J. Meehan, "Record-Keeping Practices."

30. Garfinkel, *Studies in Ethnomethodology*; Zimmerman, "Record-Keeping."

31. Best, *Threatened Children*.

32. Pollner, *Mundane Reason*, 77–81.

33. Massachusetts General Laws, Chapter 1076.

34. Garinger and Hyde, "Child Abuse," 171–73.

35. Flango, "Central Registries," 404. In the state of Iowa alone, six thousand names are added to the register per year (see "Joy Brown's Ordeal, *Des Moines Register*, 29 Nov. 1994, 6a).

36. Flango, "Central Registries," 404.

37. Rosenhan, "On Being Sane in Insane Places."

38. D. E. Smith, "Social Construction," 259.

39. Santiago, "Fighting the System," 1a, 10a.

40. Kriesberg et al., *Incarceration of Minority Youth*, 86.

41. Lévi-Strauss, *Tristes Tropiques*, 291.

42. This is illustrated most vividly in Zimmerman, "Record-Keeping," an ethnography of a public welfare agency. The author notes that statements by applicants were treated as inherently problematic (only as claims). By contrast, the content of official records was seen as inherently nonproblematic. Thus, applicants' statements needed to be verified through reference to records, but the contents of records needed no independent verification—they were simply factual. We can see this same partiality in Richmond, *Social Diagnosis* (53). There, she lists a continuum of evidence, from least reliable, such as the testimony of relatives, friends, and employers, to the most reliable, the records of social agencies, a data source she considers totally unimpeachable.

43. Lyttkens, *Of Human Discipline*, 90.

44. Derrida in *On Grammatology* (136–37) quotes this passage from Levi-Strauss's *Tristes Tropiques* to illustrate how writing is a condition of social inauthenticity: "In this respect it is, rather, modern societies that should be defined by a private character. Our relations with one another are now only occasionally and fragmentarily based on global experience, the *concrete 'apprehension'* of one *person by another*. They are largely the result of a [indirect] construction, through written documents. We are no longer linked to our past by an oral tradition which implies *direct [vécu] contact* with others (storytellers, priests, wise men, or elders), but by books *amassed* in libraries, books from which criticism endeavors—with extreme difficulty—to form a picture of their authors. And we communicate with the immense majority of our contemporaries by all kinds of intermediaries—written documents or administrative machinery—which undoubtedly vastly extend our contacts but at the same time make those contacts somewhat *'unauthentic.'* This has become typical of the relationship between the citizen and the public authorities. We should like to avoid describing negatively the tremendous revolution brought about by the invention of writing. But it is essential to realize that writing, while it conferred vast benefits on humanity, did in fact deprive it of something fundamental."

10. The New Record

1. Public Law 93–579.
2. Wilson, *Confidentiality in Social Work*, 26.
3. Abel and Johnson, "Clients' Access to Records," 42.
4. Gelman, "Client Access to Agency Records," 194.
5. Pippen, *Developing Casework Skills*, 41.
6. Gelman, "Risk Management," 77.
7. Ibid.
8. Badding, "Client Involvement in Case Recording," 546.
9. Gelman, "Risk Management," 77.
10. Dewar, "Professionalization of the Client," 5.
11. Gambrill, *Casework*, 104–5.
12. Kane, "Look to the Record," 412.
13. Kagle, "Restoring the Clinical Record," 46.
14. Ibid.
15. Karls and Wandrei, "PIE," 81–82.
16. Gould and Lewontin, "Spandrels of San Marco," 341.
17. Sheafor, Horejsi, and Horejsi, *Techniques and Guidelines*, 299.
18. W. J. Reid, *Task-Centered System*, 275–83.
19. Foucault, *Discipline and Punish*, 139.
20. Siporin, *Introduction to Social Work Practice*, 331.
21. Fischer, *Effective Casework Practice*, 286–87.
22. Ibid., 79.
23. Siporin, *Introduction to Social Work Practice*, 327.
24. Fischer, *Effective Casework Practice*, 252.
25. Hartman and Wickey, "Person-Oriented Record," 296.

26. Murdach, "Avoiding Errors in Clinical Prediction," 382.
27. Ibid., 381–82.
28. Fischer, *Effective Casework Practice*, 64.
29. Hepworth and Larsen, *Direct Social Work Practice*, 179.
30. Wood and Middleman, *Structural Approach*, 38.
31. Anderson and Mandell, "Use of Self-Disclosure," 263.
32. Hepworth and Larsen, *Direct Social Work Practice*, 110.
33. Ibid., 115.
34. Hoffman and Sallee, *Social Work Practice*, 88.
35. Fischer, *Effective Casework Practice*, 200.

11. Self-Inoculations

1. Barthes, *Mythologies*, 41–42.
2. Joseph, "Ain't I a Woman?" 103–4.
3. Ibid.
4. Ibid., 194.
5. Ibid., 104.
6. Pozatek, "Problem of Certainty," 396.
7. Ibid., 401–2.
8. Ibid., 402.
9. Bricker-Jenkins, introduction to *Feminist Social Work Practice*, 5.
10. Fook, "Feminist Contributions to Casework," 56.
11. Palmer, "Feminist Practice," 65.
12. Cabot, *Social Work*, 188.
13. Simon, "Rethinking Empowerment."
14. Ibid., 32.
15. Pollner, *Mundane Reason*, 114.
16. Mehan and Woods, *Reality of Ethnomethodology*, 9.
17. Holmes and Saleeby, "Empowerment," 74.
18. Barthes, *Mythologies*, 42.

12. Penetration

1. Schorr, *Within Our Reach*, xxiii.
2. Belville et al., "Community as a Strategic Site," 11–13.
3. Foucault, "Life of Infamous Men," 84.
4. Belville et al., "Community as a Strategic Site," 11–13.
5. Ronnau and Marlow, "Family Preservation," 539.
6. National Resource Center on Family Services, *Annotated Directory*.
7. Weisman, "Best Interests of the Child," 60.
8. Schorr, *Within Our Reach*, 156.
9. Hodges and Blyth, "Improving Service Delivery," 260.
10. Kinney, Haapala, and Booth, *Keeping Families Together*, 56.

11. Ibid., 138.
12. Ibid., 56.
13. Lloyd and Bryce, *Placement Prevention and Family Reunification*, 138.
14. Kinney, Haapala, and Booth, *Keeping Families Together*, 60.
15. Janis, *Groupthink*.

WORKS CITED

Abbott, Edith. *The Tenements of Chicago, 1908–1935*. Chicago: Univ. of Chicago Press, 1936.

Abel, Charles M., and H. Wayne Johnson. "Clients' Access to Records: Policy and Attitudes." *Social Work* 23 (1978): 42–46.

Addams, Jane. *Democracy and Social Ethics*. New York: Macmillan, 1902.

———. "The Objective Necessity of Social Settlements." 1893. Reprinted in *Jane Addams: A Centennial Reader*, ed. Emily Cooper Johnson, 14–21. New York: Macmillan, 1960.

———. "The Subjective Necessity for Social Settlements." 1893. Reprinted in *Jane Addams: A Centennial Reader*, ed. Emily Cooper Johnson, 10–14. New York: Macmillan, 1960.

American Association of Social Workers. *Interviews: A Study of the Methods of Analyzing and Recording Social Case Work Interviews*. New York: American Association of Social Workers, 1931.

———. *Social Case Work: Generic and Specific (A Report on the Milford Conference)*. New York: American Association of Social Workers, 1931.

American Humane Association. *National Analysis of Official Child Neglect and Abuse Reporting*. Denver: American Humane Association, 1978.

———. *National Analysis of Official Child Neglect and Abuse Reporting*. Denver: American Humane Association, 1988.

Anderson, Sandra C., and Deborah L. Mandell. "The Use of Self-Disclosure by Professional Social Workers." *Social Casework* 70 (1989): 259–67.

Arendt, Hannah. *The Origins of Totalitarianism*. New York: Harcourt, Brace & World, 1958.

Axinn, June, and Herman Levin. *Social Welfare: A History of the American Response to Need*. New York: Harper and Row, 1978.

Badding, Nancy C. "Client Involvement in Case Recording." *Social Casework* 70 (1989): 539–48.

Bandler, Louise. "Casework with Multiproblem Families." In *Social Work Practice*, ed. Elizabeth Meier, 158–71. New York: Columbia Univ. Press, 1964.

Banks, Louis Albert. *White Slavery; or, the Oppression of the Worthy Poor*. Boston: Lee and Shepard, 1893.

Barthes, Roland. *Mythologies*. Comp. and trans. Annette Lavers. New York: Hill and Wang, 1972.

Bell, Winifred. *Aid to Dependent Children*. New York: Columbia Univ. Press, 1965.

Belville, Renate, Debbie Indyk, Vivian Shapiro, Tracey Dewart, Jane Z. Moss, Gail Gordon, and Sister Susanne Lachapelle. "The Community as a Strategic Site for Refining High Perinatal Risk Assessments and Interventions." *Social Work in Health Care* 16 (1991): 5–19.

Best, Joel. *Threatened Children: Rhetoric and Concern about Child-Victims*. Chicago: Univ. of Chicago Press, 1990.

Birtwell, Mary L. "Investigation." *The Charities Review* 4 (1895): 129–37.

Bittner, Egon. "The Concept of Organization." *Social Research* 32 (1965): 239–55.

Boquet, Rudolf F. "The Use of an 'Intrusive' Technique in Casework with Chronic Mentally Ill Patients." *Journal of Psychiatric Social Work* 24 (1954): 31–35.

Bosserman, Eleanor V. "Trends in Casework Treatment in In-Patient Service in Hospital Settings." *Journal of Psychiatric Social Work* 22 (1952): 61–66.

Brace, Charles Loring. *Dangerous Classes of New York*. New York: Wynkoop & Hallenbeck, 1872.

Breckenridge, Sophonisba P. *Family Welfare Work: Selected Case Records*. Chicago: Univ. of Chicago Press, 1924.

Bricker-Jenkins, Mary. Introduction. In *Feminist Social Work Practice in Clinical Settings*, ed. Mary Bricker-Jenkins, Nancy R. Hooyman, and Naomi Gottlieb, 1–13. Newbury Park CA: Sage, 1991.

Brieland, Donald. "The Hull-House Tradition and the Contemporary Social Worker: Was Jane Addams Really a Social Worker?" *Social Work* 35 (1990): 134–38.

Brisley, Mary S. "An Attempt to Articulate Processes." *The Family* 8 (1924): 153–57.

Bruno, Frank J. "What a Case Record Is For." In the *Proceedings of the National Conference on Charities and Correction*, Indianapolis, 1916.

Buell, Bradley. *Community Planning for Human Services*. New York: Columbia Univ. Press, 1952.

Burgest, David R. *Social Work Practice with Minorities*. Metuchen NJ: Scarecrow Press, 1989.

Buzelle, George B. "Charity Organization in Cities." *The Charities Review* 2 (1892): 3–10.

———. "Individuality in the Work of Charity." In *Proceedings of the National Conference of Charities and Correction*, Boston, 1886.

Byington, Margaret F. *The Confidential Exchange: A Form of Social Cooperation*. New York: Russell Sage Foundation, 1912.

Cabot, Richard C. *Social Work: Essays on the Meeting-Ground of Doctor and Hospital*. Boston: Houghton Mifflin, 1919.

Cahoon, Herbert A. "Discussion [of psychiatric casework and its relationship to prefrontal lobotomy]." *Journal of Psychiatric Social Work* 21 (1952): 139–41.

Campbell, Helen. *Darkness and Daylight in New York; or, Lights and Shadows of New York Life*. Hartford CT: A. D. Worthington, 1891.

Cannon, Ida M. *Social Work in Hospitals.* New York: Russell Sage Foundation, 1923.

Castel, Robert, Francoise Castel, and Anne Lovell. *The Psychiatric Society.* Trans. Arthur Goldhammer. New York: Columbia Univ. Press, 1982.

Cherniss, Cary. *Staff Burnout: Job Stress in the Human Services.* Beverly Hills CA: Sage, 1980.

Chilman, Catherine S. "Social Work Practice with Very Poor Families." *Welfare in Review* 4 (1966): 13–22.

Cohen, Stanley. *Visions of Social Control: Crime Punishment and Classification.* Cambridge: Polity Press, 1985.

Cole, William I. "Introductory." In *The City Wilderness,* ed. Robert A. Woods, 1–9. Boston: Houghton Mifflin, 1899.

Connery, Maurice F. "The Climate of Teamwork." *Journal of Psychiatric Social Work* 22 (1952): 59–60.

Conrad, Peter, and Joseph W. Schneider. *Deviance and Medicalization.* St. Louis: C. V. Mosby, 1980.

Cowger, Charles D. "Assessing Client Strengths: Clinical Assessment for Client Empowerment." *Social Work* 39 (1994): 262–68.

Davis, Kingsley. "Mental Hygiene and the Social Class Structure." *Psychiatry* 1 (1938): 55–65.

Dax, E. Cunningham. "The History of Prefrontal Leucotomy." In *Psychosurgery and Society,* ed. J. Sydney Smith and L. G. Kiloh, 19–24. Oxford: Pergamon Press, 1977.

Deihl, Nannie E., and Robert S. Wilson. "Can Listening Become a Case Work Art?" *The Family* 14 (1933): 99–105.

Derrida, Jacques. *Of Grammatology.* Trans. Gayatri Chakavorty Spivak. Baltimore: Johns Hopkins Univ. Press, 1976.

De Schweinitz, Karl. *The Art of Helping People Out of Trouble.* Boston: Houghton Mifflin, 1924.

Devine, Edward T. *Principles of Relief.* London: Macmillan, 1904.

———. *Social Work.* New York: Macmillan, 1922.

———. "The Value and the Dangers of Investigation." In *Proceedings of the National Conference of Charities and Correction,* Boston, 1897.

———. *When Social Work Was Young.* New York: Macmillan, 1939.

Dewar, Thomas R. "The Professionalization of the Client." *Social Policy* 8 (1978): 4–9.

Dick, Kenneth, and Lydia J. Strnad. "The Multi-Problem Family and Problems of Service." *Social Casework* 39 (1958): 349–55.

Douglas, Jack D. "Deviance and Respectability: The Social Construction of Moral Meanings." In *Deviance and Respectability,* ed. Jack D. Douglas, 3–30. New York: Basic Books, 1970.

Dunst, Carl J., Carol M. Trivette, and Angela G. Deal. "Enabling and Empowering Families." In *Supporting and Strengthening Families,* ed. Carl J. Dunst, Carol M. Trivette, and Angela G. Deal, 2–11. Cambridge MA: Brookline Books, 1994.

Eberle, Paul, and Shirley Eberle. *The Politics of Child Abuse.* Secaucus NJ: Lyle Stuart, 1986.

Edelman, Murray. "The Political Language of the Helping Professions." *Politics and Society* 4 (1974): 295–310.

———. *Politics as Symbolic Action: Mass Arousal and Quiescence.* New York: Academic Books, 1971.

Edelwich, Jerry, and Archie Brodsky. *Burn-out: Stages of Disillusionment in the Helping Professions.* New York: Pergamon Press, 1983.

Ellis, Mabel Brown. *The Visiting Teacher in Rochester.* New York: Joint Committee on Methods of Preventing Delinquency, 1925.

Elsing, W. T. "Life in New York Tenement-Houses as Seen by a City Missionary." In *The Poor in Great Cities*, ed. Robert A. Woods, 42–85. New York: Charles Scribner's Sons, 1895.

Fischer, Joel. *Effective Casework Practice: An Eclectic Approach.* New York: McGraw-Hill, 1978.

Flango, Victor Eugene. "Can Central Registries Improve Substantiation Rates in Child Abuse and Neglect Cases?" *Child Abuse & Neglect* 15 (1991): 403–13.

Fook, Jan. "Feminist Contributions to Casework Practice." In *Gender Reclaimed: Women in Social Work*, ed. Helen Marchant and Betsy Wearing, 54–63. Sydney: Hale and Iremonger, 1986.

Foucault, Michel. *Discipline and Punish: The Birth of the Prison.* Trans. Alan Sheridan. New York: Vintage, 1977.

———. "The Life of Infamous Men." In *Power, Truth, Strategy*, ed. Meaghan Morris and Paul Patton, 76–91. Trans. Paul Foss and Meaghan Morris. Sydney: Feral Publications, 1979.

———. "Nietzsche, Genealogy, History." In *Language, Counter-Memory, Practice*, ed. Donald F. Bouchard. Trans. Donald F. Bouchard and Sherry Simon. Ithaca: Cornell Univ. Press, 1977.

———. *Power/Knowledge.* Ed. Colin Gordon. Trans. Colin Gordon, Leo Marshall, John Mepham, Kate Soper. New York: Pantheon, 1980.

———. "The Subject of Power." In *Michel Foucault: Beyond Structuralism and Hermeneutics* by Hubert L. Dreyfus and Paul Rabinow, 208–28. Chicago: Univ. of Chicago Press, 1983.

Fox, Anna B. "Focusing the Lines of Social Contact." *The Survey* 25 (1911): 1035–37.

Franklin, Donna L. "Mary Richmond and Jane Addams: From Moral Certainty to Rational Inquiry in Social Work Practice." *Social Service Review* 60 (1986): 504–25.

Franks, Virginia. "Shall We Sneak Up on Our Clients?" *Public Welfare* 9 (1951): 106–9, 123.

Freeman, Walter, Hiram W. Davis, Isaac C. East, Sinclair Tait, Simon O. Johnson, and Weaver B. Rogers. "West Virginia Lobotomy Project." *Journal of the American Medical Association* 156 (1954): 939–43.

Freeman, Walter, and James W. Watts. "Prefrontal Lobotomy: Convalescent Care and Aids to Rehabilitation." *American Journal of Psychiatry* 99 (1943): 798–806.

Friedman, Sonya. Casework Treatment of Relatives of Lobotomized Patients. Master's thesis, New York School of Social Work, Columbia Univ., 1951.

Froman, Creel. *Language and Power*. Vol. 1. Atlantic Highlands NJ: Humanities Press, 1992.

G. H. "The Bad Penny." *The Family* 3 (1922): 94–95.

Gambrill, Eileen. *Casework: A Competency Based Approach*. Englewood Cliffs: Prentice-Hall, 1983.

Garfinkel, Harold. *Studies in Ethnomethodology*. Englewood Cliffs: Prentice-Hall, 1967.

Garinger, Gail, and James N. Hyde. "Child Abuse and the Central Registry." In *Child Abuse: Intervention and Treatment*, ed. Nancy B. Ebeling and Deborah A. Hill, 171–75. Acton MA: Publishing Sciences Group, 1975.

Garvin, Charles D., and Brett A. Seabury. *Interpersonal Practice in Social Work*. Englewood Cliffs: Prentice-Hall, 1984.

Gelman, Sheldon R. "Client Access to Agency Records: A Comparative Analysis." *International Social Work* 34 (1991): 191–204.

———. "Risk Management through Client Access to Case Records." *Social Work* 37 (1992): 73–79.

George, S. I. "Minutes and Discussions." In *Proceedings of the National Conference of Charities and Correction*, (Portland OR), 1905.

Gil, David G. *Violence against Children*. Cambridge: Harvard Univ. Press, 1970.

Glasser, Ira. "Prisoners of Benevolence: Power versus Liberty in the Welfare State." In *Doing Good: The Limits of Benevolence*, ed. William Gaylin, Ira Glasser, Steven Marcus, and David J. Rothman, 97–170. New York: Pantheon Books, 1978.

Goffman, Erving. *The Presentation of Self in Everyday Life*. Garden City NY: Doubleday, 1959.

Gordon, Linda. *Heroes of Their Own Lives: The Politics and History of Family Violence*. New York: Viking, 1988.

Gould, Stephen Jay, and R. C. Lewontin. "The Spandrels of San Marco and the Panglossian Paradigm." 1979. Reprinted in *Understanding Scientific Prose*, ed. Jack Selzer. Madison: Univ. of Wisconsin Press, 1993.

Gray, Emily. "Investigation of Applications for Relief." In *Proceedings of Minnesota State Conference of Charities and Correction*, Minneapolis, 1894.

Greenblatt, Milton. "Psychosurgery: A Review of the Literature." In *Studies in Lobotomy*, ed. Milton Greenblatt, Robert Arnot, and Harry C. Solomon, 7–56. New York: Grune & Stratton, 1950.

Gurteen, S. Humphreys. "A Plan for Charity Organization." Reprinted in *The Heritage of American Social Work*, ed. Ralph E. Pumphrey and Muriel W. Pumphrey, 170–73. New York: Columbia Univ. Press, 1961.

Gutridge, A. W. "Investigation." In *Proceedings of the National Conference of Charities and Correction*, Portland OR, 359–62, 1905.

Haas, Walter. "Reaching Out: A Dynamic Concept in Casework." *Social Work* 4 (1959): 41–51.

Halbert, L. A. *What Is Professional Social Work?* New York: Columbia Univ. Press, 1923.

Hall, Fred S., ed. *Social Work Year Book, 1929*. New York: Russell Sage Foundation, 1930.

———, ed. *Social Work Year Book, 1933*. New York: Russell Sage Foundation, 1933.

Hallinan, Helen W. "Coordinating Agency Efforts in Behalf of the Hard-to-Reach Family." *Social Casework* 40 (1959): 9–17.

Hallowitz, David. "Counseling and Treating the Poor Black Family." *Social Casework* 56 (1975): 451–59.

Hamilton, Gordon. *Theory and Practice of Social Case Work.* Rev. ed. New York: Columbia Univ. Press, 1951.

Hamlin, Leonora. "Friendly Visiting." *The Charities Review* 6 (1897): 322–25.

Harlin, Luella. "The Fields for the Social Service Exchange." *The Family* 1 (Dec. 1920): 21–22.

Hartman, Barbara L., and Jane M. Wickey. "The Person-Oriented Record in Treatment." *Social Work* 23 (1978): 296–99.

Henry, Charlotte S. "Motivation in Non-Voluntary Clients." *Social Casework* 39 (1958): 130–36.

Hepworth, Dean H. "Managing Manipulative Behavior in the Helping Relationship." *Social Work* 38 (1993): 674–82.

———, and Jo Ann Larsen. *Direct Social Work Practice: Theory and Skills.* 4th ed. Chicago: Dorsey Press, 1993.

Hewitt, John P., and Randall Stokes. "Disclaimers." *American Sociological Review* 40 (1975): 1–11.

Hodges, Vanessa G., and Betty J. Blythe. "Improving Service Delivery to High-Risk Families: Home-Based Practice." *Families in Society* 73 (1992): 259–65.

Hoffman, Kay S., and Alvin L. Sallee. *Social Work Practice.* Boston: Allyn & Bacon, 1994.

Hollingshead, August B., and Fredrick C. Redlich. *Social Class and Mental Illness.* New York: John Wiley, 1958.

Holmes, Gary E., and Dennis Saleeby. "Empowerment, the Medical Model, and the Politics of Clienthood." *Journal of Progressive Human Services* 4 (1993): 61–78.

Hutchins, M. L. "The Best Mode of Investigation." *Proceedings of the Minnesota State Conference of Charities and Correction*, St. Paul, 1895.

Hyde, Robert W., Beatrice Talbot, Milton Greenblatt, and Robert Arnot. "Problems in Rehabilitation of Patients after Lobotomy." In *Studies in Lobotomy*, ed. Milton Greenblatt, Robert Arnot, and Harry C. Solomon, 229–45. New York: Grune Stratton, 1950.

Janis, Irving L. *Groupthink: Psychological Studies of Policy Decisions and Fiascoes.* Boston: Houghton Mifflin, 1983.

Johnson, Harriet M. *The Visiting Teacher in New York City.* New York: Public Education Association, 1916.

Jones, James A., and Abraham Alcabes. "Clients Don't Sue: The Invulnerable Social Worker." *Social Casework* 70 (1989): 414–20.

Joseph, Barbara. "Ain't I a Woman?" In *Women's Issues and Social Work Practice*, ed. Elaine Norman and Arlene Mancuso, 91–116. Itasca IL: Peacock, 1980.

Kadushin, Alfred. *The Social Work Interview.* New York: Columbia Univ. Press, 1983.

Kagle, Jill Doner. "Restoring the Clinical Record." *Social Work* 29 (1984): 46–50.

Kahn, Alfred J. *A Court for Children.* New York: Columbia Univ. Press, 1953.

Kane, Rosalie A. "Look to the Record." *Social Work* 19 (1974): 412–19.

Kaplaw, Barbara. The Role of the Social Worker in Preparing Patients and Their Relatives for Mental Hospitalization." Master's thesis, New York School of Social Work, Columbia Univ., 1951.

Karls, James M., and Karen E. Wandrei. "PIE: A New Language for Social Work." *Social Work* 37 (1992): 80–85.

Katz, Michael B. *In the Shadow of the Poorhouse: A Social History of Welfare in America*. New York: Basic Books, 1986.

———. *Poverty and Policy in American History*. New York: Academic Press, 1983.

———. *The Undeserving Poor: From the War on Poverty to the War on Welfare*. New York: Pantheon, 1989.

Keiser, Laura Jean. "Analysis of an Interview." *The Family* 8 (1927): 17–20.

Kempe, C. Henry, et al. "The Battered-Child Syndrome." *Journal of the American Medical Association* 181 (1962): 17–24.

Kempton, Helen P. "The First Contact and Social History." *The Family* 13 (1932): 111–15.

———. "Skill in Case Work." *The Family* 9 (1928): 260–62.

King, Charles H. "Family Therapy with the Deprived Family." *Social Casework* 48 (1967): 203–8.

Kinney, Jill, David Haapala, and Charles Booth. *Keeping Families Together*. New York: Aldine de Gruyter, 1991.

Kirkham, Juanita, and George N. Thompson. "The Relationship between Practicing Psychiatrist and Psychiatric Social Worker." *Mental Hygiene* 35 (1951): 104–17.

Kriesberg, Barry, Ira Schwartz, Gideon Fishman, Zvi Eiskovits, Edna Guttman, and Karen Joe. *The Incarceration of Minority Youth*. Minneapolis: Hubert Humphrey Institute, University of Minnesota, 1986.

Lance, Evelyn A. "Intensive Work with a Deprived Family." *Social Casework* 50 (1969): 454–60.

Lasch, Christopher. *The New Radicalism in America, 1889–1963*. New York: Alfred A. Knopf, 1966.

Lee, Joseph. "Why Have School Visitors?" *The Survey* 31 (1913): 302.

Lee, Judith A. B. *The Empowerment Approach to Social Work Practice*. New York: Columbia Univ. Press, 1994.

———. "The Helping Professional's Use of Language in Describing the Poor." *American Journal of Orthopsychiatry* 50 (1980): 580–84.

Lee, Porter R. "The Future of Professional Social Work." *The Compass* 7 (1926): 2–3, 5.

Lemert, Edwin M. "Records in Juvenile Court." In *On Record: Files and Dossiers in American Life*, ed. Stanton Wheeler, 355–89. New York: Russell Sage Foundation, 1969.

Levi, Harry. "Religion and Social Service." In *The Field of Social Service*, ed. Philip Davis, 299–314. Boston: Small, Maynard, 1915.

Lévi-Strauss, Claude. *Tristes Tropiques*. Trans. John Russell. New York: Atheneum, 1964.

Levine, Rachel A. "Treatment in the Home." *Social Work* 9 (1964): 19–28.

Levine, D. *Jane Addams and the Liberal Tradition*. Madison: State Historical Society of Wisconsin, 1971.

Lindenberg, Ruth Ellen. "Hard to Reach: Client or Casework Agency?" *Social Work* 3 (1958): 23–29.

Litwak, Eugene, and Lydia F. Hylton. "Interorganizational Analysis: A Hypothesis on Co-ordinating Agencies." *Administrative Science Quarterly* 6 (1962): 395–420.

Lloyd, June C., and Marvin E. Bryce. *Placement Prevention and Family Reunification: A Handbook for the Family Centered Service Practitioner*. Iowa City: National Resource Center on Family Based Services, 1984.

Lowell, Josephine Shaw. *Public Relief and Private Charity*. 1884. Reprint, New York: Arno Press & New York Times, 1971.

Lubove, Roy. *The Progressives and the Slums*. Pittsburgh: Univ. of Pittsburgh Press, 1962.

Lum, Doman. *Social Work Practice and People of Color*. Monterey CA: Brooks/Cole, 1986.

Lyttkens, Lorentz. *Of Human Discipline: Social Control and Long-Term Shifts in Values*. Trans. Roger Tanner. Philadelphia: Coronet Books, 1989.

Maisel, Albert Q. "Bedlam 1946." *Life* (6 May 1946): 102–10, 112, 115, 116, 118.

Marcus, Grace. "Social Attitudes as They Are Affected by Financial Dependency and Relief-Giving." *Journal of Social Case Work* 9 (1928): 135–40.

Margolin, Leslie. "Deviance on Record: Techniques for Labeling Child Abusers in Official Documents." *Social Problems* 39 (1992): 58–70.

McKinney, Geraldine E. "Adapting Family Therapy to Multideficit Families." *Social Casework* 51 (1970): 327–33.

McMahon, Anthony, and Paula Allen-Meares. "Is Social Work Racist? A Content Analysis of Recent Literature." *Social Work* 37 (1992): 533–39.

McMurry, Nan Marie. *"And I? I Am in a Consumption": The Tuberculosis Patient, 1780–1930*. Ann Arbor: Univ. Microfilms International, 1985.

Meehan, Albert J. "Record-Keeping Practices in the Policing of Juveniles." *Urban Life* 15 (1986): 70–102.

Mehan, Hugh, and Houston Woods. *The Reality of Ethnomethodology*. New York: Wiley, 1975.

Merleau-Ponty, Maurice. *Phenomenology of Perception*. London: Routledge & Kegan Paul, 1962.

Meyer, Carol H. *Assessment in Social Work*. New York: Columbia Univ. Press, 1993.

Middleman, Ruth R., and Gale Goldberg Wood. *Skills for Direct Practice in Social Work*. New York: Columbia Univ. Press, 1990.

Mills, C. Wright. "Situated Actions and Vocabularies of Motive." *American Sociological Review* 5 (1940): 904–13.

Murdach, Allison D. "Avoiding Errors in Clinical Prediction." *Social Work* 39 (1994): 381–86.

Murray, Agnes L. "Case Work above the Poverty Line." In *Proceedings of the National Conference of Social Work*, Kansas City MO, 1918.

Myrick, Helen L. "Psychological Processes in Interviewing," *The Family* 7 (1926): 25–29.

National Resource Center on Family-Based Services. *Annotated Directory of Selected Family-Based Programs*. Iowa City: School of Social Work, Univ. of Iowa–Oakdale Campus, 1988.

Nelson, Barbara J. *Making an Issue of Child Abuse*. Chicago: Univ. of Chicago Press, 1984.

Nietzsche, Friedrich. *The Genealogy of Morals*. Trans. Horace B. Samuel. 1887. Reprint, London: George Allen & Unwin, 1910.

———. "On Truth and Lying in an Extra-Moral Sense." 1873. Reprinted in *Friedrich Nietzsche on Rhetoric and Language*, ed. and trans. Sander L. Gilman, Carole Blair, and David J. Parent, 246–57. New York: Oxford Univ. Press, 1989.

Norton, A. K. "Friendly Visiting—The True Charity." In *Proceedings of the Minnesota State Conference of Charities and Correction*, Minneapolis, 1894.

Odencrantz, Louise C. *The Social Worker*. New York: Harper and Brothers, 1929.

Oppenheimer, Julius John. *The Visiting Teacher Movement*. New York: Joint Committee on Methods of Preventing Delinquency, 1925.

Orcutt, Ben A. "Casework Interventions and the Problems of the Poor." *Social Casework* 54 (1973): 85–95.

Orwell, George. *1984*. New York: New American Library, 1949.

Overton, Alice. "Aggressive Casework." In *Reaching the Unreached*, ed. Sylvan S. Furman, 51–61. New York: New York City Youth Board, 1954.

———. "Serving Families Who 'Don't Want Help.'" *Social Casework* 34 (1953): 304–9.

———, and Katherine H. Tinker. *Casework Notebook*. St. Paul: Family Centered Project, 1957.

Palmer, Nancie. "Feminist Practice with Survivors of Sexual Trauma and Incest." In *Feminist Social Work Practice in Clinical Settings*, ed. Mary Bricker-Jenkins, Nancy R, Hooyman, and Naomi Gottlieb, 63–82. Newbury Park CA: Sage, 1991.

Pear, William H. "Social Values in Public and Private Relief." In *The Field of Social Service*, ed. Philip Davis, 205–24. Boston: Small, Maynard, 1915.

Pearrson, Geoffrey. *The Deviant Imagination: Psychiatry, Social Work, and Social Change*. New York: Holmes & Meier, 1975.

Pelton, Leroy H. *For Reasons of Poverty: A Critical Analysis of the Public Child Welfare System in the United States*. New York: Praeger, 1991.

Perman, Joshua M. "Role of Transference in Casework with Public Assistance Families." *Social Work* 8 (1963): 47–54.

Pfohl, Stephen J. "The 'Discovery' of Child Abuse." *Social Problems* 24 (1977): 310–23.

Pinderhughes, Elaine B. "Teaching Empathy in Cross-Cultural Social Work." *Social Work* 24 (1979): 312–16.

Pines, Ayala, and Ditsa Kafry. "Occupational Tedium in the Social Services." *Social Work* 23 (1978): 499–507.

Pippen, James A. *Developing Casework Skills*. Beverly Hills CA: Sage, 1980.

Platt, Anthony M. *The Child Savers: The Invention of Delinquency*. Chicago: Univ. of Chicago Press, 1969.

Pollner, Melvin. *Mundane Reason: Reality in Everyday and Sociological Discourse.* New York: Cambridge Univ. Press, 1987.

Poole, Ernest. *The Plague in Its Stronghold.* New York: Committee on the Prevention of Tuberculosis of the Charity Organization Society of the City of New York, 1903.

Pozatek, Ellie. "The Problem of Certainty: Social Work in the Postmodern Era." *Social Work* 39 (1994): 396–403.

Proctor, Enola K., and Larry E. Davis. "The Challenge of Racial Difference: Skills for Clinical Practice." *Social Work* 39 (1994): 314–23.

"Public Records." *The Family* 3 (1922): 183.

Pumphrey, Muriel W. "Mary E. Richmond—The Practitioner." *Social Casework* 42 (1961): 375–85.

Ralph, Georgia G. *Record Keeping for Child-Helping Organizations.* New York: Survey Associates, 1915.

Rannells, Marion E. "The Psychiatric Social Worker's Technique in Meeting Resistance." *Mental Hygiene* 11 (1927): 78–123.

Ratliff, Nancy. "Stress and Burnout in the Helping Professions." *Social Casework* 69 (1988): 147–54.

Rauch, Julia. Unfriendly Visitors: The Emergence of Scientific Philanthropy in Philadelphia, 1878–1880. Ph.D. diss., Bryn Mawr College, 1974.

Reamer, Frederic G. "The Concept of Paternalism in Social Work." *Social Service Review* 57 (1983): 254–71.

———, and Marcia Abramson. *The Teaching of Social Work Ethics.* New York: Institute of Society, Ethics, and the Life Sciences, 1982.

Regensburg, Jeanette. "Reaching Children Before the Crisis Comes." *Social Casework* 35 (1954): 104–11.

Reich, Charles A. "Searching Homes of Public Assistance Recipients: The Issues under the Social Security Act." *Social Service Review* 37 (1963): 328–39.

Reid, Kenneth E. "Nonrational Dynamics of the Client-Worker Interaction." *Social Casework* 58 (1977): 600–606.

Reid, William J. *The Task-Centered System.* New York: Columbia Univ. Press, 1978.

Richmond, Mary E. *Friendly Visiting among the Poor: A Handbook for Charity Workers.* New York: Macmillan, 1899.

———. "The Social Caseworker in a Changing World." *Proceedings of the National Conference of Charities and Correction*, Baltimore, 1915.

———. *Social Diagnosis.* New York: Russell Sage Foundation, 1917.

Riis, Jacob A. *Children of the Poor.* New York: Charles Scribner's Sons, 1893.

———. *How the Other Half Lives: Studies among the Tenements of New York.* 1890. Reprint, New York: Dover, 1971.

Robinson, Virginia. *A Changing Psychology in Social Case Work.* Chapel Hill: Univ. of North Carolina Press, 1930.

Ronnau, John P., and Christine R. Marlow. "Family Preservation, Poverty, and the Value of Diversity." *Families in Society* 74 (1993): 538–44.

Rooney, Ronald H. *Strategies for Work with Involuntary Clients.* New York: Columbia Univ. Press, 1992.

Rosen, Aaron, and Shula Livne. "Personal versus Environmental in Social Workers' Perceptions of Client Problems." *Social Service Review* 66 (1992): 85–97.

Rosen, Aaron, Enola K. Proctor, and Shula Livne. "Planning and Direct Service." *Social Service Review* 59 (1985): 161–77.

Rosenhan, D. L. "On Being Sane in Insane Places." *Science* 179 (1973): 250–58.

Rosenwaike, Ira. *Population History of the City of New York.* Syracuse: Syracuse Univ. Press, 1972.

Rue, Alice W. "The Case Work Approach to Protective Work." *The Family* 18 (1937): 277–82.

Ryan, William. *Blaming the Victim.* New York: Pantheon Books, 1971.

Salsberry, Pearl. "Techniques in Case Work." *The Family* 8 (1927): 153–57.

Santiago, Frank. "Fighting the System That Calls Her an Abuser." *Des Moines Register,* 29 Nov. 1993: 1, 10a.

Schlesinger, Benjamin. *The Multi-Problem Family: A Review and Annotated Bibliography.* Toronto: Univ. of Toronto Press, 1970.

Schorr, Lisabeth B. *Within Our Reach—Breaking the Cycle of Disadvantage.* New York: Doubleday, 1988.

Scott, Marvin B., and Stanford M. Lyman. "Accounts." *American Sociological Review* 33 (1968): 46–62.

Sears, Amelia. *The Charity Visitor: A Handbook for Beginners.* Chicago: Chicago School of Civics and Philanthropy, 1917.

Sennett, Richard. "Middle-Class Families and Urban Violence: The Experience of a Chicago Community in the Nineteenth Century." In *Nineteenth Century Cities,* ed. Stephan Thernstrom and Richard Sennett, 386–420. New Haven: Yale Univ. Press, 1976.

Sheafor, Bradford W., Charles R. Horejsi, and Gloria A. Horejsi. *Techniques and Guidelines for Social Work Practice.* Boston: Allyn & Bacon, 1994.

Sheffield, Ada Eliot. *The Social Case History: Its Construction and Content.* New York: Russell Sage Foundation, 1920.

Shutts, David. *Lobotomy: Resort to the Knife.* New York: Van Nostrand, 1984.

Simcox, Beatrice R., and Irving Kaufman. "Treatment of Character Disorders in Parents of Delinquents." *Social Casework* 37 (1956): 388–95.

Simmel, Georg. "Sociology of the Senses: Visual Interaction." In *Introduction to the Science of Sociology,* ed. R. E. Park and F. W. Burgess, 356–61. Chicago: Univ. of Chicago Press, 1921.

Simmons, Harold E. *Protective Services for Children.* Sacramento: General Welfare Publications, 1968.

Simon, Barbara Levy. *The Empowerment Tradition in American Social Work.* New York: Columbia Univ. Press. 1994.

———. "Rethinking Empowerment." *Journal of Progressive Human Services* 1 (1990): 27–39.

Siporin, Max. *Introduction to Social Work Practice.* New York: Macmillan, 1975.

Slear, Genevieve Sennett. "Helping Psychotic Patients toward Reality through the Application of Professional Ethics." *Journal of Psychiatric Social Work* 23 (1954): 169–71.

Smith, Dorothy E. "The Social Construction of Documentary Reality." *Sociological Inquiry* 44 (1974): 257–68.

Smith, Zilpha D. "The Education of the Friendly Visitor." *Proceedings of the National Conference of Charities and Correction,* Denver, 1892.

Solomon, Barbara Bryant. *Black Empowerment: Social Work in Oppressed Communities*. New York: Columbia Univ. Press, 1976.

Spaulding, Frank E. "The New Immigration: A Problem in Education." In *The Field of Social Service*, ed. Philip Davis, 101–14. Boston: Small, Maynard, 1915.

Specht, Harry, and Mark E. Courtney. *Unfaithful Angels: How Social Work Has Abandoned Its Mission*. New York: Free Press, 1994.

Spencer, Anna Garlin. "The Sociological and Practical Value of Our Accumulated Knowledge." In *Proceedings of the National Conference of Charities and Correction*, Portland ME, 1904.

Springer, Gertrude. "How We Behave in Other People's Houses." *The Survey* 69 (June 1922): 218–19.

Steele, Brandt F., and Carl B. Pollack. "A Psychiatric Study of Parents Who Abuse Infants and Small Children." In *The Battered Child*, ed. Ray E. Helfer and C. Henry Kempe, 103–47. Chicago: Univ. of Chicago Press, 1968.

Stempler, Benj L. "Effects of Aversive Racism on White Social Work Students." *Social Casework* 56 (1975): 460–67.

Stevenson, Charles. "Children without Fathers." *Reader's Digest* 79 (Nov. 1961): 72–80.

Strode, Josephine. "Client Co-operation." *The Family* 20 (1939): 24–25.

———, and Pauline R. Strode. *Social Skills in Case Work*. New York: Harper & Brothers, 1942.

Sunley, Robert. "New Dimensions in Reaching-Out Casework." *Social Work* 13 (1968): 64–74.

Sykes, Gresham M., and David Matza. "Techniques of Neutralization: A Theory of Delinquency." *American Sociological Review* 22 (1957): 664–70.

Taft, Jessie. "The Social Worker's Opportunity." *The Family* 3 (1922): 149–53.

Tenney, S. E. "Aids to Charity Visitors." *The Charities Review* 5 (1895): 202–10.

Thompson, Craig. "Indiana Stops Federal Welfare Abuses." *Reader's Digest* 65 (July 1954): 7–10.

Thompson, R. E. "General Suggestions to Those Who Visit the Poor." In *The Heritage of American Social Work*, ed. Ralph E. Pumphrey and Muriel W. Pumphrey, 176–81. 1879. Reprint, New York: Columbia Univ. Press, 1961.

Thomson, Ellen M., Norman W. Paget, Doris W. Bates, Morris Mesch, and Theodore I. Putnam. *Child Abuse: A Community Challenge*. East Aurora NY: Henry Stewart, 1971.

Tidwell, Bill J. "The Black Community's Challenge to Social Work." *Journal of Education for Social Work* 7 (1971): 59–65.

Tinker, Katherine H. "Casework with Hard-to-Reach Families." *American Journal of Orthopsychiatry* 29 (1959): 165–75.

Tolson, Eleanor Reardon, William J. Reid, and Charles D. Garvin. *Generalist Practice: A Task Centered Approach*. New York: Columbia Univ. Press, 1994.

Trower, Kristine D. "Consumer-Centered Social Work Practice: Restoring Client Self-Determination." *Social Work* 39 (1994): 191–96.

Tucker, William Jewett. "The Work of the Andover House in Boston." In *The Poor in Great Cities*, ed. Robert A. Woods, 177–95. New York: Charles Scribner's Sons, 1895.

Tufts, James H. *Education and Training for Social Work*. New York: Russell Sage Foundation, 1923.

Valenstein, Elliot S. *Great and Desperate Cures.* New York: Basic Books, 1986.

Van Krieken, Robert. "Social Theory and Child Welfare: Beyond Social Control." *Theory and Society* 15 (1986): 401–29.

Viorst, Judith. Foreword. In *Within Our Reach* by Lisabeth B. Schorr. New York: Doubleday, 1988.

Walker, Wilma, ed. *Child Welfare Case Records.* Chicago: Univ. of Chicago Press, 1937.

Wall, Phoebe, Howard. "Mom Called an Abuser." *Des Moines Register,* 27 Nov. 1994: 1.

Ward, David. *Poverty, Ethnicity, and the American City, 1840–1925: Changing Conceptions of the Slum and the Ghetto.* Cambridge: Cambridge Univ. Press, 1989.

Warner, Amos G. *American Charities.* New York: Thomas Y. Crowell, 1894.

Warren, Marjorie. "A Voyage of Discovery." *The Family* 3 (1922): 170–71.

Waters, Miriam Van. "Philosophical Trends in Modern Social Work." In *Proceedings of the National Conference of Social Work,* Minneapolis, 1931.

Watson, Frank Dekker. *The Charity Organization Movement in the United States.* New York: Macmillan, 1922.

Weaver, Donna R. "Empowering Treatment Skills for Helping Black Families." *Social Casework* 63 (1982): 100–105.

Weick, Ann, and Loren Pope. "Knowing What's Best: A New Look at Self-Determination." *Social Casework* 69 (1988): 10–16.

Weisman, Mary-Lou. "When Parents Are Not in the Best Interests of the Child." *Atlantic Monthly* 274 (July 1994): 43–63.

Wilson, Susanna J. *Confidentiality in Social Work: Issues and Principles.* New York: Free Press, 1978.

———. *Recording: Guidelines for Social Workers.* New York: Free Press, 1980.

Wiltse, Kermit T. "The 'Hopeless' Family." *Social Work* 3 (1958): 12–22.

Wood, Gale Goldberg, and Ruth R. Middleman. *The Structural Approach to Direct Social Work Practice.* New York: Columbia Univ. Press, 1989.

Woodroofe, Kathleen. *From Charity to Social Work: In England and the United States.* London: Routledge & Kegan Paul, 1962.

Woods, Robert A. *Handbook of Settlements.* New York: Russell Sage Foundation, 1911.

———. University Settlements as Laboratories in Social Science. Paper presented at International Congress of Charities, Correction, and Philanthropy, Chicago, 1893.

Young, John Wesley. *Totalitarian Language: Its Nazi and Communist Antecedents.* Charlottesville: Univ. Press of Virginia, 1991.

Young, Leontine. *Wednesday's Children: A Study of Child Neglect and Abuse.* New York: McGraw-Hill, 1964.

Young, Pauline V. *Interviewing in Social Work.* New York: McGraw-Hill, 1935.

Zimmerman, Don H. "Fact as a Practical Accomplishment." In *Ethnomethodology,* ed. Roy Turner, 128–43. Middlesex, England: Penguin Books, 1974.

———. "Record-Keeping and the Intake Process in a Public Welfare Agency." In *On Record: Files and Dossiers in American Life,* ed. Stanton Wheeler, 319–54. New York: Russell Sage Foundation, 1969.

KNOWLEDGE:
Disciplinarity and Beyond

Knowledges: Historical and Critical Studies in Disciplinarity,
edited by Elen Messer-Davidow, David R. Shumway, and David J. Sylvan

**The Recovery of Rhetoric: Persuasive Discourse and Disciplinarity
in the Human Sciences,**
edited by R. H. Roberts and J. M. M. Good

**Modern Skeletons in Postmodern Closets: A Cultural Studies Alternative
to the Disciplining of Literary Studies,**
by James J. Sosnoski

Crossing Boundaries: Knowledge, Disciplinarities, and Interdisciplinarities,
by Julie Thompson Klein

Under the Cover of Kindness: The Invention of Social Work,
by Leslie Margolin